Harriet Atkinson was educated at University of York, the Courtauld Institute and the Royal College of Art. She was co-editor of *The Banham Lectures* (2009) and contributor to Findling and Pelle's *Encyclopedia of World's Fairs and Expositions* (2008). She has written for various journals of art and design, as well as for *The Guardian* and *The Independent*. She is Research Fellow at the University of Brighton and lives in London with her husband and two children.

'Harriet Atkinson provides an excellent account of a key event in twentieth-century British cultural history. Her book is marked by attention to the complex senses of place shaping the events of 1951, and detailed scrutiny of the exhibition spaces conveying the Festival's spatial stories. Richly illustrated from original sources, *The Festival of Britain: A Land and Its People* is an insightful study of the geographies of British identity.'

David Matless, author of *Landscape and Englishness*

'Most studies of the Festival of Britain have concentrated on "the Festival style" (atoms and whimsy), or on the ways in which the buildings of the South Bank exhibition introduced visitors to modern architecture for the first time. Harriet Atkinson's book is about something deeper: the relationship between the 1951 exhibitions across the country and "love of land and history", a modern urban version of the Picturesque which aimed to reconcile tradition and modernism and in the process reconstruct British identity after the disfigurements of war. The book is original, well researched, judiciously illustrated and very revealing. The Festival of Britain will never seem quite the same again.'

'This highly successful exhibition, which amazingly took place throughout the UK although centred on London's Southbank, underscored Britain as the most creative nation in the world and at a time when it was smashed, grey and desolate.

It demonstrated British talent in not only architecture and design but sculpture and painting, literature, poetry, theatre and music – all activities that had lain pretty dormant during five years of grim and damaging war. The great thing about the exhibition was that it demonstrated that there was a better life to be lived which could be achieved by intelligent creativity and pointed the way to a better quality of life. This made people happy, cheerful and optimistic and made even a spam sandwich taste quite good – well not really – but it put a smile on visitors' faces. Some of them even cried with excitement and it demonstrated that the UK had the ideas and know-how to create a modern world.

As the book admirably demonstrates, much of the credit must go to the Government of the time and the two people given day to day control. Gerald Barry, a newspaper editor, and Hugh Casson, an architect and designer, ran the show and selected outstanding creative people who were responsible for every tiny detail. They were quite clear about what they wanted to achieve and were backed by the socialist politicians and most of the civil servants. They saw the Festival as a great opportunity to demonstrate that the country was not down and out but filled with energy and creativity which could be the UK's strength in the future. It succeeded for those people who were not politically biased or cynical and Britain's subsequent success in the creative world can be directly linked to the Festival – it was a turning point for the UK.

This book does a wonderful job of describing what went on behind the scenes and why the exhibitions were such a great success. What a shame it was not written before the Millennium disaster as it really is a perfect primer on how to create an inspirational festival. It shows that dedicated leadership knew how to select and direct the best team of creative people, encourage their talents and correct them when necessary without losing their energy or enthusiasm. Why Churchill, who I always thought rather admired creativity, wanted to smash it all down as soon as possible, especially the Skylon, I never really quite understood.

That is why every politician of every party, every architect and designer and every creative person should read this excellent and intensely researched book from cover to cover and look for the next Barry, Casson and Morrison if ever another Festival appears on the horizon. Full marks Dr. Atkinson, you have researched and written a really useful book.'

Terence Conran

'P.S. I worked on the Southbank site for several weeks before the exhibition opened so I have firsthand experience of its wonders!'

THE FESTIVAL OF BRITAIN

A LAND AND ITS PEOPLE

HARRIET ATKINSON
WITH A FOREWORD BY MARY BANHAM

I.B. TAURIS
LONDON · NEW YORK

Published in 2012 by I.B. Tauris & Co Ltd
6 Salem Road, London W2 4BU
175 Fifth Avenue, New York NY 10010
www.ibtauris.com

Distributed in the United States and Canada Exclusively by Palgrave Macmillan
175 Fifth Avenue, New York NY 10010

ISBN   978 1 84885 792 6

A full CIP record for this book is available from the British Library
A full CIP record is available from the Library of Congress

Library of Congress Catalog Card Number: available

Cover designed by Will Webb: www.willwebb.co.uk
Typeset by Paul Tompsett: www.freerangeproduction.com

Printed and bound by CPI Group (UK) Ltd, Croydon, CR0 4YY

For Valerian, Joseph and Martha

CONTENTS

ILLUSTRATIONS

ILLUSTRATION CREDITS

The author and publishers wish to express their thanks to the following for giving permission to use illustrative material.

National Archives, Kew: Front cover; 0.4 (both); 0.6 (below); 1.3 (both); 3.1 (all); 3.2 (both); 4.1 (both); 4.6; 5.1 (below); 5.3 (below, left and right); 5.4 (below, left and right); 5.5; 5.6 (all); 6.1 (above, right and below); 7.4 (both). Colour plates 1, 25, 26, 27, 28, 29 and 30.

Design Archives, Brighton (www.brighton.ac.uk/designarchives): 0.3; 0.6 (above); 0.7 (above); 0.8 (both); 1.4 (both); 2.1 (both); 2.2 (both); 2.4 (both); 4.2 (above and middle, centre and right); 4.3 (all); 4.4 (both); 4.5 (both); 5.1 (above); 5.3 (above); 5.4 (above); 6.1 (above, left); 6.2 (all); 6.4; 7.1 (all); 7.2 (all); 7.3 (above and below, right). Colour plates 8, 9, 10, 11 and 12.

Scott Brownrigg, with kind permission: 1.1.

The Estate of Abram Games, with kind permission of Naomi Games: 2.3

Michael Cooke-Yarborough, with kind permission of The C20 Society: colour plates 32 and 33.

Clifford Hatts, with kind permission: 8.1 (both).

Public Records Office of Northern Ireland: 5.2 (all).

LIST OF ILLUSTRATIONS

COLOUR PLATE SECTION

NOTES AND ABBREVIATIONS

NOTES

There is slippage between national labels in Festival discussions. 'England', 'Britain' and 'the United Kingdom' are all at times elided. 'Britain' is used in this book as shorthand to describe the four nations of England, Wales, Scotland and Northern Ireland, which more accurately should be described as either 'the United Kingdom' or 'Britain and Northern Ireland'. 'England', 'Wales', 'Scotland' or 'Northern Ireland' is used here to mean those nations individually.

The typefaces used in this book are Sentinel, Perpetua and Gill Sans.

ABBREVIATIONS

AA	Architectural Association
AAD	Archives of Art & Design, Victoria and Albert Museum
ABCA	Army Bureau of Current Affairs
ACP	Architects' Co-operative Partnership
AD	*Architectural Design*
AIA	Artists' International Association
AJ	*The Architects' Journal*
AR	*Architectural Review*
BBC	British Broadcasting Corporation
BFI	British Film Institute
BIF	British Industries Federation

CEMA	Council for Encouragement of Music and the Arts
CIAM	Congrès Internationaux d'Architecture Moderne
CL	*Country Life*
COI	Central Office of Information
COID	Council of Industrial Design
DA	Design Archives, University of Brighton
DIA	Design and Industries Association
DRU	Design Research Unit
EMB	Empire Marketing Board
GB	Gerald Barry
HMSO	His Majesty's Stationery Office
ICA	Institute of Contemporary Arts
LCC	London County Council
LSE	London School of Economics
MARS	Modern Architectural Research Group
MOI	Ministry of Information
NA	National Archives, Kew
NBL	National Book League
PRONI	Public Records Office of Northern Ireland
RCA	Royal College of Art
RIBA	Royal Institute of British Architects
RSA	Royal Society of Arts
TLS	*Times Literary Supplement*
V&A	Victoria and Albert Museum

ACKNOWLEDGEMENTS

Over the decade since I started the work towards this book, I have been helped by many dozens of people. Warm thanks must go first to Jeremy Aynsley and David Crowley at RCA who supervised my doctorate and were kind and generous mentors, always inspiring me to look further; to my PhD examiners, David Matless and Barry Curtis, with Hilary French chairing, who offered constructive criticism and pointed the way towards publication; to my editor, Philippa Brewster, who believed in this book and offered wise advice all the way through; and to Cecile Rault and others at I.B.Tauris who made it happen. Many thanks to Will Webb for designing the cover and to Paul Tompsett at Free Range Book Design & Production Limited for typesetting and Robert Bullard for copy-editing. Many thanks also to colleagues at the RCA, V&A and University of Brighton, in particular Jonathan Woodham, Catherine Moriarty, Lesley Whitworth, Sirpa Kutilainen and Carolyn Thompson.

Many who worked on the Festival gave me extraordinary insights (as well as welcoming me with cups of tea): Pauline Baines, Gordon and Ursula Bowyer, the late Jim Cadbury-Brown, Trevor Dannatt, the late Michael Grice, Clifford and Barbara Hatts, Alan Irvine, Willie Landels, Ray Leigh, Bob Maguire, Leonard Manasseh, Charles Plouviez, the late Ruari McLean, the late Philip and Philippa Powell, Jean Symons, the late Paul Wright, and the late Peter Youngman. Their children have also been very generous in sharing memories and collections: Jackie Barry, Julia Black, Richard and Mireille Burton, Dinah Casson, Faith Clark, Naomi Games, Henrietta Goodden, Kate Irvine, Mary-Lou Jennings and Carola Zogolovitch, as was Anthony Raymond, previously studio assistant to Barbara Jones. John and Frances Sorrell generously lent me their collection of Festival catalogues and ephemera, while Joanna Cox gave me material owned by her late father Anthony Cox, all of which has been invaluable.

Several very kind friends commented on draft chapters: Clare Oliver, in particular, and also Annie Atkins, Lisa Godson, Aasiya Lodhi, Alan Powers, Susanna Rustin, Chris Wild and Rachel Wrangham. Thanks also to the following, who have given help, support and insights during the years of research and writing: Rebecca Arnold, Juliet Ash, Richard Atkinson, Mary Banham, Andrew Barrow, Nick Beech, Rob Boddice, Barnabas Calder, Annette Carruthers, Emily Churchill, Becky Conekin, Michelle Cotton, Catherine Croft, Elizabeth Cumming, Elizabeth Darling, Rika Devos, Georgia Dickson, Konstanze Sylva Domhardt, Erdem Erten, Martin Francis, Annabel Freyberg, Christina Freyberg, Ivry Freyberg, David Gentleman, Sue Gilkes, Miles Glendinning, Michael Graham-Jones, Denise Hagströmer, Elain Harwood, Simon Houfe, the late Stanley Hunter, Lesley Jackson, Josie Kane, Peter Larkham, Belinda Lawley, Katri Lento, Jo Littler, Jack Lohmann, Harriet Mackay, Hugh Maguire, Eilish McGuinness, Nancy McLaren, Richard McLaren, Conor Mullan, Patricia Nicol, Stephanie Olsen, John Pendlebury, Fred Peskett, Mike Pitts, Michael Proudfoot, the late George Simner and members of the Festival of Britain Society, Sarah Quarmby, Paul Rennie, Livia Rezende, Deborah Sugg Ryan, Linda Sandino, Jana Scholze, Gill Scott, Annie Sutherland, Barry Turner, Richard Wentworth, Katharine Whitehorn and Ken Worpole.

I have been helped throughout by many knowledgeable people in libraries and archives: colleagues at Brighton University's Design Archives; staff at the National Art Library and Archive; National Archives at Kew; BFI; National Sound Archive; Public Records Office of Northern Ireland; Royal Society of Arts; RIBA; Museum of London; Book Trust; Mitchell Library and Archive in Glasgow; Museum of the Domestic Interior; and British Library. This has all cost a lot: many thanks to the Arts & Humanities Research Council for funding my doctoral study, thanks to The Wingate Foundation, the RCA and University of Brighton for invaluable smaller sums for pictures and materials. Thanks to all at KTMS and at Montpelier Community Nursery and to Mum and John for looking after Joe and Martha while I worked on this, and to Anna, Rachel, Sarah, Jess and Julia who kept me afloat. Lastly, innumerable thanks go to Valerian for being a wonderfully wise and patient critic and for giving me time and space to write it.

FOREWORD

In my twenties I visited London's South Bank several times with my late husband, Reyner Banham, who was then working at the *Architectural Review*. The magazine was long established and took a rather 'English' view of architecture of the period. The contributors, however, held open views and represented many opinions. We, and our friends, were far more interested in the work of European architects, Le Corbusier particularly, rather than what we considered somewhat 'tame' British work. As soon as travel was possible again after the Second World War, we all trooped over the Channel and visited as many monuments of the Modern Movement as we could.

The Festival of Britain buildings were a mixture of those by pre-war admirers of the International Style, who had been fighting for recognition in Britain pre-war, and more traditional styles. Some of the artefacts shown inside the pavilions though, particularly the Lion and Unicorn, representing Britain in its many manifestations, were hard to swallow, being too 'cute' for words. There was much, however, that was forward-looking and tough-minded.

The Festival of Britain was, of course, originally intended to celebrate the centenary of 1851, as well as being an International Expo. As things turned out, largely because Europe was on her knees in 1951, it could only be a celebration of peace in Britain alone, but because Britain had committed herself to assisting the USA with her postwar problems, she found herself helping with the Korean War and the Festival budget was cut in half. There was talk of cancelling it altogether, but it was clearly too far along for there to be any kind of saving of money or resources.

In the end the Festival was presented as a 'cheer up' effort and 'let's see some colour' after the greyness of the war and long depression before it. The South

Bank undoubtedly supplied this last element. The newspapers and magazines talked of screens of colour 'hiding filthy old Victorian London' – a sacrilegious statement only a few years later. In fact 'Festival prose' is hard to believe now and could not have been acceptable had the nation not wanted to hear it. The propaganda worked partly, I believe, because such cajoling was seen as one of the successful tools that pulled us through the war. Admittedly many of the design ideas and use of materials were borrowed from the Continent, especially Italy, but the British people had not seen them and were thrilled.

A foreseen shortage of materials for building after the war meant that the South Bank pavilions needed to be frugal with traditional house building bricks, slates etc. Many of the pavilions used steel and glass and were carefully designed to be dismantled and used again off-site. Bids were made to achieve this end but politics got in the way and only one pavilion – the Country – managed to escape to Edgware where it became a synagogue. All the other structures were smashed and carted away the day after the Festival closed – an act of vandalism claimed to have been ordered by Churchill, then back in power, who was convinced that the Festival was a Labour Party plot, an advertisement for the Welfare State.

In 1974 I was invited to curate a show on the Festival at the Royal Institute of British Architects' (RIBA) Heinz Gallery. While working on the show, there were many amusing moments. One I particularly recall was when my husband and son borrowed a Jeep and transported a huge figure of a boxer from Hugh Casson's house to the Heinz Gallery at Portman Square, avoiding traffic and street furniture by inches and attracting astonished crowds all the way. In the 1970s I was also approached to help organize an exhibition at the Victoria and Albert Museum to mark the twenty-fifth anniversary of the Festival. The then Director, Dr Roy Strong, thought that it would be interesting to look again at an event which covered the whole of Britain and was the last time a truly concerted effort was made to present a countrywide view of itself. Visitors and contributors to that exhibition retained detailed memories of 1951 in its many forms and threatened to make it an exercise in nostalgia. It was very well attended and was accompanied by a book *A Tonic to the Nation*, which has been in great demand from scholars looking at the period ever since.

I was struck at the time by the noticeably international quality of the sculpture and felt sure that future generations would find a fascinating PhD subject there. Certainly younger scholars are increasingly showing an interest in the whole postwar period, as I know from students and lecturers who still ask me for interviews as a survivor, and as this book reveals.

Mary Banham, London

THE MAJOR FESTIVAL EXHIBITIONS

A Brief Introduction

The Festival of Britain was held across the four nations of the United Kingdom in 1951. This is an introduction to the major events. The central focus of the celebrations was the seven large government-sponsored exhibitions and the Battersea Pleasure Gardens, open between May and September 1951.

SOUTH BANK EXHIBITION, LONDON
(4 MAY TO 30 SEPTEMBER 1951)

The major South Bank Exhibition, the Festival's spectacular centrepiece, was held on the bank of the River Thames across from Westminster. The site was divided across the middle by a railway bridge and designed around 22 freestanding pavilions all showing 'The Land and People of Britain'. The only building designed to be permanent was the London County Council's Royal Festival Hall. The only pre-Festival building that remained on the site was the Shot Tower, which had been used in the industrial production of shot and which became a radar tower during the Festival. In addition to the major pavilions, the 1851 Centenary Pavilion recalled the Crystal Palace, and many restaurants, cafés and bars were set around them. The site was landscaped with fountains and water features, freestanding sculpture set within it.

KEY

FESTIVAL OF BRITAIN

Exhibitions

Arts Festivals

LONDON
May 4 - September 30
South Bank Exhibition
May 3 - October 31
Festival Pleasure Gardens, Battersea Park
May 3 - September 30
Exhibition of Science, South Kensington
Exhibition of Architecture, Lansbury, Poplar
Exhibition of Books, Victoria & Albert Museum
May 3 - June 30. Festival Season of the Arts

EDINBURGH
August 19 - September 8
International Festival of Music and Drama
July - September: Exhibition of Scottish
Architecture and Traditional Crafts
August 3 - September 15
Exhibition of 18th Century Books

BELFAST
June 1 - August 31
Ulster Farm and Factory Exhibition
May 7 - June 30
Arts Festival

Map labels:
INVERNESS June 17-30 · ABERDEEN July 30-Aug 13 · PERTH May 27-June 16 · EDINBURGH See Key Panel · GLASGOW May 28-Aug · DUMFRIES June 24-30 · BELFAST See Key Panel · YORK June 3-17 · LIVERPOOL July 22-Aug 12 · NORWICH June 18-30 · LLANGOLLEN July 3-8 · ALDEBURGH June 8-17 · LLANRWST Aug 6-11 · CAMBRIDGE July 30-Aug 18 · WORCESTER Sept 2-7 · STRATFORD-UPON-AVON April-Oct · CHELTENHAM July 2-14 · LONDON See Key Panel · CANTERBURY July 18-Aug 10 · St. DAVIDS July 10-13 · SWANSEA Sept 16-29 · OXFORD July 2-16 · BATH May 20-June 2 · BRIGHTON July 16-Aug 25 · BOURNEMOUTH June 3-17

Exhibitions and Arts Festivals

0.1 FESTIVAL OF BRITAIN MAP (see also colour plate 1)
A 'constellation of events' across the nation. Map
drawn by Eric Fraser showing nationwide Festival
events, including exhibitions and arts festivals.

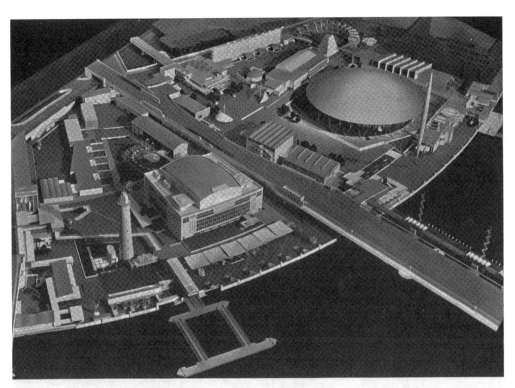

THE
SOUTH BANK SITE

0.2 SOUTH BANK EXHIBITION
Model of site from *South Bank Exhibition Guide*.

0.3 SOUTH BANK EXHIBITION
South Bank at dusk looking from the Station Gate
entrance towards the Thames; Dome of Discovery is to
the left, Transport to the right.

1951 EXHIBITION OF SCIENCE AT SOUTH KENSINGTON, LONDON (4 MAY TO 30 SEPTEMBER 1951)

The Exhibition of Science at South Kensington showcased the latest advances in science, telling a visual 'story' through working models and displays, developing its theme, according to the exhibition guide, 'by means of things you can see and believe'. The theme was developed by Science Director Ian Cox, co-ordinating designer Brian Peake, with captions by popular scientist Jacob Bronowski. Sections included: 'What Matter Is', 'Atomic Structure' and 'How Atoms Form Substances'. The show attempted to put on display abstract scientific ideas and theories in a wider context and included a mock-up of a chemical laboratory and a science cinema that showed British films about science and industry.

1951 EXHIBITION OF ARCHITECTURE AT LANSBURY, POPLAR (3 MAY TO 30 SEPTEMBER 1951)

The exhibition of town planning and building research at Poplar in East London enabled visitors to experience 'live' architecture as they visited an area comprised of two churches, various housing estates, schools and shopping centres. A plan for navigating through the streets was offered to visitors who were invited to make a comparison between the interiors of one new, model building which had been furnished for the occasion and another, older house – 'Gremlin Grange' – providing an example of so-called 'bad' design. The exhibition had been one catalyst for redevelopment of this former slum area of the East End as part of a broader vision for development set out in Abercrombie's *Greater London Plan* of 1944. London County Council planning officer Arthur Ling oversaw the Exhibition. Architects including Frederick Gibberd and Yorke, Rosenberg and Mardall were invited to design elements.

1951 EXHIBITION OF INDUSTRIAL POWER, GLASGOW (28 MAY TO 18 AUGUST 1951)

After the South Bank, the largest and most ambitious Festival of Britain exhibition was that of Industrial Power in Glasgow. The show's theme was the 'conquest of power' as seen through the two main sources of that power: coal and water. It was intended to hold 'a magnifying glass over the power, shipbuilding and heavy engineering sequences in the South Bank Exhibition'.[1]

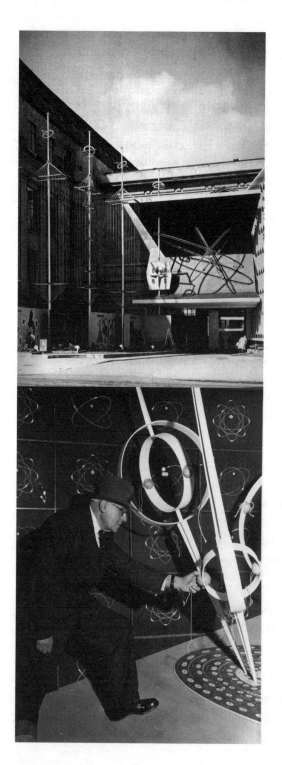

0.4 EXHIBITION OF SCIENCE, SOUTH KENSINGTON (see also colour plate 3) (Above) Entrance to the exhibition in the new museum wing before opening; (Below) Arranging one of the illustrative exhibits of 'What Matter Is'. Display designer: Brian Peake.

Shopping Centre and Market Place seen from Chrisp Street

Plan views of a maisonette over a shop, showing lower and upper floors

0.5 *LIVE ARCHITECTURE EXHIBITION, LANSBURY
ESTATE, POPLAR* (see also colour plate 4)
(Above) Model of shopping centre and Market Place,
with clock tower in foreground, seen from Chrisp Street;
(Below) Model showing double arcade of shops and
paved Market Place. Architect: Frederick Gibberd.

0.6 EXHIBITION OF HEAVY INDUSTRY,
KELVIN HALL, GLASGOW (see also colour plate 5)
(Above) The Hall of Power, exhibition entrance, designed
by Basil Spence with Thomas Whalen's 'Coal Cliff';
(Below) Architect Victor Prus and Glasgow University
lecturer J.R. Atkinson discussing their model atomic
energy display – a 30 feet high million volt lightning
machine – for the Hall of the Future.

Designed by architect Basil Spence and organized by journalist Alastair Borthwick and held at Kelvin Hall, which at the time boasted of being the largest exhibition space in the British Empire, the exhibition covered 100,000 square feet. On the way in, visitors arrived in the Hall of Power and passed beneath a vast sculptured mural of a coal cliff, which reached from floor to roof in a giant crescent (the biggest piece of sculpture ever executed in Scotland, being 105 feet long). A symbolic sun was created by a 'stroboscopic' flash contained in a Perspex sphere. In the water section, 20,000 gallons of water cascaded over the roof of a bright glass tunnel leading into halls devoted to hydroelectricity, civil engineering and irrigation. Halls were also devoted to shipbuilding, railways and atomic energy.[2]

1951 ULSTER FARM AND FACTORY EXHIBITION, BELFAST
(1 JUNE TO 31 AUGUST 1951)

The Ulster Farm and Factory Exhibition was held at Castlereagh, a suburb of Belfast, telling a story of 'how Ulster earns its living through agriculture and industry'.[3] The exhibition, designed by Willy de Majo and L. Bramberg, with R. Ferguson and S. McIlveen as architects for the factory building and Henry Lynch-Robinson as architect to the agricultural exhibits, was 'set out amid lagoons and gardens', according to the Guide, and built around a new model factory on a four-acre industrial estate at Castlereagh. The site belonged to the government of Northern Ireland, which also financed the exhibition, and had as its central theme the continuing tradition of skill and craftsmanship in farm and factory, especially in the linen industry. Outside were the Old Farmhouse of 1851, thatched and with a turf-burning fireplace, set next to the Farm of the Future. There was also a Children's Play Centre. Inside the factory building was the Linen Hall, which included displays of various other textiles including rayon, cotton, silk, wool and nylon and a large agricultural section.

1951 LAND TRAVELLING EXHIBITION
(MAY TO OCTOBER 1951)

Designed by Richard Levin, 3,000 objects were carried on a fleet of lorries to four sites in Britain: Manchester, Leeds, Birmingham and Nottingham. These venues were chosen based on their population, accessibility and the limited opportunities that inhabitants might have to visit London.

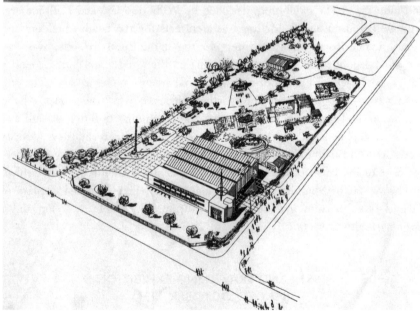

0.7 ULSTER FARM AND FACTORY EXHIBITION, BELFAST
(Above) New model factory built at Castlereagh for the
Farm and Factory Exhibition, designed by R. Ferguson and S.
McIlveen;
(Below) Drawing of site from Ulster Farm and Factory Guide.

In Manchester, the exhibition was held at the City Hall and in Birmingham at Bingley Hall, but in Leeds and Nottingham there were no permanent buildings in which the exhibition could be displayed, so a rigid structure covered by 100,000 square feet of canvas was erected to contain it. The exhibition aimed to be eye-catching: in the Corridor of Time section 16 large pendulums swinging over the heads of visitors illuminated and demonstrated the progress of the British 'throughout the ages'.

1951 FESTIVAL SHIP *CAMPANIA* SEA TRAVELLING EXHIBITION (MAY TO OCTOBER 1951)

The Festival Ship *HMS Campania* was a miniature replica of the South Bank Exhibition, telling the same 'story' for those unable to get to London, and was carried to ten sites: Southampton, Dundee, Newcastle, Hull, Plymouth, Bristol, Cardiff, Belfast, Birkenhead and Glasgow. Built at Harland and Wolff's shipyard in Belfast, the ship had been an escort aircraft carrier during the Second World War. Designed principally by James Holland, the theme had been devised by the Director of Science and Technology, Ian Cox, and showed Britain's contribution to world civilization particularly in science, technology and industrial design.

FESTIVAL PLEASURE GARDENS, BATTERSEA, LONDON (3 MAY TO 3 NOVEMBER 1951)

The Pleasure Gardens at Battersea in London gave relief and relaxation to weary visitors who had been round the South Bank Exhibition. Chief Designer was James Gardner. A boat ferried visitors up and down the River Thames between the South Bank and Battersea Park. The Pleasure Gardens offered a six-acre amusement park, including a children's zoo and pet corner; a miniature railway line; two theatres: one dedicated to music hall performances, the other to ballets, revues and marionettes; a tree-top walk; a Mississippi Show Boat and a huge tented dance pavilion. The Pleasure Gardens were run by a private company and kept open for five years after the Festival to ensure they paid their way.

0.8 *FESTIVAL PLEASURE GARDENS, BATTERSEA*
(Above) Aerial view of site by Aerofilms;
(Below) The Far Tottering and Oyster Creek Railway
booking office.

Introduction

'IT WAS NICE, WASN'T IT'

It was nice, wasn't it ... Festival year? It was the nicest thing that happened in England in the whole of my life.

Marghanita Laski, *The Observer*, Sunday 6 July 1952

The Millennium Dome was a gigantic, surreal, Ruritanian folly. It made Tony Blair look like a reincarnation of Mad King Ludwig. For a mere £1 billion, he gave the British people a tent filled with nothing in particular in a forgotten, inaccessible part of London.

Bryan Appleyard, *The Sunday Times*, 9 May 2010

I am too young to have been one of the many who visited the Festival of Britain in 1951. I was, though, one of the four and a half million that went to the Millennium Dome at Greenwich during the year 2000, the event that sparked my interest in the earlier Festival. For, from early on in the gestation of the Greenwich Dome, media commentators were making a crude comparison between the two. While both events had as their centrepiece a Thames-side Dome, the similarities ended there; 1951 was cast as hero, 2000 as villain.[4] The Festival had – journalists believed – served a solid purpose: to cheer people up after the war, run by politicians with a mission to put Britain back on her feet and designed by architects inspired by a laudable vision to rebuild Britain. The Dome's purpose, meanwhile, was unclear, beyond marking a change in the Christian calendar and providing another vehicle for a New Labour government pitifully enthusiastic about rebranding the nation as 'cool Britannia'. And, so the characterization went, it was overseen by a dubious politician (minister without portfolio Peter Mandelson) dubbed the 'Prince of Darkness', who, like any comic-book villain got his just deserts when he became embroiled in a loans scandal and had to step down; it was managed by an incompetent civil servant who was replaced partway through by a Disneyland manager. The Greenwich exhibition was immortalised in daily newspaper headlines about '£1m vacuum cleaners' and '120 ft magic mushrooms' celebrating 'hippie drug culture'. Meanwhile, the Richard Rogers building itself looked like it might become a white elephant, standing forlornly empty for several years after the Millennium celebrations, an extended metaphor for its purposelessness.

While the Dome was being loudly and uncompromisingly assigned to the 'fiasco zone' (even by *The Guardian*, which might otherwise have been assumed to be its natural ally), the Festival was remembered as successful and popular.[5] How strange, it seemed to me, that attitudes to two occasions only five decades apart, staged by two Labour governments, might be so polarised. The work towards this book started soon after the Greenwich Dome closed its doors in 2000, a journey that has taken me around the United Kingdom, to visit collections in museums and archives, to see buildings still standing, and landscapes where buildings once stood. It has seen me welcomed into the houses of many dozens of people who worked on, or were influenced by, the events between May and September 1951.

Memory is central to this book. The Festival provided an occasion on which to remember conquests past and to project a sense of national identity back to the very beginning of 'British' time. It was an occasion on which to forget recent terrible times and to rethink a national sense of place, to fall in love with the land again, in the face of the rebuilding of Britain. And it is people's memories of the Festival – their passions for it, their scepticism about it, their reasoning about it, gathered in the past decade – that provide the backbone to this history.

The Festival of Britain: A Land and Its People is an account of the Festival imagination – the sense of place that inspired its organization and design – rather than a singular account of its buildings, objects or politics. It shows how architects' and designers' visions of the future set out in exhibition landscapes were strongly shaped by their attachment to the land of Britain and the history of that land. This was manifest in the Festival's exhibitions, events, films and books. This book also shows how these exhibitions, organized by an ex-newspaper editor, became spatial stories. Their visual and spatial qualities were inextricably bound up with words and texts. This form of mass-communication, this 'propaganda in three-dimensions', was a dying medium. It had been evolved from the interwar period and was widely used during the Second World War to disseminate public information. Only a few years after the Festival of Britain, television would replace exhibition as the universal medium of mass communication. Ultimately, the Festival of Britain, which centred on the idea of 'the land and people of Britain' and showed every aspect of British life, was an occasion on which British people could fall in love again with their land.[6]

Ask a visitor to the Millennium Dome at Greenwich what they remember of it and many shrug and ask what it was all for. It provoked a sense of dislocation and detachment, of a space without substance for its visitors. Filled with the furniture of non-place: coffee chains, a McDonald's restaurant, and embryonic cyber cafés, the Greenwich building left many feeling bewildered and bemused. Ask a visitor to the Festival of Britain in 1951 what they remember of it and passions are aroused: oh! the enormity of the mushroom-shaped Dome of Discovery, the soaring beauty of the statuesque Skylon and the gaiety of the Battersea Funfair! Those strikingly bright colours that were unlike anything seen for years in drab homes and monotone cities! That heavenly feeling of liberation at leaving home for a day-trip to London, where eating and drinking in the open-air and waltzing after dark were not censored, but positively encouraged. Oh, the very wonder of it all!

Photo albums from 1951 yield a similar impression, of a wonderful new world in which anything was possible. Vera and Jack's family album, found discarded in a Winchester junk shop, perhaps like many thousands of albums lovingly compiled across the country, holds five tiny black-and-white photographs of a late summer visit to London's Festival at the South Bank and Battersea, nestled beside their snaps of a summer holiday at Bournemouth Sands.[7] Their photos are long views of the structures that have become synonymous with 'Festival': the Dome, Skylon, and fountains that are defining features of this strange new landscape. Derek and Jean Baker's album, with its tiny snaps, also records a trip to the South Bank. The Dome and Skylon are seen from several angles; Jean stands on the South Bank's concourse wearing a smart two-piece tweed suit and carrying a picnic basket; Derek wears a dark, double-breasted suit while posing at the base of the towering Skylon.[8] The photograph album of the Holland family from Newcastle-upon-Tyne repeats this pattern: images of the Skylon and fountains mingle with shots of the family, dressed up in smart suits, eating sandwiches beneath the Dome of Discovery. These are images of emancipation, of a populous reconnecting with itself after severe and extended privation, of people, many still in demob clothes – the ones issued to help servicemen make the transition back into civilian life – enjoying their first day out in years.

0.9. VERA AND JACK'S ALBUM
Page from a family album recording a visit to the South
Bank Exhibition and Battersea, September 1951.

Festival snaps are a visual record of a population awakening from the trauma of war. Memories rely on a common condition: on absence of opportunity experienced in the wake of war. They focus on the smell, the taste, the sound and, most often, the sight of the Festival. Remembering a childhood visit one woman said 'I don't remember a lot. It was the excitement of going and getting a new dress and new shoes. I do remember it being clean and white after the drabness of London, and getting candyfloss,'[9] while another said 'my palate still remembers the shock of tasting its first-ever chilled drink – a glass of cold milk in one of the pavilions.'[10] Yet another asked 'Do you remember the colours that glared across the river, olive and scarlet and yellow and blue, balls and windmills and walls and doors, dabs of pure colour such as we didn't know we had always hungered for until at last they were there?'[11] The Festival allowed people feelings and experiences that had long been missing.

Beyond the appeal to the four senses, Festival-goers also recall the strong emotional response it sparked in them. 'The excitement and euphoria which [the Festival] produced were, for me, irresistible,' wrote one young Londoner.[12] But beside recollections of delight and elation, another emotion is also present. 'When I stood on the Embankment at the bottom of Northumberland Avenue, and saw the lights and colours of the Festival across the river on that first morning', one man wrote later, 'it was so utterly beautiful and exciting that I wept.'[13] Alongside the relief at the presence of sensory stimulation after its absence for many long years, are recollections of grief and loss. Intermingled with joy is sorrow. As much as the Festival was a celebration, it was an occasion on which to forget, to consign the misery of the previous years to a state of oblivion. It provided a chance to grieve what was lost, as much as a chance to imagine again. And the recollection of the Festival, which at the time had seemed to be a vivid augury of future happiness, is enough to inspire mourning for a future that never, perhaps, materialised.

The Festival is remembered in retrospect by its visitors as an occasion on which they experienced waves of feeling: of sorrow, joy, relief, elation, optimism, a feeling that it had been, well, just 'nice', a sense that all was right with the world. This reconnection was provided through the creation of temporary places – populated with buildings, landscapes and things – allowing visitors to dream of their battered country made new. Inheriting characteristics of the old but inspired by the new, by a vivid technical futurism, the Festival of Britain set out to provide a sense of place for a British people in need of location.

While in 2011, the Festival's sixtieth anniversary year, there was much enthusiasm for remembering the occasion as a party at the South Bank, much of the detail of Festival events organized up and down the country had been forgotten. The majority of the hundreds of advisers, designers and administrators employed to set the scene for 'one united act of national reassessment and one corporate reaffirmation of faith in the nation's future' made contributions that are no longer relevant to visitors recalling the events. But this memory loss was part of the occasion, which was about healing, 'a tonic to the nation', in the now well-known words of its organizers, about getting better and moving on.[14] For if the Festival was remembered by many as an uplifting party, pointing the way forward, it was designed as a reconstruction of the British land and built by people with a deep love of that land.

This love of the British land went to the very heart of the Festival. Its organizers decided early on that all the events would be structured around the pivotal idea of the 'Land and People' of Britain. The focus therefore became re-forging the link between people and place that had been severed by war and – going deeper – by the perceived impact of the Industrial Revolution, a recurring theme of discussions. The Festival's architects and designers, defending the postwar space of Britain as they did through these exhibitions, were shaped by a particular attachment to landscape and environment, a topophilia. It was this attachment that poet W.H. Auden described as shaping poet and writer John Betjeman's work, the year Festival planning started. Auden had distinguished 'topophilia' from love of nature, 'wild or unhumanised nature holds no charms for the average topophil because it is lacking in history', he wrote.[15] A topophils' love of place, according to Auden's definition, was shaped by the memory and history of that place. This topophil love of the land and the history of that land may initially seem a long way from the modernism of Festival architects who aspired to rebuild the world in aluminium, glass and concrete. But as this book will demonstrate, there was a deep vein of topophilia running through the thinking and design of the Festival. Again and again modernist Festival architects, landscape architects and designers illustrating the 'land and people' showed themselves to be in tune with the past, not at odds with it.[16] They had developed a tempered modernism, suited to the needs of the moment.

The Festival of Britain: A Land and Its People explores the way these unparalleled nationwide events, to which so many hundreds of people contributed, were a ground for experimentation with what it meant to be modern and British. The models for a newly reconstructed country that were offered – which looked 'modern' – were shaped by a deep engagement with the British land and its history. The book is spread across eight chapters. It starts by tracing the Festival from its origins in Chapter 1; Chapter 2 traces the development of the Festival exhibitions from their roots in nineteenth century world's fairs, inter-war national exhibitions and wartime information shows; Chapter 3 explores the evolution of the architecture and landscape of the exhibitions, in particular the strong influence that came from the English Picturesque and ideas about visual planning; Chapter 4 shows how land and people were brought together in the exhibitions; Chapter 5 looks at how productivity was exhibited; Chapter 6 discusses displays of English language; Chapter 7 explores homes and neighbourhoods on show; Chapter 8 concludes by looking at the closure, aftermath and legacy of the exhibitions. In each, the way the 'land and people of Britain' became both subject and object of the exhibitions is the overriding focus.

1

'THIS FESTIVAL OF OURS
IS A DEADLY SERIOUS AFFAIR'

If anyone should still argue that the money spent on an exhibition could be better spent these days on armaments, I can only answer him that a great people's survival does not simply depend on a naïve choice between guns and butter.

Gerald Barry, *Flair*, September 1950

By 1945, the year the Second World War ended, the United Kingdom had been ravaged by six years of war. With the explosion of atomic bombs at Nagasaki and Hiroshima, a new threat was unleashed on the world: a war to end all wars. Clement Attlee's Labour administration entered government that same year, with a fearsome amount to achieve in rebuilding and re-housing Britain, and an ambitious programme for sweeping nationalization of major industries and public utilities that included the Bank of England, coal, gas, electricity, the railways, canals, road haulage and iron and steel, and an aspiration to nationalize the land itself.[1]

The same year, industrial design consultant John Gloag repeated an idea broached privately a couple of years earlier by the Royal Society of Arts (the organization that encouraged arts, manufactures and commerce and had initiated the Great Exhibition in 1851). In a September letter to *The Times*, Gloag proposed a centenary be held of the Great Exhibition at Crystal Palace in Hyde Park of 1851. This would, he believed, provide an occasion upon which to boost trade, gain prestige and show off national inventiveness.[2] Three days later, Gerald Barry, Editor of Liberal broadsheet *News Chronicle*, echoed this proposal. In an open letter addressed to the President of the

Board of Trade, Sir Stafford Cripps, he urged that the country needed to stimulate British exports through 'a great Trade and Cultural Exhibition,' a centenary of 1851. This project, Barry believed, would be 'an opportunity for the Labour Government to give an imaginative lead to the nation and the Empire'.[3] Barry's enthusiasm for an event in 1951 had been sparked just after war ended when, he recalled, seasoned exhibition designer Misha Black had visited his News Chronicle office 'with the drawings for a magnificent new Exhibition building which was to be constructed, as it seems to me now, as a kind of interplanetary edifice more or less suspended in the sky'.[4] Black's futuristic exhibition site, drawn by Hilton Wright and later published in The Ambassador magazine, ingeniously anticipated the choice of the South Bank as central site of the 1951 events by several months. Its single structure was based around the framework of a spiral ramp from which the buildings would rise in terraces reaching 1,500 feet, topped by a vertical feature that anticipated the Festival's Skylon.

Where Barry's initial letter had addressed the trade advantage of such an event, successive articles published in News Chronicle focused on its potential value for international diplomacy in the face of the developing Cold War. 'Great Exhibition would assist world unity' ran a headline quoting London County Council (LCC) Leader Lord Latham, declaring that 'In view of the terrifying possibilities of the atomic bomb, the common bonds of culture will be the greatest insurance against future war.'[5] As the threat of the atomic war became increasingly magnified, from late 1945, the idea of a universal exhibition in 1951 evolved in the pages of News Chronicle.

Responding to Gerald Barry's open letter in October 1945, Stafford Cripps declared he was in favour of the idea of a major exhibition in 1951 and the Board of Trade would investigate the subject further in a committee under the chairmanship of prominent industrialist Lord Ramsden, its brief 'to consider the part which Exhibitions and Fairs should play in the promotion of Export Trade in the Post-War Era'. The Ramsden Committee believed fervently in the economic value of major exhibitions. Reporting in 1946, they unequivocally recommended a 'Universal International Exhibition' be held in central London in 1951 'to demonstrate to the world the recovery of the United Kingdom from the effects of the war in the moral, cultural, spiritual and material fields', and as a demonstration of international progress. The process of reconstruction should happen on the level of morale-building and cultural and spiritual enrichment, as well in actual rebuilding, with a major exhibition as the perfect showcase for this. As added justification for the expenditure, the Committee recommended, during the same period, notable progress should be made in the provision of public institutions, industrial

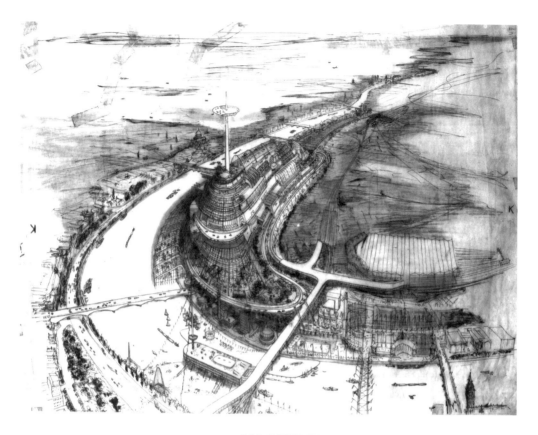

1.1 'A PROJECT FOR THE UNIVERSAL INTERNATIONAL EXHIBITION OF 1951', IMAGINED BY MISHA BLACK, DRAWN BY HILTON WRIGHT
Black explained, 'The great spiral ramp forms a framework on which the buildings rise in terraces to the sky platform fifteen hundred feet above London. Here the exhibition is shown sited on the South Bank of the Thames, but it could be positioned equally well in Hyde Park or Regent's Park.'

buildings, dwelling houses and schools.[6] This way the impact would be very tangible.

By 1947, the legacy of war continued to take its toll on Britain. Extreme shortages and extraordinary deprivation prevailed and nearly 2 million people were officially out of work. After a horrendous winter at the start of the year British manufacturing virtually ground to a halt. At the same time, industrial action meant coal production was half a million tons short and steel also in short supply, partly due to a scarcity of skilled labour. In spring 1947, heavy flooding had washed away crops, producing the threat of food shortages, and continuing rations in Britain fell well below the wartime average. More serious even than rationing, since it affected Britain's ability to buy provisions, was the shortage of foreign exchange currency. This was a result of depleted reserves and extensive national borrowing from North America. Loans from the USA and Canada, agreed after the war had ended, which, it had been hoped, would last until recovery could be achieved in 1951, were almost entirely exhausted by 1947. By September the dollar-poor Labour government had virtually no convertible currency, a situation that precipitated an exchange crisis in government, to be repeated soon after, in 1949 and again in 1951.

The British were in no doubt at the end of the Second World War, with conferences at Yalta and Potsdam, then bombings at Nagasaki and Hiroshima, that they needed their own atomic project. Through this they could fight the potential threat emerging as the division between Western democratic, capitalist countries and communist states of the East widened. The British government's public response started as the development of fissile material that could either be used for nuclear power or for nuclear weapons. But in 1947 Prime Minister Clement Attlee's Labour administration decided, under a veil of secrecy, to develop an atomic bomb for Britain. That year Attlee also set up his first Cabinet Committee on Subversive Activities. So Britain began in earnest to construct a Cold War state alongside the existing one.

Into the developing context of suspicion and fear, and in close proximity with discussions about the worsening international climate taking place in Whitehall, came the arrangements for this unprecedented nationwide celebration in 1951. Clement Attlee's administration accepted the recommendations of the Ramsden Committee and Herbert Morrison was put in charge of events, combining positions as Lord President of the Council, Deputy Prime Minister and Leader of the House of Commons. Professing 'we ought to do something jolly ... we need something to give Britain a lift,' Morrison took a close interest in supporting and promoting centenary celebrations for 1951.[7] But despite the government's professed light-hearted gesture in staging these events, Attlee and Morrison's interest in marking the centenary focused on its potential instrumental value in improving national morale, boosting trade and in displaying Britain as exemplar democracy to the world. This was an impoverished administration, already under enormous financial strain, and such expenditure had to be justified.

Herbert Morrison formally presented the idea of an event to mark the 'Centenary of the Great Exhibition of 1851' to Parliament on 5 December 1947. These events, he announced, would be accompanied by no new building and, in spite of Ramsden's recommendations for an international exhibition, all would be focused on Britain alone.[8] An international trade fair had been ruled out for 1951 as the possibilities of attracting foreign trade were considered limited and, as Morrison later explained to Parliament, shortages of manpower and materials had dictated that Commonwealth governments and administrations could not be invited to take part.[9] This British focus also reflected the restricted budget available. Ultimately, it better served the government's propaganda purpose: Britain's past achievements and future promise could be shown off to best advantage. MPs raised various concerns: about the use of already restricted materials, the diversion of labour from key building projects, the events' dubious benefits beyond London, and the danger of Sunday openings; but despite these continuing issues the proposal attracted cross-party support and a pledge of budget. To direct the events a new temporary department – the Festival Office – was set up in Whitehall, the heart of British government.

Gerald Barry (1898–1968) was appointed Director-General in 1947.[10] For 11 years editor of *News Chronicle*, he strongly believed that a new Britain should not only be planned in government, through policy and principle, but that architects and designers had as crucial a part to play by building it in three-dimensions. Before the war he had been a patron for new building in his own right: The Forge House, a cottage which Barry had commissioned English modernist architect F.R.S. Yorke (1906–62) to convert and extend, was an extraordinary convergence of old and new and considered one of Yorke's most successful and subtle interwar commissions. Barry had considered it crucial that readers of *News Chronicle* be given the chance to engage with contemporary architectural practice. Open architecture competitions, run in the pages of the *Chronicle*, encouraged radical architectural solutions.[11] Architectural columns run in the paper were also Barry's innovation. The first of their kind, they caught the imagination of a public hungry to be informed about a world under reconstruction.

Barry brought with him a conviction that people should be privy to reconstruction as work-in-progress. In his first public statement as Director-General, Barry proclaimed that these events – by now named 'The Festival of Britain'[12] – would show 'The British contribution to civilization past, present and future, in the arts, in science and technology and in industrial design' and not be confined to London, but, with a 'strong measure of devolution'.[13] This devolution would, he hoped, stop activity from being focused solely in the capital, and ensure its manifestations be dispersed across the country. To fit with this devolved model, eight major government-funded events were planned across Britain and Northern Ireland. Committee discussions indicate that the title 'Festival' was chosen to try to keep the definition of events as loose as possible. Having a nationwide form, the Festival became an occasion on which to focus on, and celebrate, the place of Britain.

PROJECTING BRITAIN

This focus on the four nations of England, Wales, Scotland and Northern Ireland – the United Kingdom, but almost always described in Festival rhetoric as 'Britain' – allowed the Labour government to determine the ideological terms of the Festival. These events were to be more than a simple appeal to buy and sell, not merely the opportunity for a modern industrial expansionist nation to set out its stall. Refuting connotations of international trade or commercialism, Barry decided the focus would, instead, be on telling a national 'story'. In the light of Britain's retreat from empire with the granting of self-government to India, Pakistan, Burma and Ceylon by the Attlee government from 1947 to 1949, the Festival's form limited the possible references to Britain's waning international influence. By making the Festival coterminous with the physical boundaries of the four nations of England, Scotland, Wales and Northern Ireland, the internal logic was put in place for excluding the British Empire from the exhibition's content.[14]

Various sites across the length and breadth of London were mooted for a spectacular centrepiece to the Festival of Britain. Hyde Park was an obvious contender for its commemorative significance as the site of the 1851 Exhibition, but after deliberation the Festival Council agreed on London's South Bank.[15] The South Bank worked well on a practical level, being close to the historic centre of London. Becoming even more accessible from the heart of London via newly built bridges, the South Bank of the Thames had already been marked out in 1943 and 1944 LCC plans as ripe for development into a cultural quarter.[16] This was, in fact, returning it to an earlier use: the South Bank had been the site of several short-lived pleasure gardens during the eighteenth century. The South Bank also worked on a symbolic level, as its organizers acknowledged. With the site's rapid transformation from a wasteland populated by the old Lion Brewery (built in 1836–7 and operating until 1931), disused industrial buildings and slum dwellings into a 'magical city', populated with new buildings and landscapes, the South Bank would become a vivid metaphor for reconstruction in action.[17] The new site would include 4½ acres reclaimed from Thames mud. Twinned with a funfair downriver at Battersea, the Festival Pleasure Gardens, to give South Bank visitors light relief, the South Bank served as not only the centre of an extended web of national exhibitions but also as a microcosm of the island nation itself where people could see Britain at work, at play and everything in between.

Elsewhere, at Lansbury in east London, an exhibition of 'Live Architecture' was proposed, showing the possibilities for areas under reconstruction through the building of new housing, schools, churches and shops; a major science exhibition would be mounted at South Kensington to show the potential of future technology; and beyond London an exhibition of Farm and Factory was to be held in Belfast to put industrial and agricultural production on show. Glasgow was to be the site of an Exhibition of Heavy Industry, while two travelling exhibitions were to take the Festival further afield, one focused on industrial production, the other a miniature version of the South Bank.

By 1948 a plethora of committees, supported by the Festival Office, had started organizing events. The Festival Council was the most senior of these, chaired by Winston Churchill's wartime confidant, the Conservative General Lord Ismay. Ismay had held various senior defence roles, including, as Head of the Committee of the Chiefs of Staff, being central to the development of nuclear capability in Britain. Ismay's committee had overseen the establishment of the Department of Scientific and Industrial Research to direct this work, known, for purposes of secrecy as 'The Directorate of Tube Alloys'. Ismay's Festival appointment was a strategic masterstroke for the Labour government, arresting the carping of the right wing press and Conservative parliamentarians and giving a semblance of cross-party support to events mounted by a Labour administration.

Ismay's Festival Council was made up of luminaries, amongst them planner Sir Patrick Abercrombie, poet T.S. Eliot, art historian Sir Kenneth Clark and actor John Gielgud.[18] At its first meeting in May 1948, the young Princess Elizabeth spoke, as President of the Royal Society of Arts, to welcome the Council, encouraging them to follow the example set in 1851 of emphasizing the application of the arts to industrial design. She alluded to the precarious international situation, observing that 'at a time when the world is racked with uncertainties there is a special virtue in dwelling upon the arts of peace'.[19]

As propaganda in a new war, the Cold War, the Festival needed to speak both to home and international audiences. This was well-trodden territory, squarely in the spirit of earlier interwar projects of national projection, in particular those undertaken by the short-lived but highly influential Empire Marketing Board (EMB). Set up in 1926 under the aegis of the Dominions Office to market Empire products in the United Kingdom, the EMB had provided an important platform from which the government could project messages to the British public through advertisement, posters and films. Through the enlightened policies of patronage of its Chairman, Sir Stephen Tallents, the EMB Film Unit became influential in the development of the British documentary film movement and on the shape of Second World War information films.

Tallents' revelation about how to market the country, which he set out in his book *The Projection of England* in 1932, had come about as a result of a week-long visit to the 1929 Barcelona International Exhibition. Tallents had been overwhelmed by the impression of Germany's 'expression of a lonely, powerful and forward-looking spirit' transmitted through the architecture of its Mies van der Rohe Pavilion and 14 other sections enforcing this 'sense of the industrial power of modern Germany'. He explained:

> You passed through exhibits of books and typewriters and office furniture, of electrical equipment and toys, till you came to the display of German machinery, black and dustless, displayed in a horizontal and rectangular order which successfully conveyed the sense of a powerful present and a yet more powerful future. So spoke at Barcelona the industrial ambition of Germany; and the voice was clearly the voice of one who had summoned the arts of architecture and painting and sculpture, of stage design and skilled lighting and fine lettering to the unified projection of a nation's excellence.

Tallents recognized Germany's success in projecting itself as a nation, through the medium of exhibition, as 'the industrial leader of Europe' and the place to find 'efficient, modern manufactured goods', an art of national projection that he set out to emulate.[20] He drew a fine distinction between cultural propaganda that promoted 'national aims and achievements' and other types of propaganda, such as political or economic propaganda. Tallents' formulation of how the nation of the 1930s should set out to be perceived as a civilised, stable, peaceful country in an increasingly volatile world remained extremely influential for at least two decades.[21] Indeed, the curiously subdued British contribution to an exhibition such as Paris 1937 was in the spirit of Tallents.[22] Incredulous *New Statesman* and *Nation* Editor Kingsley Martin was to describe his visit to the Paris Exhibition as follows:

> When you went in, the first thing you saw was a cardboard Chamberlain fishing in rubber waders and, beyond, an elegant pattern of golf balls, a frieze of tennis rackets, polo sets, riding equipment, natty dinner

jackets and, by a pleasant transition, agreeable pottery and textiles, books finely printed and photographs of the English countryside. I stared in bewilderment. Could this be England?

This quaint attempt to project England as a civilised country at the Paris International Exhibition of 1937, staying true to itself and unruffled by an increasingly hostile world was also the message projected by the Festival of Britain's publicity.[23] Indeed, the Britain Martin described in the Paris displays would be echoed in the Festival a few years later.

The Festival of Britain was driven by the desire of Attlee's government to demonstrate the viability of British democracy whether in peaceful times or when threatened by enemies. In December 1948 the General Assembly of the United Nations was to adopt the Universal Declaration of Human Rights, calling upon member countries to publicise it. One Article proclaimed 'Everyone has the right freely to participate in the cultural life of the community, to enjoy the arts and to share in scientific advancement and its benefits.'[24] The Festival obediently fulfilled this idea: war had had a deep impact on the way that peace was to be preserved. This peace was to be participative and a vibrant cultural life was an important part of this. In the Festival, Britain would be shown as a cohesive, singular nation where diverse cultures were part of a seamless whole symbolized by a common language, English, to be enjoyed by all. Essentially, Britain was to be shown too as a classless society, where all were as one, but this was characterized by liberal, gentlemanly values, a country peacefully 'at home to the world', as if waiting for visitors at a polite drinks party. Director-General Gerald Barry declared the Festival's exclusively national focus offered opportunities to transmit significant messages, which justified its support at a time of financial crisis. 'It was obvious ...', he declared,

> ... that a worthy *national display*, through its challenge to every branch of creative effort, and with its proclamation of confidence in ourselves and in the future, would bring much credit and profit to the country.[25]

Barry's idea of 'national display' was vital: this was not simply an exhibition but an important chance to communicate ideas about Britain through any number of means.

In the run-up to the Festival MPs regularly called upon Morrison to justify spending. Sir Waldron Smithers MP, in particular, pursued this, requesting Morrison disclose to Parliament the amount the Festival Council were requesting in 1949. When turned down on grounds of confidentiality,

Smithers replied, 'are we to assume that the Government do not wish to make public more than is necessary their policy of squandermania?'[26] For critics like Smithers, the government's support for the Festival was emblematic of their perceived financial mismanagement. Morrison fought back, characterizing Festival doubters as 'croakers' and 'grumblers'.[27]

In June 1950, North Korean forces invaded South Korea and any hopes that the government had had of concentrating solely on rebuilding domestic affairs – achieved elsewhere by limited engagement with developments in Europe – were shattered as Britain was drawn into the conflict.[28] There were questions in the House of Commons about whether the Festival should at this point be abandoned, postponed or modified. Morrison's justification that the Festival was about showing peace in an uncertain world was amplified.[29] 'When the Festival of Britain began to be planned three years ago, the international skies were not dark as now,' wrote Gerald Barry in an article for the *English Speaking World*, magazine of the English Speaking Union in late 1950.

> But the worsening of the situation lends the Festival of Britain a deeper significance. For a world given to violence, it is important to show that a free nation still has a mind to the creative virtues, on which the health of many people must ultimately depend. It is important to demonstrate to the unfree world that one of the privileges of democracies is to enjoy freedom of travel and intercourse and the exchange of knowledge and ideas. There are those in another part of the world who find it useful to claim a monopoly of peace, and to pretend that Britain and her partners in the West are occupied solely with plans of destruction. Next summer British democracy will give its own answer in its own way to such nonsense.[30]

The Festival, so Barry said, should go ahead not in spite of the hardships that Britons were experiencing at the time, but because of them. In an article for New York magazine *Flair*, Barry wrote:

> How can you organise exhibitions while men are dying in Korea? To which I respectfully but very firmly answer that Korea, and all that Korea implies, makes our plans more timely than ever. Fighting, I mean, not necessarily with tanks and bazookas, but with every moral and spiritual weapon in our democratic armoury. This Festival of ours is a deadly serious affair.[31]

The Festival was increasingly presented by Barry and Morrison as one of the moral and spiritual weapons in a 'democratic armoury', celebrating the

British way of life with the intention of demonstrating its moral and spiritual superiority, part of a propaganda battle focused towards itself, Western allies and as a challenge to non-democratic states.

For Attlee and his Cabinet it was not only foreign nations who were potentially 'the enemy'. The enemy was evidently also within. The highly visible arrest and conviction of British scientist Dr Alan Nunn May in 1946, having been found spying for Russia while working in Ontario on the joint US-UK-Canada atomic project during the Second World War, had caused a shock reassessment of national allegiances. Only a matter of months before the Festival, in February 1950, the arrest of Dr Klaus Fuchs, a senior scientist working on the British atomic weapons project, also exposed as a Soviet agent, had again sent shock waves. Speaking in a public broadcast to the nation late in 1950, Attlee cautioned 'I would ask you all to be on your guard against the enemy within. There are those who would stop at nothing to injure our economy and our defence. The price of liberty is still eternal vigilance.'[32] Likening Communists and other so-called enemies of democracy to armed burglars fighting the 'peaceful householder', Attlee made Britain a metaphorical home, under siege from those near at hand who might attack its comfort and security. To Attlee, as indeed to many Britons, the threat of a devastating atomic war to end all wars felt all too close. All efforts should be focused towards avoiding it.

Gerald Barry's private diary from this period records his pessimism at the worsening international situation, describing his exchanges with publisher and writer Victor Gollancz on the loss of faith in Communism and change in perception of the USSR, and ruminations on the increasingly fraught relationship between the USA and Britain. In this climate of fear even the Festival might be a target. Three weeks before the Festival opened MI5 were called in. Intelligence had come through that a bomb was hidden in the Dome of Discovery. This proved to be a false alarm but special counter-measures were hurriedly put in place to guard against last-minute sabotage.[33]

While Herbert Morrison dealt with continuing parliamentary opposition to the Festival, a wider public relations campaign was doggedly pursued. This was aimed at countering fierce domestic opposition from British newspapers in the months leading up to May 1951. Gerald Barry took comfort from the parallel with the Great Exhibition a century earlier, which had also faced fierce criticism that had melted away after its opening. In 1851 parliamentary opposition had been led by an MP named Colonel Sibthorpe, and venomous criticism had come from *The Times*. 'Every kind of complaint and prophecy of doom was made about the 1851 project,' Barry wrote,

It was too costly, it was badly designed, it was wrongly sited. It would ruin the neighbourhood, it would import hoards of unruly vagabonds, 'the finger of the Almighty would infallibly descend on so presumptuous an enterprise.' Not only were secret societies plotting to assassinate the Queen, but there would be a disastrous influx of Papists bent upon ruining the country with idolatory, schism, bubonic plague and venereal disease.[34]

But the doubters had been converted once the Crystal Palace opened. He hoped the same would happen in 1951.

Countering criticism and producing leaflets and posters to appeal to visitors from all corners of the United Kingdom, as well as from abroad, was a major job. Paul Wright was appointed the Festival's Director of Public Relations (PR) in 1948, to lead this campaign and ensure that the Festival's messages were sent to audiences at home and abroad. Previously Assistant Director of PR of the National Coal Board, Wright was a friend and Sussex neighbour of Barry's. This familiarity carried on into the planning process when Wright and the other organizers made important decisions, as he later commented, over 'pints of beer and pipes', during congenial country weekends away, staying at Barry's Sussex house.[35] Not only did he have PR experience, but Wright also shared something with Barry and the rest of the Festival team that was more significant: a love of the British land and a strong sense of its history. Wright, like Barry, was a lover of the countryside around their Sussex homes and the twenty mile walks of the planning committees through the Downs, followed by 'mustard baths', were a deep part of the experience of planning.

This immersion in the English countryside strongly shaped and informed the Festival and was central to Barry's idea of the origins of the Festival events. Recalling the early planning Barry said,

We spent the first week-end of that first May in my house in West Sussex and occupied the time in almost continuous session, beginning to hammer out the shape of things to come. Weather and company were in their best form. In the daytime we worked on the terrace or paced the lawn. Below us rolled away in succeeding folds of green and gold a landscape of English parkland inherited from an age of men who had such faith in the future of their country, and so robust a sense of responsibility to their successors, that they planted not for themselves but for their great-grandchildren. Here was our incentive. The Festival of Britain was to be made not only round committee tables. It was made on hill-tops, in gardens, round a log fire, tearing through the English landscape.[36]

This experience of walking, of being immersed deep in the English countryside, became a crucial source of inspiration for the Festival. Gerald Barry and Paul Wright's love of the great outdoors was shared with others who contributed to the Festival, not least the Festival's designers and architects; indeed, some contemporaries saw such a passion for the countryside as an essential part of national identity, the very essence of Britishness.[37] This deep appreciation of the national countryside married with a practical concern for shaping a new Britain was shared by Max Nicholson, the civil servant in charge of the Festival as head of Herbert Morrison's office. In 1931 Nicholson, then working with Barry at *Weekend Review,* had penned *A National Plan for Great Britain.* Through this he aimed to improve the country's economic, political and social conditions. It contained pioneering ideas that were widely adopted. Nicholson was also a formidable conservationist and naturalist. In 1951 he wrote the critically acclaimed *Birds and Men,* about the bird life of British towns, villages, gardens and farmland.[38]

In the run up to the Festival, Wright and Barry fought their PR campaign with gentlemanly diplomacy. They tackled the vociferously anti-Festival Editor of the *Evening Standard,* for example, through a charm offensive that included talking him round to their plans over dinner.[39] Barry's insider's knowledge of the newspaper industry meant he was adept at handling the press. Correspondence between Tom Hopkinson, *Picture Post*'s Editor, his Assistant Editor Lionel Birch and Barry in the second half of 1950 suggests Barry hoped to plant coverage of the Festival in the *Picture Post* to tackle opposition specifically from the Beaverbrook newspapers – the *Daily Express* and *Evening Standard* – but that opposition was dying down towards the end of the year.

The Festival Office needed a symbol that could be used to overbrand the celebrations, in all their chaotic diversity. In late 1948 Barry ran a competition for a Festival symbol that could be used universally across exhibitions, in books and on approved souvenirs. The winning symbol, designed by graphic designer Abram Games (1914–96), was a master-stroke of economy in keeping with Games' own maxim 'maximum meaning, minimum means' by expressing much through seemingly little.[40] The symbol beat eleven other entries by a mix of established and fledgling designers (including Milner Gray, Richard Guyatt, Lynton Lamb, Robin Day and F.H.K. Henrion). It was Britannia in profile, mounted on the points of a compass in red, white and blue, referencing the Union Jack. It expressed, through the four cardinal points, a sense of the whole nation mapped and included in this nationwide Festival. This sense of the whole land was extended by the Games symbol's incorporation into in a widely reproduced Festival publicity poster by illustrator Eric Fraser (1902–83) entitled 'Verdant Isle', in which Fraser painted the British Isles as if from a bird's eye view of a geographer's model (the cover image of this book). Fraser also drew a number of maps setting out the extent of Festival events.

Games's emblem was an extraordinarily popular and immediately recognizable means of branding with the Festival insignia – at any size, on any material – all manner of things. Some nervous criticism was voiced about the symbol's French or Teutonic quality, according to the Council of Industrial Design (COID)'s Paul Reilly. But Reilly's overall assessment was that it had been 'successful as a maid of all work, even to the point of ennui; its loyal colouring in the long run became tedious, for there are few more obvious combinations than our national red, white and blue'.[41] As Games later wrote, the emblem was used everywhere and in every form, 'from postage stamps to police registrations, spoons to cartoons, bread to flowerbeds, pub signs and ensigns, information to deformation'. 'Its representations were too numerous to record', he went on, 'ranging from the amusing to the bizarre … a bromide showing the emblem made up of 604 gallstones from one patient and displayed in the Histological Laboratory of a London hospital'.[42] Games's emblem showed the potential of universal branding for uniting products of many types.

The Festival PR campaign focused on winning domestic visitors as well as those from Europe and North America. Although the exhibitions and events of the Festival focused on British achievements alone, they were conceived to appeal to an international audience, to draw in tourist revenue from outside the country. London was short of tourist accommodation so the authorities set about providing for potential visitors. Deep shelters last used during the Blitz were spruced up. In the Clapham shelter, for example, 4,000 beds were lined up through a tunnel one mile long.

Two million Festival advertising leaflets were produced in eight languages and press advertising undertaken in 34 countries.[43] A significant part of this advertising drive was the European tour of four London double-decker buses, dispatched in three stages from February to April 1951 and carrying on board sample Festival displays, as well as showing the film specially produced for the Festival, Family Portrait (Humphrey Jennings, 1950), a meditation on British achievement through the centuries. The buses visited Scandinavia, Germany, Switzerland, Belgium, Holland and Portugal.[44] The British Broadcasting Corporation (BBC) signed up enthusiastically to the Festival project, seeing in it a wealth of opportunities for radio broadcasts from Festival sites around the country.[45]

Other English-speaking countries were a particular focus for the PR campaign, especially the USA. Little of the British fear of Americanization that was a subject of much debate elsewhere can be detected in the marketing activities of the Festival Office or, indeed, in Barry's diaries which record his lengthy marketing visits to the USA in 1950.[46] While in Washington on a pre-Festival trip Barry met Ed Barrett, an official in the State Department, to discuss the best way to get propaganda value for the Festival due to be publicised through the government-funded radio station Voice of America. Barry and Wright focused on wooing visitors from the USA based on a hope that Americans would bring tourist revenue.[47] Important, too, was Barry's strong belief that the US had a bond with Britain through the use of a common language, through a common cause in the Second World War, and through the rapidly evolving new international war.

Festival publicity constantly repeated the claim that these exhibitions and events, staged across the whole nation, were throwing Britain's metaphorical doorways wide open to let everyone come in and have a look round. Visitors were invited, in publicity slogans and advance guides to the festivities, to go anywhere they wanted in the country in 1951. An advertisement placed in US magazine *Life*, inviting Americans to visit Britain in 1951, bears this out. It was decided the whole of the Festival's US$100,000 publicity budget for North America should be spent on this, the first four-page full colour advert to appear in the magazine and, according to the magazine's own publicity, circulated to around 5.2 million people.[48] As the first of its size, it attracted much attention.

The *Life* advert carried drawings by Eric Fraser comparing 1851 with 1951, placing the Festival in a great tradition of major exhibitions. The central spread was an illustrated aerial view of the South Bank, taken from a black-and-white photograph that was widely used elsewhere, drawn by J.D.M. Harvey. As a drawing, it provided a warmer, more enticing view of a site that was in fact bordered on all sides by railway cuttings and unreconstructed industrial sites. The *Life* advert illustrated just two elements of the many exhibitions: Glasgow's 'Hall of the Future', a display about atomic energy, and the Science Exhibition's atomic entrance screen. Hundreds of other examples of Festival displays could have been the focus, but Barry and Wright considered that these elements – the Festival's presentation of atomic science – would capture the imagination of an American audience most vividly. It was not the potential of atomic science to divide the world, but rather its ability to cause wonder and to improve the future, that was the subject of these exhibitions.

FESTIVAL OF BRITAIN

MAY 3—SEPTEMBER 30, 1951

BRITAIN'S FESTIVAL

AN OCCASION WHICH COMES ONLY ONCE IN A CENTURY

WHEN King George VI declares the Festival open on the morning of May 3 he will start a chain of activities extending through the country from the heart of London to the remotest village green.

In London the focal point will be the South Bank Exhibition. Here, exciting new buildings and broad terraces have replaced the rubble and squalor left by 19th Century slums and the bombs of World War II. Two of these works will remain as permanent features: one is the fine new embankment terrace, reclaiming five acres of Thames mudflats in a part of the city where land is valued by the square inch; the other is the Royal Festival Hall, embodying in its design the latest results of acoustical research. Here, world-famous orchestras and conductors will give concerts throughout the five months of the Festival. The South Bank Exhibition, dominated by the giant Dome of Discovery, reveals the story of the land and people of Britain from the earliest times. Here you will see a concise picture of the British people at work and at play — in factory and laboratory, at sea and in the air, in all those fields of exploration and research in which Britons are helping to build the world of tomorrow.

WHERE PRESENT AND FUTURE MEET; the Tesla million volt lightning machine which will be seen in the final section of the Exhibition of Industrial Power, at Kelvin Hall, Glasgow, Scotland. This Exhibition tells the story of the development of power from coal and water with many examples of past and present achievement in heavy engineering.

AN ATOM ENLARGED 10,000,000,000 TIMES is one of the first things you will see on entering this novel Exhibition of Science in South Kensington, London. It is part of many special displays showing what we know nowadays of the ways in which matter, the substance of the world about us, is built up, and what use we are making of this knowledge.

1.2 LIFE *MAGAZINE*

Details from four-page colour Festival advertisement in *Life* magazine, 22 January 1951, focusing on displays about the atom including sketches by Eric Fraser of (above) 'The Hall of the Future' at Glasgow and (below) the entrance to the Science Exhibition at South Kensington.

Euphemistically referring to the developing antagonism between East and West, the advertisement's accompanying text exhorted people to visit Britain in 1951, 'At a time when the peoples of many nations are living behind a veil of secrecy and fear, Britain will open her doorways wide. Visitors will have an opportunity as never before to get to know the work of her technicians, scientists and architects.' The unique selling point of the Festival, so the line went, was Britain's total transparency, her having nothing whatsoever to hide, unlike many other nations, living as they were 'behind a veil of secrecy and fear'. Unfettered access would be given even to Britain's science laboratories, so the advert boasted, although in fact the British government was still smarting from the arrest of British spies, Alan Nunn May and Klaus Fuchs.

This government's Festival of Britain, taking place in the early years of Britain's Cold War, was developed in Whitehall, close to the key players in that conflict. Suffusing, as they did, the imagination of the nation, Cold War anxieties also shaped the way the Festival was planned. This was to be part of the British government armoury, defending her people from aggressors by robustly showing off her traditions and achievements. These festivities were also, of course, intended to give people a good time, to help them forget terrible times past and to allow them to get close to reconstruction in action. In Whitehall the work of social reconstruction was focused through the setting up of a Welfare State, which could provide for the population, to ensure that there would be no return to the grimness of the 1930s Depression. Reconstruction was further enabled by legislation governing planning and land use. The 1946 New Towns Act allowed new towns to be built across the country in fixed areas. The Festival married these ideas, showing how Britain was recovering from war and how the future was being planned and organized. The form this would take was up for grabs.

While Morrison and Barry fought to justify the Festival in Parliament or in the press, the work of designing this exemplary Britain, to be displayed to the world in 1951, was to be led by architects and designers. Gerald Barry set up two Festival committees that gave form to the Festival. The Executive Committee was made up of the Directors of Architecture, Exhibitions and Science working across the Festival sites who came together to discuss ideas uniting the exhibitions. Meanwhile, the Exhibition Presentation Panel planned their design. The Panel included 38 year-old Cambridge and Bartlett trained architect Hugh Casson (1910–99) as Director of Architecture and 36 year-old Architectural Association (AA) School architectural graduate Ralph Tubbs (1912–96). Despite being a seasoned exhibition designer Misha Black (1910–77) was still only 38 at the time of his Festival appointment. Other members included experienced exhibition designers Cecil Cooke (1899–1991), James Gardner (1907–95) and James Holland (1905–96).[49]

The ambitions of recently trained, demobbed architects to build a brave new world after the war had largely been frustrated. The combination of materials shortages, building licences, the worsening international situation and the economic downturn meant only a few had had much actual building experience. Here, in the Festival of Britain, was their chance to demonstrate the pioneering role that architects and designers might have in rebuilding a postwar Britain. How this newly built Britain should look and feel, what would allow for national distinctiveness and what were 'appropriate' building designs, were questions already being vigorously debated. Popular periodicals such as *Architectural Review* and *Architects' Journal* were an influential focus for such discussions, as were art and architecture schools and local authority architecture departments up and down the country. The Modern Architecture Research Group, known as MARS, had also contributed to these debates by producing the MARS Plan for London (published in *Architectural Review* in 1942). MARS was set up in 1933 by architects Wells Coates and Maxwell Fry as the British branch of international modern architecture group CIAM (Congrès Internationaux d'Architecture Moderne), formed earlier in 1928 by, among others, Le Corbusier and Sigfried Giedion. The CIAM conference at Bridgewater in 1947 was evidence of Britain's growing importance as a home for international modernism. Many of those who would contribute to the Festival were members of the MARS Group including Misha Black, H.T. (known as 'Jim') Cadbury-Brown, Ralph Tubbs, Frederick Gibberd, Hugh Casson, Maxwell Fry and Jane Drew.

As well as MARS, which was mainly populated with architects, Festival designers were active members of other pioneering groups. The most prominent of these was the Artists' International Association (AIA, initially the Artists' International), co-founded in 1933 by a small group that included Festival designers Misha Black and James Holland. AIA held regular exhibitions and talks with the intention of promoting the 'Unity of Artists for Peace, Democracy and Cultural Development'.

A number of architects had inspired debate in the architectural columns of papers such as *News Chronicle* by holding exhibitions about city planning and by publishing architectural booklets. Ralph Tubbs, who went on to design the Dome of Discovery and who, as a young architect, was also central to the MARS group, grappled with ideas about how to rebuild and develop this complex 'organism' the city through the medium of exhibition and writing. His ideas about rebuilding had developed through his 'Living in Cities' exhibition of 1940 for the Army Bureau of Current Affairs (ABCA), evolving into his influential 1942 Penguin pamphlet *Living in Cities*, and again in 1945 in his book *The Englishman Builds*.[50] Jane Drew, who would go on to contribute to the Festival at the South Bank, had organized a 1943 exhibition at the National Gallery entitled 'Rebuilding Britain', which was based on ideas of the RIBA reconstruction committee about how modern design could tackle societal ills. Discussions over the design of the Festival of Britain offered a new locus for these debates over the appropriate visual form for reconstruction.

Early visions of the Festival's South Bank Exhibition, as drawn by Hugh Casson and James Holland, bore little resemblance to the look of the final exhibition. In Casson's 1948 bird's eye sketch, which included the LCC building and Royal Festival Hall, there were almost no other buildings that would later be Festival landmarks, such as the Dome or Skylon. Holland's sketch, drawn at a similar moment, is recognizable as the South Bank Exhibition only by the Shot Tower.[51]

'AN INTERWOVEN SERIAL STORY OF BRITAIN'

Early on, Barry, working closely with Ian Cox, decided that to give a semblance of unity to all these many activities; they should be understood as an 'interwoven serial story' unfolding across the nations. According to the thinking of the Festival's organizers, all designers, architects, scriptwriters and theme convenors were working together to tell the 'story'. The Festival was not simply designed by architects and designers and run by civil servants, or even by architects, designers and civil servants side-by-side, but at every level it was a collaboration of architects and designers with scriptwriters.

For each part of the Festival, scriptwriters were employed to work alongside the section's designers and architects, to ensure the proposed 'story' of the Festival was properly told. Captions were written by freelance writers, 'delivered and subbed by the editor'.[52] Editor-in-chief was *Picture Post* journalist Lionel Birch, replaced during the planning period by *Picture Post* Editor Tom Hopkinson; the Chief Caption Writer was novelist Laurie Lee. To achieve the envisaged cohesion of events, each designer and architect was asked to work very closely to their theme, display designers bringing to life visually written briefs they had been given. Festival architect Hugh Casson described the experience of design work being carried out 'with the script in one hand and a map of the site in the other'.[53]

As well as sticking to scripts, all eight government exhibitions used labels written by scriptwriters to tell their stories. By presenting a story through

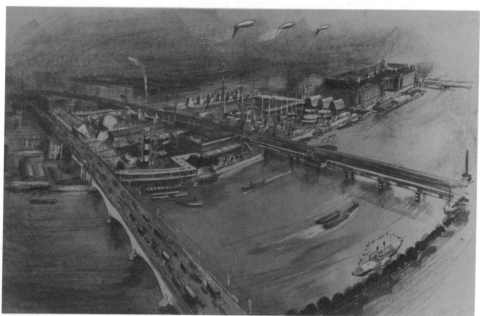

1.3 SOUTH BANK EXHIBITION PRELIMINARY SKETCHES
(Above) Hugh Casson;
(Below) James Holland – both *c*.1948.

the exhibition 'to be told in narrative form, chapter by chapter', there was an impact on the layout of the exhibition sites, in particular at the South Bank where pavilions had to be placed in correct relationship to those which preceded and followed them, as Casson explained. The script dictated not only the order in which visitors should reach pavilions, but also how the visitors punctuated, or planned, their visits around the site. Notably, too, each Festival exhibition was accompanied by a plethora of lengthy written catalogues and guides that mediated the direct impact that these exhibitions might have had. They informed visitors in more detail about the ideas behind sections, and, important to the Festival's organizers, set out 'correct' routes round the exhibitions on maps with circulation routes. Poet Dylan Thomas, writing after the Festival opened, made fun of these routes, 'Most people who wish, at the beginning, anyway, to make sense of the Exhibition, follow the course indicated in the official Guide-book – a series of conflicting arrows which lead many visitors who cannot understand these things slap-splash into the Thames ... other visitors begin, of course, at the end.'[54] Whether the prescribed routes 'worked' or not, the exhibitions were not designed to produce a spectacular but short-lived effect. They were intended to present a narrative about the greatness of Britain's past and to predict an illustrious future. This story, Barry hoped, would resonate in the collective imagination long after the Festival closed.

When Barry, previously Editor of *News Chronicle*, came to the Festival Office he brought some ex-newspaper colleagues with him. According to one observer, he had the concerns of an editor with arranging content and for fast turnaround, setting up the Festival Office 'like he would have set up a newspaper'.[55] Barry's experience as editor of written content – keeping to deadlines, thinking up attention-grabbing headlines and captions from longer stories – had a clear impact on the visual content of the Festival, which was always accompanied by a written version. Barry chose people who were adept both visually and at using the written word. Architect Hugh Casson later remarked on this. Although a qualified architect, Casson believed Barry had given him the job of Architecture Director because he wrote for the *News Chronicle*. Casson also thought Ralph Tubbs probably got his job as Dome designer since he had advised Barry's paper on architecture and had written 'an excellent Penguin paperback on architecture'.[56] Casson had also worked extensively as journalist on *Night and Day* magazine (1937–8) and as the main contributor to gossip column 'Astragal' in *Architects' Journal* in the 1930s.[57] Barry had also given Antony Hippisley Coxe, COID's representative in the Festival Office, his first job as Features editor on *News Chronicle*.

'The Festival of Britain will be a British event, telling the story of British contributions to civilization ...,' declared a Festival information leaflet.[58] This structure gave coherence to a jumble of Festival activities with no internal logic, except they were taking place in Britain and Northern Ireland from May to September 1951. The whole of Britain was itself on show and the story of the British people might take any form or aspect but using nothing 'that is not entirely British', according to the organizers.[59] The 'story' was everything that was in Britain and visitors would be able to 'read' it all around them during the Festival months. The conceit operated on many levels. The 'one, continuous, interwoven story ... about the British people and the land they live in and by' was claimed to unite all the sites across the country, the single element that knitted together the 'constellation of events'.[60] It also operated on the level of the seven major exhibitions, each being accompanied by a 'guide to the story it tells', and the narrative only being legible if visitors followed the prescribed circulation route. Poetic licence was used to overcome two immediate problems of definition; first that the territory covered by the Festival was actually the 'United Kingdom' (not 'Britain'), and second that the nation was not a single 'island' but at least two land masses. From the start of planning, overarching constructions of 'Britishness' vied with constructions of 'Scottishness', 'Irishness', 'Englishness' and 'Welshness'. By focusing on an ascendant British identity, the Festival created a problematic elision of ideas such as 'the local', English 'regions', more precise national identities (such as English or Scottish) and an overall place summarised as 'Britain'. Notable, too, was the fact that many emigre designers were employed to tell this, supposedly exclusively 'British', story of the 'British people'.

According to the Festival guides, a story was being told 'not only through the objects which these buildings will contain, but through the language of the craftsmen, architects, designers and artists who have made or embellished them', positing an imaginary link between objects in the Festival and the people from different locales across Britain, who had made them.[61] This narrative continued into objects too; Edward Bawden's mural *Country Life* in the Lion and Unicorn pavilion showed the focus and pace of farming changing through its annual cycle and Constance Howard's appliquéd and embroidered mural *The Country Wife* in the Country pavilion showed a Women's Institute meeting in a church hall surrounded by vignettes of the same women engaging with other aspects of village life.

This presentation of a story helped the Festival's organizers to set it apart from trade fairs focused on selling products. Stories were the ideal carriers of the Festival message, being infinitely flexible constructions. They enabled the Festival's polyvalent meanings to be offered and presented as if they added up to a singular account. They permitted those responsible for the overall planning of the Festival to present an agreed series of ideas as one account, one object across the scattered Festival sites where spoken or written accounts extended visual displays into the realm of the imagination. The imagined, singular nature of 'the' Festival was paralleled in another regular description of the events by their organizers as the 'autobiography of a nation', presenting the idea of a nation united in telling one tale about 'itself'.[62] Lodged somewhere between story and history, being based on an idea of historical chronology, but allowing for an endless amount of personal mythologizing, 'autobiography' worked well as a metaphor for the Festival. The 'story' was not told through one medium or another, but, according to the ideas of these organizers, through the structures of the Festival as a whole, with each of the Festival's designers telling an episode in a single history.

The Festival's story also operated as spatial practice, a method of transporting visitors from place to place in the Festival; from site to site across geographies and topographies; imaginatively from one place to another; and from historical moment to future triumph. All Festival exhibitions around the country were notionally telling part of the wider 'story'. This might be a tiny element or else a more all-encapsulating version, as at the South Bank. Ian Cox, who developed the theme, later explained 'We were going to tell a consecutive story, not industry by industry, still less firm by firm, but the story of the British people and the land they live in and by.'[63] The structure of the story could be distinguished from the exhibition displays themselves, some of which, as at Glasgow, were structured industry by industry. To negotiate the 'story' being told through the Festival, its visitors needed to navigate the physical spaces between buildings, within exhibits and through landscapes. Cox explained,

> It was on the spatial relationship between exhibit and exhibit, section and section, building and building … (coupled with a persuasive route or circulation) – a 'way to go round' that the Festival largely depended for the conveyance of its theme.[64]

The close correlation between and interdependence of the written, textual (or, in his phrase, 'intellectual plan') and the architectural or spatial one was important. Hugh Casson, Festival Architecture Director, described the contributions of designers and architects in linguistic terms, they 'spoke the same language but each with enough variety of intonation to make it interesting'.[65] Both scriptwriters and designers needed to consider the impact of the story.

The written narrative made it possible to put the exhibitions on an axis of continuing British development, suggesting the future would be even better. It drove visitors towards one conclusion: that Britain had been, and would continue to be, a significant and successful force in the world. Awkward facts or criticism could be edited out. Britain's diminishing Empire could be left out of this story. And despite the Festival organizers' claims to complete transparency, among all the many references to atomic power across Festival sites, there was only one very brief reference to the potential danger of the atom.

The Festival of Britain was both edited and designed, its constituent parts presented as an irreducible whole that made sense only when considered together, in their entirety. Such an equal interdependence or 'relay' between visual medium and written text, creating entire environments, was central to the Festival, where the story-telling conceit relied on words integrated into the exhibition environment to communicate meanings.[66] This intention was summarised by Misha Black,

> We believe for the first time the buildings in which this story is told will not be buildings in the normal sense of the word. They are not, so to speak, merely decorative pavilions, with labels on the outside saying Industry, Fashion, Agriculture, or whatever it may be, but actual three-dimensional expressions of the story they contain.[67]

How text became part of the three-dimensional story of the Festival is evident from a close look at one section of a Festival exhibition.

'The Pantechnicon' was the name given to the introduction to the South Bank's Homes and Gardens pavilion. 'Pantechnicon', a van used for furniture removals, suggested a place in transit, rather than the settled place of home. Reflecting this, the section was built of canvas stretched over a metal frame, designed by Denis Clarke Hall.[68] The section encouraged people to pause and consider philosophical ideas about home, before inviting them to look at the roomsets that followed. Inside a collage of media introduced the theme (brought together by architects Neville Conder and Patience Clifford). The focus was on what constituted a 'good' family and on the limited 'commodity' of space. The visitor, the guide declared, 'finds himself face to face with one of the main problems of modern housing – the problem of space'. Endeavouring to help visitors understand this, the designers used every medium at their disposal.

1.4 THE PANTECHNICON
Introductory section to Homes and Gardens, South
Bank Exhibition showing the way exhibition designers
combined text, murals, photographs and mannequins.

Standing in the centre of the warehouse-like space, slogans surrounded visitors on all sides in the Festival's house-style, a modernised Egyptian script. In the centre, under a large sign with raised lettering declaring the section's title:

'PANTECHNICON'

a sub-heading summarised the area as focusing on

'THINGS ABOUT THE HOME'

Turning to look at the wall behind, beside a subject board entitled:

'THE CROWDED ISLAND'

a slogan superimposed over a black and white photograph of a crowd of people stated,

'50,000,000 PEOPLE CROWD THIS COUNTRY – 4 OUT OF 5 LIVE IN TOWNS'

Below this large wall banner, another smaller slogan stated,

'SPACE IS LIMITED AND COSTLY'

This was placed near to a projecting board with an arrow down to the ground below, pointing to the turf extending in to this covered section from the landscaped lawns outside. The board set out in words and statistics national comparisons of the price of a piece of turf. To follow the argument, visitors needed physically to follow the letters, turning to their right, to look at the text above the entrance, which read,

'YET EVERY HOME DEMANDS SPACE FOR ALL THIS …'

The words were superimposed over, and referred to, a mural by artist James Fitton, showing whimsical illustration scenes of domestic life: a girl playing a piano, a woman ironing, a mother bathing her child, on top of which was traced the ghostly outline of a terraced house – the place where each activity occurred. Turning right again, following the direction of a three-dimensional arrow curling round the corner, another slogan read

'... AND ALL THESE ...'

Pointing visitors back round to their starting point, the title of the section

'PANTECHNICON'

The arrows encouraged visitors to look at the activities referenced by a dolls-house-like shallow tableau of the front of a house. It used techniques that resembled contemporary shop-window displays, animating limited numbers of goods to make them appear alive. In this section, as in other Festival displays, statistics, murals, collages, photographs, text and objects were used to communicate its message. All were equal carriers of the meaning, performing the verbal-visual relay (in Barthes' sense of being interdependent and mutually reinforcing.) The origins of this 'three-dimensional' form of expression and why the Festival exhibitions came to look as they did are the subject of the next chapter.

2

TOWARDS A FESTIVAL EXHIBITION STYLE

*While architecture languished in Great Britain during the war, exhibitions,
Government-sponsored as a propaganda medium, attracted to themselves the
flattering attention of architectural critics whose judgment was perhaps influenced
by the lack of other new building with which the talents of the exhibition designers
could be compared.*

Misha Black, *Exhibition Design*, 1950

Hundreds of architects, designers, landscape architects, artists and craftsmen
collaborated on the events of 1951. For the South Bank alone contributions
were listed from 40 architects or practices and 99 designers. Many dozens
more were involved with designing the other major exhibitions.[1] Their
interests and alliances were shaped by backgrounds in art and architecture
schools, and by their service during the Second World War. This chapter
examines in more detail how the visual style of the Festival – this 'three
dimensional propaganda' – evolved.

MINISTRY OF INFORMATION EXHIBITIONS

During the Second World War in Britain exhibitions mounted by public
bodies such as the Army Bureau of Current Affairs and the Council for
the Encouragement of Music and the Arts (CEMA, later the Arts Council)
had become a widely used official means through which to educate, inform
and entertain the public. In central government the Ministry of Information

(MOI) Exhibitions Branch pioneered exhibition as a form of wartime communication.

The MOI had been formed the day after Britain's declaration of war, on 4 September 1939, as the central department responsible for developing publicity and propaganda in support of Britain's war effort and to sustain national morale. The initial functions of the MOI were threefold: news and press censorship; home publicity; and overseas publicity in allied and neutral countries. In MOI there were teams producing photographs, posters, films, displays and exhibitions, as well as Kenneth Clark's War Artists' Advisory Committee. Many designers worked at MOI who would go on to be Festival luminaries. Headed by graphic designer Milner Gray, with Misha Black supporting him, the Exhibitions Branch drew contributions from designers F.H.K. Henrion, Peter Ray, James Holland, Bronek Katz, Richard Levin, as well as architects Peter Moro and Frederick Gibberd, all of whom later worked on the events for 1951. They were strongly influenced by currents within European Modernism, Surrealism and by *The New Typography* (the seminal treatise on book and graphic design in the machine age, written by Jan Tschichold in 1928). The importance of this experience of collaborative working in influencing the content and structure of displays mounted for the Festival cannot be overestimated.[2] Many artists and designers who had started the war in one of the forces were recalled from the services to work for the MOI in 1942, a year in which £4 million was spent on publicity, of which £120,000 was spent on posters, art and exhibitions.[3]

The MOI Exhibitions Branch was a service department for all Whitehall departments and, as such, its impact was diffuse. The enormous number of exhibitions it organized ranged from small display units to full-scale exhibitions, a number of which were travelling shows, although the MOI's strategy of invisibility meant it was not always clear that they had designed the exhibitions. There was an anomaly at the heart of the exhibitions: that their subjects, often involving highly abstracted technical or economic ideas, did not immediately lend themselves to visual interpretation, but were explained through visual means.[4] The inaugural MOI Exhibition was entitled 'London Pride'. This aimed to give Londoners a morale boost, and was held at Charing Cross Underground Station, a convenient location for passers-by going about their daily routine. Milner Gray, the lead designer on 'London Pride', used enormous portrait photographs as the focus of his displays and as background, showing crowds and individuals with up-lifted expressions. This was an approach that would not have seemed out of place in the pages of British photo-news magazine *Picture Post*, which had been presenting stories and articles about 'ordinary' Britons in written and pictorial form side-by-side since its inception in 1938. The photography of 'London Pride' used a similar visual language for expressing abstracts such as pride and allegiance. Ignoring local problems, it asserted an image of one nation, united despite barriers of class or culture.

The Ministry of Agriculture's 'Dig for Victory' campaign (originally entitled 'Grow More Food') had called for every man and woman in Britain to keep an allotment. This not only ensured that British people had access to fresh food, but also freed up space on ships to carry essential wartime machinery. In response, lawns and flowerbeds were turned into vegetable gardens and chickens, rabbits, goats and pigs reared even in very confined domestic spaces, turning Britain, by the end of the Second World War, into a nation of farmers. The Ministry of Agriculture's 'Dig for Victory' campaign was publicised widely through information posters, but it was also fought through the medium of exhibition. From 1940 Milner Gray, Peter Ray, Bronek Katz and F.H.K. Henrion collaborated on the 'Dig for Victory' touring show. The exhibition stands were designed with striped awnings resembling grocers' stalls and a combination of text, diagrams and basic drawings of food and planting techniques were used to instruct visitors on how to 'Dig Well,' 'Sow Thinly,' 'Plant Carefully' and 'Tackle Pests Early'. Exhibition stands constructed out of poles carved as gigantic garden spades and a section on garden pests that showed wireworms, slugs and leatherjackets carrying Nazi insignia added humour to the didactic presentation.

A section in 'Dig for Victory' set out to demonstrate how productive one person could be using isotype diagrams. Isotype diagrams, the system of pictograms developed by Viennese émigré planner and housing consultant Otto Neurath (1882–1945), were an important way of conveying complex information within these wartime shows. Isotypes – acronym for International System of TYpographic Picture Education – were symbols representing, for example, people, food or transport types, to show complicated statistical data about production, distribution or planning and reconstruction in a simplified visual form. From 1940 until his death, Neurath had worked in England, setting up the Isotype Institute, which produced exhibitions, film documentaries (including those with notable documentary filmmaker Paul Rotha) and a series of popular books on subjects such as food production, health, women at work and democracy. Neurath's influence on visual presentation of complex ideas was profound. He was associated with the 'Vienna method of picture statistics' that had evolved since the 1920s through exhibitions of subjects such as hygiene, health, social care and sport. This was

2.1 MINISTRY OF INFORMATION: FOOD EXHIBITIONS
(Above) Display from 'Off the Ration';
(Below) Display from 'Dig for Victory'.

a visual language developed with the intention of communicating complicated plans to mass public audiences at a glance, provoking broad public discourse and discussion.

The MOI's 'Life Line' travelling exhibition was about the contribution of Britain's ships. It was first shown in 1941 with the aim of explaining the contribution that ordinary householders could make to the war effort. The message was that simply by using food and other materials sparingly, civilians would allow ships to be freed up to focus on the war effort. Designed by a team including F.H.K. Henrion, the exhibition used a combination of captions, isotypes, documentary photographs of ships at work and much magnified photographs of the faces of named seamen, such as 'John Reid – Able Seaman' and 'Willem Hermans Trotzenbergh – Fireman'. Accompanied by biography and testimony, these gave a sense of intimacy and proximity, which allowed a move from statistical data to the stories of individuals, a typical formula that twinned collective achievement with individual social responsibility.[5] Other Ministry of Information exhibitions included 'Private Scrap Builds a Bomber' as part of a salvage drive; 'Poison Gas' (on behalf of the Ministry of Home Security) to demonstrate the range of poison gases and how to respond to each; 'Gangway Please' about War Transport; 'Comrades in Arms' about the war in Russia; 'The Unconquerable Soul' about resistance in occupied countries; 'Off the Ration' at Charing Cross and London Zoo; and 'Fuel Exhibition' at the Dorland Hall.

One of the Ministry's most ambitious shows was 'The Army Exhibition', designed for the War Office and staged on the bombed Oxford Street site of the John Lewis department store in 1943 (and later on a blitzed site in New Street, Birmingham and in Cardiff in 1944). Ministry of Information publicity turned the terror of the Blitz to advantage in exhibition publicity, which announced 'German Bombs Provide Exhibition Site'.[6] It covered 56,000 square feet and showed 23,000 exhibits, its aim to give the public a general idea of how the army was organized, explaining communications, food, transport, clothes, munitions and medical services through sections such as 'A gun's life – and yours,' 'Every bit of fuel counts' and 'Every ounce of salvage counts.' Contributors were a glittering line-up of those who would go on to dominate the Festival's design: Milner Gray, Misha Black, F.H.K. Henrion, Bronek Katz (designer of the South Bank Homes and Gardens), Frederick Gibberd (lead designer for the Festival's Live Architecture Exhibition), Peter Moro (designer on the LCC's Royal Festival Hall) and Richard Levin (lead designer of the Festival 'Land Travelling' exhibition). The exhibition ranged 'from Churchill tanks to optical lenses'.[7] It used a mixture of means to communicate its message about the might and modernity of the British army, including graphs,

2.2 MINISTRY OF INFORMATION: 'THE ARMY EXHIBITION'
(Above) Aerial view of 'The Army Exhibition' at its
Oxford Street site;
(Below) Inside the Exhibition.

full-sized military equipment, striking enlarged graphics and integrated text panels built out of the rubble of the site, in the open air, under small awninged display boxes and panels. A 30 feet high tower of jerry cans suspended in a metal frame built by designer Richard Levin was a visual illustration of the amount of fuel used by an armoured division in 2½ minutes.

Assessing the impact of MOI exhibitions a few years later, graphic designer Ashley Havinden saw a strong influence coming from the 'dynamism' of 'abstract and constructivist art', in particular in what he described as 'the new asymmetric typography'.[8] Although those designing these MOI shows were trained as architects, exhibition designers or so-called 'commercial artists', many had strong links with organizations across the boundaries of medium, collaborating on exhibitions outside MOI.

PROPAGANDA POSTERS

Just as in peacetime exhibition designers had worked on stands for trade fairs focused towards promoting products, poster designers had largely focused on product advertising and marketing. From the start of the Second World War poster designers were again called upon to be propagandists, focused outwards on fighting the enemy and inwards on inciting a home audience to certain behaviours in support of the war effort: how to eat, to avoid waste or not to drop their guard while talking to friends and neighbours.[9] Posters were powerful and, according to designer Austin Cooper, served as 'a reminder, a stimulus, a missionary; as propaganda in pictorial form'. The poster artist had a key role in society, producing work that embodied 'spiritual, humanitarian and political truths in visual terms'.[10] The poster implied a command, 'In every good poster there is an implied 'Do'! or 'Don't'!' wrote a contemporary critic,

> It must convince one that to invest in War Savings or to grow cabbages is desirable – to indulge in careless talk or to sneeze without a handkerchief in front of one's face undesirable. And it must persuade rather than bully … The poster artist is the modern propagandist's most potent agent.[11]

Where in peacetime billboards had been covered with posters advertising products for sale – beer, cigarettes, bars of soap – during the Second World War they became the vehicle for public information posters.

Wartime posters, with their limited size and space, relied on the art of 'integration', as graphic designer Abram Games, designer of the Festival's emblem and advertising posters for the Festival described it: integration of combinations of word and image to convey meanings.[12] Games's poster 'Grow Your Own Food,' of 1942, was designed as part of the MOI's wider 'Dig for Victory' campaign. It entreated military personnel in barracks to 'supply your own cookhouse', keeping them healthy and saving transport and personnel to concentrate on the war effort. Playing with imagery – garden implements as the legs of a dining table (echoed in the design of 'Dig for Victory' exhibition stands) and the vegetable patch as carpet – the poster communicated the message with extraordinary elegance. This impetus towards inducing a particular action, sequence of behaviours, or emotional response in the onlooker, marked out the arts of poster and exhibition design as distinctive. Instead of focusing on aesthetic considerations in isolation, the idea was the thing. It was this sensibility that designers who had worked on wartime propaganda brought to their work on the Festival of Britain. No distinction was drawn between words, things, murals, sculptures, buildings, landscapes: all were subservient to the greater Festival idea.

That graphic and exhibition designers were given such prominence during the Festival is testament to the important role that poster designers – previously known by the pejorative term 'commercial artists' – were considered to have played during the Second World War. In the Festival's technocracy, architects, exhibition designers and graphic designers would sit as equals, as would painters, sculptors, landscape architects, interior designers, product and engineering designers, typographers, illustrators, modelmakers, photographers, lighting experts, craftsmen and structural engineers. This was despite the different training that each had received and the inflection of class difference that went with this. Festival designer Clifford Hatts, who as a young RCA-trained designer was invited to work with design consultancy Design Research Unit (DRU) on the Dome of Discovery displays would characterize this difference as 'the round boys' – the architects who had been to architecture colleges – versus 'the flat boys' – the graphic artists who had come through the technical college system.[13] Designer Richard Guyatt – who went on to collaborate on the design of the South Bank Lion and Unicorn pavilion – is credited with coining the phrase 'graphic design' as a name for the discipline. As Professor at the Royal College of Art from 1948, he had started off presiding over the School devoted to 'design for publicity' but this was soon changed to 'graphic design', the first time such a title had been used in an educational setting.[14] Guyatt influenced the development of the wider design profession, acknowledging that the visual language of graphic design was tempered both by aesthetic considerations and the

2.3 MINISTRY OF INFORMATION: 'GROW YOUR
OWN FOOD'
Poster designed by Abram Games as part of the 'Dig
for Victory' campaign.

pressures of industry. Graphic designers were quick to absorb developments in architecture, painting, sculpture and photography into their work, focused as they were on the art of communication.

Wartime and early postwar projects were a training ground for designers who would go on to work on the Festival of Britain. Aside from exhibition design, several Festival contributors had come from another area of wartime civil defence: developing patterns of deception as camouflage designers. Festival Architecture Director Hugh Casson worked for four years as a Camouflage Officer at the Air Ministry alongside James Gardner as Chief Deception Officer at the Camouflage Training School from 1941–6. Gardner went on to design parts of the South Bank, as well as the Festival Pleasure Gardens. Meanwhile, Robert Goodden who went on to design the Festival's Lion and Unicorn pavilion, had worked at the Naval Camouflage Unit. These projects were significant sites of collaboration and provided training in group practice that would feed into the teamwork that characterised the later Festival. As well as this wartime work experience, a number of Festival designers had worked together as students. Jim Cadbury-Brown and Ralph Tubbs were together at the AA, for example. Some had worked together in architectural offices pre-Second World War: Bronek Katz, Reginald Vaughan and Ralph Tubbs had all worked for Maxwell Fry, for example. Some had collaborated for some time through formalized partnerships: Black and Milner Gray had collaborated from the early 1930s, and the Architects' Co-operative Partnership (ACP), a group of former AA students, had formed in 1939.

After the Second World War ended, MOI was reorganized to become Central Office of Information (COI).[15] Deriving mainly from the production division of the wartime MOI, including its film unit, COI provided information services for all government departments at home and overseas. Many who had worked on exhibitions for the wartime MOI stayed on to design exhibitions in the aftermath of war and these had the hallmarks of the wartime shows' work of sharing factual material with the public through visually appealing means. Focused on defeating a new Cold War enemy, working methods developed during the Second World War continued to be used in COI exhibitions.

'BRITAIN CAN MAKE IT'

Skills that designers had honed through wartime exhibition work were used in the design of 'Britain Can Make It,' the first great postwar British exhibition. Held at the Victoria and Albert Museum from September to December 1946, the exhibition set out to show Britain's manufacturing capability through the display of British goods. Sir Stafford Cripps described the show as 'British industry's first great postwar gesture to the British people and the world' and 'a record of the strikingly rapid changeover from war to peace production in Great Britain'.[16] Only five years before the Festival and attracting many of the same contributors, 'Britain Can Make It' was an important testing ground for ideas used in 1951. Indeed Cecil Cooke, who was to become Director of Exhibitions for the Festival of Britain organized 'Britain Can Make It' with James Gardner, who was also pivotal to the later Festival. Cooke had previously worked at MOI then COI as Director of Exhibitions.[17]

Demonstrating the value of 'good' design and telling a story about how design could be ever improved was the intention of 'Britain Can Make It' organizing body, the Council of Industrial Design (COID). Set up in 1944, COID was pivotal to developing and projecting 'good design' in the UK. The exhibition's main focus was on showing domestic products separated into groups such as radio, dress fabrics, furniture and furnishing fabrics, books and travel goods. The furnished rooms, set up according to the class and profession of their imagined inhabitants, such as 'the Suburban Living Room for a hard-up curate,' were particularly popular and would be echoed in the various homes sections of the Festival of Britain. The exhibition's 'Quiz Bank', where visitors were handed coins so that they could record their favourite designs, gave visitors an experience of passing judgement on quality of design, albeit superficial.

'Britain Can Make It' was extraordinarily popular, attracting nearly 1.5 million people despite covering a mere 90,000 square feet, and captured the imagination of a public hungry for new products after years of privation and keen to see the signs of a return to normal, peacetime manufacturing. This popularity did not, however, equate to success for the manufacturers involved and the reception for trade buyers was unsatisfactory. Goods were given indicative price ranges and, because many were not yet available, indicative timings. A frustrated public dubbed the show 'Britain Can't Have It.'[18]

Importantly, because this show was not simply focused on selling goods, but on demonstrating wider ideas about Britain's productive capabilities, there was also an attempt to explain technical aspects of industrial design. A section called 'From War to Peace: Wartime technical developments applied to peacetime products' and another titled 'What Industrial Design Means' tried to enlighten visitors on issues of production, employing the

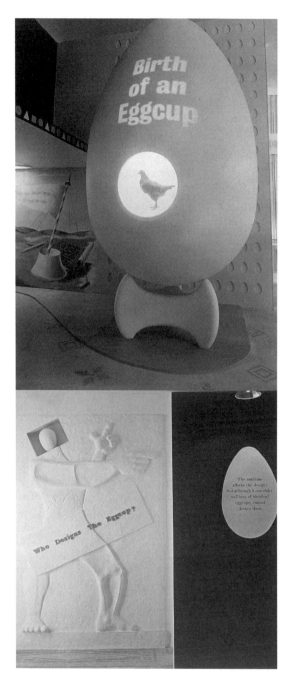

2.4 'BRITAIN CAN MAKE IT' EXHIBITION
Installation of Design Research Unit's 'Birth of an Eggcup'
showing integration of text with image.
(Above) Entrance to section;
(Below) Detail of displays.

story-telling technique favoured in wartime MOI exhibitions. A section put together by Design Research Unit (DRU)'s Misha Black, in association with Austin Frazer and Bronek Katz, was entitled 'Birth of an Egg Cup.' The eggcup became a vehicle for explaining the 'principles' of industrial design, in a display that relied heavily on written storyboards to describe how the object came to exist, alongside visual displays. Successful graphic design was key to communicating written content and was the most striking visual element in a display containing few objects. These elements would be carried into the design of the later Festival of Britain.[19]

Wartime and postwar exhibitions used 'three-dimensional techniques of communication' but had few three-dimensional objects. This made them particularly reliant on words and graphics to conjure environments from constructed boards and divisions.[20] Such text-based or scripted exhibitions taught designers the art of integrating words with objects and images to create overall exhibition environments. In 1950, Misha Black identified propaganda exhibitions as the form the British could claim superiority in. He described them as 'the informative and story-telling type of exhibition (as differentiated from the simple display of commodities) where there was a reliance on word or script to contribute to the visual telling of stories'.[21] Acknowledging the pejorative associations of 'propaganda', in particular, in its most recent use by the Nazis, Black explained,

> If this smacks of charlatanism, it is because propaganda is usually only apparent when used as a force for mischief or evil, but the technique can be varied to work for reasonable ends, and is no less required to persuade people of the importance of town planning than it is to exploit latent racial rivalries.[22]

Making the distinction between 'reasonable' and, by implication, unreasonable 'ends' that propaganda exhibitions might be put to, Black's underlying assumption was that all exhibitions were an instrumental means of communication. Exhibitions were about ideas, structured around an argument and, as such, could not simply be associated with entertainment or short-lived festivity.

Contemporary exhibition designer Adrian Thomas went further in an essay of 1950, stating that exhibitions without text had never been satisfactorily achieved.[23] Trying to explain the necessary interplay between the scriptwriter and the designer working together on exhibitions, he set out a specimen exhibition script, as follows:

Section	Code	Visual	Text
Right-hand wall I.	RH/ I/ I	Diorama of Piccadilly Circus. Lights working.	
	RH/ I/ 2	Heading.	NIGHT LIGHT.
	RH/ I/ 3	Main caption.	When full supplies of power come back, the streets of London will resume their pre-war electric brilliance.

Specimen Exhibition Script[24]

Thomas's diagram showed the 'visual' and 'text' as closely planned, with writers and designers interdependent in mounting exhibitions, ideas that remained strongly resonant in 1951.

OTHER INFLUENTIAL EXHIBITIONS

Most Festival designers were young and had built little prior to the Festival. But some, such as Misha Black and Basil Spence, had already contributed to major international exhibitions. Émigré British exhibition designer Misha Black, who was on the Festival's Design Panel, was the most influential British exhibition designer of his day and had been commissioned to arrange British displays at many major international exhibitions, as well as writing and lecturing on their history. Aged 18, he had cut his teeth as designer of the Rio Tinto Pavilion at the 1929–30 Spanish-American Exhibition in Seville, going on to work on the Steel, Coal, Shipbuilding and Public Welfare Halls for the United Kingdom Pavilion at the Glasgow Empire Exhibition in 1938, and the Public Welfare and Maritime Halls at the British Pavilion for the New York World's Fair in 1939.

In 1938, Black had also co-ordinated the interwar exhibition that most influenced modern British architects: the MARS 'New Architecture' exhibition. Held at London's Burlington Galleries and visited by Le Corbusier and other architectural luminaries, the exhibition showed the elements of modern architecture as interpreted by MARS. It managed within a limited space to demonstrate successful exhibition design in action, combining elements of modern building using models and aerial architectural photographs, maps and plans, as well as prototypes of new building elements.[25] Black had also made contributions to dozens of other trade exhibitions and shows, both major and minor through his design consultancy DRU.[26] As a founder member of AIA, Black and fellow Festival designers James Holland and F.H.K. Henrion were prominent in organizing the AIA exhibition 'For Liberty', that was held in 1943 on the same Oxford Street site as the MOI's 'The Army Exhibition' of earlier that year, the shell of the John Lewis basement canteen. The four freedoms which 'For Liberty' represented were those set out in the Atlantic Charter: 'Freedom of Speech, Freedom of Worship, Freedom of Want, Freedom of Fear.' The exhibition, according to its catalogue, aimed to show 'that the function of art in wartime is not only to record what is happening and to give enjoyment and recreation but to stimulate and encourage by vividly representing what we are fighting for'.[27] This was a direct challenge to wartime artists' projects such as Kenneth Clark's 'War Artists' or the 'Recording Britain' scheme, which were more focused towards the work of recording the effects of the Blitz and the war effort on the Home Front. The British press, particularly journalists on the right, responded negatively, criticizing artists for producing propaganda for political or social ends. The exhibition was, however, very popular, attracting 36,000 visitors in a month.

The Great Exhibition of 1851 particularly interested Black and he amassed an extraordinary collection of 1851 ephemera during his lifetime, a collecting passion also shared by other Festival designers such as architect Jim Cadbury-Brown.[28] Black's partner at DRU, Milner Gray, responsible for signage at the Festival of Britain, had also had experience of international exhibitions, designing murals for the Coal and Steel Halls at Glasgow in 1938.

At the South Bank, 22 pavilions would be spread across the site, according to themes such as 'Sea and Ships,' 'Transport' and 'Health'. Freestanding pavilions had been the norm at every international exhibition since the 1867 Paris Exposition, when a thematic approach to structuring sections of increasingly vast sites was first adopted. In 1867 pavilions had been arranged by nation as well as by industrial themes, such as mining, electricity or agriculture. Visitors entering the South Bank site through the main turnstiles would arrive at the Fairway, another common part of the lexicon of international exhibitions. Light relief was offered at the Festival in the form of a fun fair, as it had been at exhibitions since Paris 1867, a section of the show that in the USA world's fairs, from Chicago's World's Columbian Expo in 1893 onwards, had become known as the Midway Plaisance. However, due to limitations on space at the South Bank site, these entertainments were situated a boat ride away at Battersea.

Since the Great Exhibition at the Crystal Palace in 1851 major exhibitions had combined elements of trade fairs with spectacle, education and entertainment. While the centenary of the Great Exhibition provided the occasion for the Festival, its direct impact on the conception and design of the 1951 events was limited, largely because of the Festival's alternative focus and structure, being exclusively national and spread across multiple sites. The Festival's centrepiece, the South Bank Exhibition, echoed the evolved form of the international exhibition, despite its minute scale by the standard of recent exhibitions (27 acres, as compared for example to the 1,216 acres of the 1939 New York World's Fair).

In the years leading up to the Festival, British architects had been particularly impressed by a number of national and international exhibitions. These influenced the planning and landscaping of the Festival sites, the design of exteriors and interiors, graphic and display design and subjects chosen for display. Three European exhibitions had a particular bearing on the structure and look of the Festival of Britain, sharing its singular national focus. These were the 1930 Stockholm Exhibition, held at Djurgården; the 1939 National Exhibition (the 'Landesausstellung'), held in Zurich; and the 1948 Exhibition of the Lands Regained, held in the Polish city of Wrocław, all of which were known to the Festival architects through their coverage in architectural magazines. While all three exhibitions had formal similarities with the later Festival of Britain, showcasing new landscaping techniques and providing a clear conceptual link between the people of that nation and its landmass, they also offered a structure within which designers could experiment with important ideas of identity of place in newly built buildings and landscapes.

THE STOCKHOLM EXHIBITION

The Stockholm Exhibition, held from May to September 1930, had a profound impact on British architects. Focused on Swedish national products – arts, crafts and industries – it was aimed towards stimulating the export trade. But it was not the contents of the 1930 exhibition that were of particular note – indeed, Misha Black omitted the exhibition from his discussions of the evolution of exhibition displays – but Chief Architect Gunnar Asplund's treatment of the exhibition site. Held at Djurgården, the city's natural park, the exhibition produced a pattern-book for architects in search of landscaping inspiration. Pavilions and kiosks – for many a first encounter with Swedish functionalist design – were set in a seemingly informal designed landscape, beside a stretch of water, the Djurgårdsbrunn creek. The Corso, a navigational street lined with the major exhibition halls, led into the Festival Square, which provided a central gathering point by the bunting-lined water's edge, anticipating the look and the spirit of 1951. Indeed, Asplund worked hard to satisfy the need for 'beauty and *festivitas*', a chance for people to relax and let their hair down.[29] Rather than adopting the symmetrical Beaux-Arts plan familiar from international exhibitions in Paris and the States, Asplund achieved a sense of urban intimacy of tree-lined streets and piazzas, set in green space. It was the unity of this vision that made a particular impression on P. Morton Shand, *Architectural Review* contributor (who had coined the phrase 'Swedish grace' after his encounter with Swedish contributions to the 1925 Paris Exhibition). He commented:

> 'Stockholm 1930' was the electrifying stimulus it proved to be just because it was a revelation. It revealed modern architecture, not as yet another style suitable for certain types of buildings, but as the outcome of a new approach equally valid for all types...This revelation, then, as I see it, was Asplund's great achievement. It was a contribution to modern architecture so far-reaching in its effects that any attempt to analyse in what particular details his own earlier buildings heralded its ultimate realization seems superfluous, and almost a denigration of what we owe to him.[30]

Architectural Review Editor J.M. Richards summarised the extraordinary impact of this exhibition in arousing public interest in modern architecture. Where previously modern buildings had looked strangely misplaced when surrounded by the mixed architectural styles of an average city street, he was struck by the whole sequence of buildings built together at Stockholm, 'as it might be a whole new quarter of a town – was designed and laid out in a consistently modern style, and the public, walking among them, was given its first glimpse of modern architecture not as a new fashion in design but as a newly conceived environment'.[31] Richards' and fellow architecture critics' admiration of the way that Swedish architects conceived of entire environments – buildings within landscapes – led them to publish many articles in praise of Swedish building projects. It was also a starting point for various campaigns in *Architectural Review* magazine throughout the 1940s and early 1950s.

The modern British love affair with Swedish design had been sparked by two earlier events: the Jubilee Exhibition at Gothenburg of 1923 and the completion of Ragnar Östberg's Stockholm City Hall, the same year. The Gothenburg Exhibition, held from May to September 1923, had celebrated the city's three hundredth anniversary and presented a complete review of industrial progress and expansion in Sweden, showcasing Swedish history, art, crafts and exports. Five related exhibitions ran alongside it, including one of town planning, for which English planner Raymond Unwin acted as adviser.[32] Many British visitors travelled around Sweden, Norway and Denmark for the first time that year and were struck by Östberg's City Hall, set at the water's edge, its soaring tower culminating in three crowns, a symbol derived from the old Royal Palace the City Hall. The City Hall would become the model for town halls up and down Britain. Indeed, the year Hugh Casson was appointed as Director of Architecture for the Festival of Britain, in 1948, he visited Sweden for the first time and saw Östberg's City Hall, and spoke of the deep impression it had made on him.[33]

This admiration of Nordic design also focused in other directions. The design of Alvar Aalto's monumental timber-lined Finnish Pavilions for the 1937 Paris Exposition and the 1939 New York World's Fair had been much praised in British architecture journals, as had Sven Markelius's Swedish Pavilion for the 1939 New York World's Fair. Externally, the 1939 Swedish Pavilion, which was set around a courtyard with an ornamental pool and fountain sculpted in Orrefors glass, was echoed in the Moat Café at the South Bank, while internally the Swedish Pavilion's display of homewares was echoed in the Festival's Homes and Gardens.

Gunnar Asplund and contemporaries such as Sven Markelius practiced a softened modernism, which incorporated traditional materials, allied design with potential use, showed a sensitivity to site and landscape and did not shy away from spatial intimacy.[34] Characterised as the 'New Empiricism' in the pages of *Architectural Review* magazine, their work was much admired by the new generation coming out of British architecture school in the years leading up to the Festival, their attitude to orthodox modernism having been tempered by their experience of war. This Swedish example of modernism, which at the same time evoked a cosiness and homeliness, was an attractive model.[35] Swedish architects were practising within a government system charactcrized by Reyner Banham as 'advance Welfare-State architecture', sharing common ground with British architects' work on government projects.[36]

If Asplund's 1930 Stockholm Exhibition was a very strong influence on the landscaping of the later Festival, another exhibition on the same site influenced the look of elements of the South Bank pavilions. The Stockholm World's Sports Exhibition, held in 1949 at Djurgården under the overall design control of Bengt Gate, impressed several contemporaries, including Misha Black.[37] Elements of the Exhibition found echoes in Festival displays. Strong colours and abstracted shapes including atoms formed of metal tubing with coloured balls and automated sculpture were echoed two years later. Young Festival architect Gordon Bowyer, newly commissioned to design the South Bank's Sport section, was sent on a reconnaissance trip to Stockholm in August 1949, and his report contained several images of the World's Sports Exhibition's striped awnings and atomic shapes that would directly impact on the look of his own section.

THE NATIONAL EXHIBITION, ZURICH

If the landscaping of Asplund's Stockholm Exhibition was to be an influence, the South Bank exhibition with its twinned themes of 'Land and People' also paid homage to the design language of the 1939 National Exhibition in Zurich. The 'Landesausstellung,' colloquially known as 'Landi,' was highly admired by British exhibition designers. Misha Black, writing in 1950, declared that 'little was done in Great Britain during the war years which bettered the best exhibition design at Zurich in 1939.'[38] Held on two banks of the River Limmat from May to October 1939 and overseen by principal architect Hans Hofmann, the 'Landi' had originally been planned as an industrial fair to show off recently designed objects. Opening, as it did, in a climate of extreme uncertainty, which had culminated in the Nazi invasion of Czechoslovakia of March that year, it evolved as a weapon of national propaganda or of 'spiritual national defence' against totalitarianism.

The 'Landi' exhibition focused on industrial themes that would have strong echoes in 1951: raw materials, processing, sales and distribution were a focus

2.5 NATIONAL EXHIBITIONS (facing page)
(Above) Stockholm Exhibition, 1930. Asplund's landscaping was particularly praised by the British architectural press;
(Below, left) Cover of the catalogue of the 'Landi', Zurich, 1939 showing the exhibition's site on the banks of the River Limmat;
(Below, right) Tower of zinc buckets at the 'Exhibition of Lands Regained', Wrocław, 1948.

STOCKHOLMSUTSTÄLLNINGEN 1930.
Alnarpsträdgården med skulptur av Milles.

as were the 'land and people'. A near-euphoric display of national pride, the exhibition attracted 10.5 million visitors in a nation with a population of only 4.2 million. Oscar Eberle, one of the exhibition's directors, was to admit that he had taken notes from Switzerland's German neighbours in their ability to rouse the masses. Part of the exhibition included a mountain trail, akin to a pilgrim's path, culminating in the statue 'Ready for Defence', at which male visitors took their hats off and where people deposited flowers and coins. The 'Schiffliback,' an artificial sightseeing canal, wound its way through the exhibition site.

The Zurich exhibition turned a problematic site, split as it was between the two riverbanks, into a virtue, as the architects of the South Bank would a few years later. On the right bank industries and economic activities were showcased, including heavy machines such as turbines, dynamos and locomotives and the tenth Swiss Agriculture Exhibition (or 'Landi Dorfli'), reflecting the Swiss reliance on agricultural employment and the fact that national confidence was strongly linked to their ability to produce their own food. On the left bank were agricultural activities, crafts and traditions. To connect the two parts of the site, visitors travelled over the lake in a cable-car running between two steel towers 250 feet high and over half-a-mile apart, which allowed visitors to get a bird's eye view of the site and, at the same time, a striking view of the Swiss Alps. Aerial drawings of the exhibition site, reproduced as part of the exhibition literature, show its parallels with the citing of the 1930 Stockholm exhibition and of the later South Bank Festival. Its most noted architectural feature was Robert Maillart's Cement Hall, an elliptical concrete vault only six centimetres thick. Architect Sigfried Giedion was so impressed by the Hall that he would add an afterword about it to his 1954 version of *Space, Time and Architecture*, while an editorial in *Architects' Journal* of 1949 praised Maillart's structure as, with Crystal Palace, the most notable architectural contributions to any exhibition.[39]

A celebrated aspect of the 'Landi' was Hans Hofmann's mastery of landscape and built environment, from the wide open space of the *'Festplatz'* (or 'Festival ground') to the meandering greenery around small pavilions. This provided a strong example to Festival designers, being considered resolutely modern, while also reflecting the national landscape. One of its other most well known products was 'la Landi', the aluminium chair conceived by Hans Coray of the material that was a key Swiss export. Writers at the time of the Festival saw strong parallels between the Festival and 'Landi'; one likened the structure of the exhibitions and their attempt to tell 'the story of a determined people triumphing over great difficulties, in the one case imposed by Nature, in the other by War'.[40] In 1949, Misha Black and Ralph Tubbs went on a reconnaissance mission to Zurich, reporting back on the magnificent Cycle Stadium, which was comparable in size to the Dome and which had made them more enthusiastic than ever about designing the Dome of Discovery.[41]

EXHIBITION OF THE LANDS REGAINED, WROCŁAW

Another exhibition that celebrated the national land was the Polish 'Exhibition of the Lands Regained'. Less well documented than Stockholm or Zurich, it was nevertheless known to the Festival's designers through the contemporary press. The exhibition was mounted in the city of Wrocław in 1948 as companion to the Communist International Congress for Peace of that year. Set across 150 acres, the exhibition celebrated the new territories that had been given to Poland as part of the Yalta agreement, having previously been German Breslau for 200 years. For the Congress, 500 artists, scientists, architects and intellectuals were brought together from 45 countries to discuss ways of maintaining international peace. The general coverage of the Wrocław Congress and exhibition was less than British delegates, including artist Feliks Topolski, architect Berthold Lubetkin and architectural critic J.M. Richards, believed it warranted. But those who did write or speak about the exhibition were fulsome in their praise. J.M. Richards commented:

> I saw a magnificent exhibition at Wrocław ... it was the best piece of exhibition design I have ever seen – both from the point of view of ideas and execution. It had none of that rather heavy-handed symbolic-heraldic style one associates with Russian publicity displays. The style was much more sophisticated and completely western in conception.[42]

Filmmaker Ivor Montagu, a Peace Congress delegate, was similarly enthusiastic, writing, 'Wrocław housed, simultaneously with the Conference, a wonderful exhibition showing the resources and history of the restored territory, which by originality, artistry and technical quality of presentation of the exhibits, as well as the speed and efficiency with which it was said to have been prepared entirely by voluntary labour, made a great impression on all who visited it.'[43] Editor of the *New Statesman and Nation* and Wrocław delegate Kingsley Martin, wrote: 'The Exhibition is a triumph of organized display; Gerald Barry, seeking hints for the British Exhibition of 1951, should pay it a visit.'[44]

Their reports, although reaching a limited audience, were written in the year Festival planning started in earnest. It is clear that hints were gleaned by Festival organizers from this government-funded exhibition which brought together a reputed 3,000 artists, architects, engineers, graphic designers, photographers, painters, sculptors and craftspeople, synchronizing an array of media.[45] The most striking parallel is that the 'Lands Regained' exhibition celebrated the very land on which it was situated, which would be the central preoccupation of the Festival. Moreover, the Wrocław exhibition was structured like a book, as if the visitor was following a narrative while progressing through the spaces of the exhibition, as at the Festival. Many other visual elements would also be echoed in 1951. The black coal-clad rotunda at Wrocław may well have provided the inspiration for Thomas Whalen's coal cliff in the Hall of Power at the Festival Heavy Industry Exhibition in Glasgow, and the preoccupation with cartographic imagery at Wrocław, which extended the link to the Polish land, was also a strong visual theme of 1951.

TRADE FAIRS

Since the nineteenth century major exhibitions had been an accepted international language through which the British government communicated ideas about national productivity and attendant notions of national pride and prosperity.[46] The Design and Industries Association, founded in 1915, had for several decades held exhibitions aimed towards raising the quality of industrial design in Britain, such as 'Household Things' at the Whitechapel Gallery in 1920. Many young architects also learnt about exhibition design while working as a part of a team on trade fairs such as the British Industries Federation (BIF) fairs, Ideal Home Exhibitions, Building Trades Exhibitions or agricultural shows. These annual or biennial shows were held in convention centres such as Olympia or Earl's Court in London. Festival architect Jim Cadbury-Brown, for example, cut his teeth as a designer on trade stands. Having trained at the AA and qualified in 1935, Cadbury-Brown won a competition to design a prototype ticket and luggage handling office for British Railways and completed two offices, but he also designed exhibition stands for commercial companies such as Turner's Asbestos Cement and Chance Glass at the BIF fairs, a period interrupted by war service in the Territorial Army.

The trade exhibitions that Cadbury-Brown and designers like him contributed to were, by the time they designed Festival exhibitions, their reference both for design languages and also, significantly, the focus for testing their collaborative powers. While information exhibitions used few objects but relied on variations in display lettering, combining photographs and transparencies with graphics on structures of poles with panels, these trade exhibitions, designed by trained architects, were often complex built structures in miniature.[47] An editorial survey of 1948 in *Architects' Journal*, commented on this situation as of mixed merits:

> One category of design remains in which architects have been very active, since the war put a stop to permanent building: exhibitions, which some architects have taken to for lack of other work and which some think are allowed access to too much scarce material and labour. Nevertheless, the design of exhibitions and commercial displays provides a valuable creative outlet and a testing-ground for new ideas. It is a province in which the British standard is high, and the only one in which officially sponsored design undoubtedly sets the pace.[48]

Writing a few years later, Misha Black would be more qualified in his praise for the standard of British exhibition design, seeing the design quality as very mixed.[49]

BIF fairs provided opportunities for architects to practice their craft in collaboration. Held regularly since 1915, the fairs gave British manufacturers a chance to showcase recent products in stands commissioned from design and architectural practices to create eye-catching environments. The fairs were sponsored and promoted by the government (a responsibility held by the Department for Overseas Trade, which had its own Exhibitions Division, and at other times by the Board of Trade). This work stood at the border between commercial and state exhibitions activity, being considered by the government a key element in national promotion.[50] Festival architect Basil Spence acted as adviser to the Board of Trade for the fairs of 1947, 1948 and 1949 and these exhibitions attracted a dazzling array of contributions from designers. At the 1947 fair, contributions came from designers such as Hulme Chadwick, Neville Conder, Robert Goodden, Basil Spence and from various designers on behalf of DRU, which was regularly commissioned to create stands.

Aside from BIF events, other trade fairs appealed more directly to consumers. The annual Ideal Home exhibitions, founded in 1908 by Wareham Smith, advertising manager of *The Daily Mail*, set out to showcase beautiful English domestic products. They were particularly focused towards addressing women and attracted contributions from many notable designers.[51] They were another opportunity for innovative collaborations over stands selling domestic products, as well as for major industrial displays directed towards educating consumers. At the 1950 Ideal Home, for example, established exhibition designer V. Rotter (who contributed to the Festival) was commissioned by the British Iron and Steel Federation to create a stand that showed a working model of an integrated steelworks. Spotlights picked out animated units in a model filling the centre of a hall, while loudspeakers provided a running commentary. Photographs of industrial processes in action and diagrams around the walls served to illustrate the activity of a works, while abstracted machinery made in steel was used as decoration.[52] Seasoned exhibition designer James Gardner was regularly the co-ordinator of the Ideal Home Exhibitions in the 1940s and 1950s. His designs for these shows were an interesting counterpoint to those of his contemporaries. Avowedly not a modernist, his decorative flourishes − canopies falling from the ceiling in lavish fabrics, for example − did not shy away from patterning and rich textiles that were frowned on by contemporaries who had rather plainer tastes. His setting for the 1951 Ideal Home Exhibition mimicked a facade at the Crystal Palace and halls were hung with huge crystal chandeliers.

By 1951, trade fairs were also held regularly around Europe and in the USA to showcase new industrial products and these would have a strong influence on British designers both through their visits, when politics and finances permitted, and through coverage in British design journals. In Europe, the calendar included regular fairs in Paris, Basel, Leipzig and Milan. From 1930 an International Exhibition of Decorative and Industrial Arts was held in Milan every three years. These Triennales, held in the impressive modern space of Muzio's Palazzo dell'Arte and its surrounding parkland, were intended to stimulate the relationship between industry and the applied arts. Exhibitions showcased craftsmanship, objects of everyday use, graphic arts and anything else that might be called 'design'. The Triennales soon became established as a way of predicting emerging design trends and were, at least for their first couple of decades, the most significant exhibitions to be held in Italy.[53]

The first Triennale after the Second World War was held in 1947, overseen by architect and Communist Piero Bottoni. Focused on reconstruction it promoted the creation of an experimental district on the outskirts of Milan. The 'QT8' (Quartiere Triennale Ottava), as it was called, was a pattern-book of designs for architects and town-planners building new social housing that had been gathered in Italy and abroad (building prototypes from Belgium and Finland were included). It was built on 66 hectares and focused not only on building types but, crucially, on the green spaces and parks in between. Unlike exhibitions of public housing previously showcased by the Triennale, these were built to be permanent, providing an important example to designers working on the Festival's 'Live Architecture' Exhibition at Lansbury, which was also permanent. Another important theme of the 1940s Triennales was industrial design, with a section given over to the International Exhibition of Serial Production. In Festival year the British contribution to the Triennale was organized by Robin Day.

As Festival planning got underway, designers were dispatched on reconnaissance trips to a number of European exhibitions and trade fairs. Their findings, from trips to trade fairs in Basel, London, Birmingham, Milan and Paris, as well as exhibitions in Zurich and Britain, fed straight into discussions of the Festival's Presentation Panel of 1949. These findings – written up as committee papers – included comparisons of the acreage of total sites and of covered space, attendance figures, admission charges and general impressions. Exhibition designer Misha Black and architect Ralph Tubbs, writing after their trip to the Basel Trade Fair in May 1949, observed confidently that there was 'Little evidence of an overall superiority to Great Britain in terms of industrial design excepting for handcraft work' … and that the 'Good Design' section was 'excessively purist in character,' giving the general effect of 'a solemn mortuary'. Meanwhile, architect Hugh Casson, and exhibition designers James Gardner and James Holland, were singularly unimpressed by their visit to the Milan Trade Fair of April 1949, reporting the exhibition's layout and the site's landscaping were 'unimaginative and incoherent' and buildings were old and 'few are architecturally distinguished'.[54]

All of these many sources of ideas: from world's fairs to trade fairs, from official war exhibitions to small one-off shows highlighting issues for reconstruction, from exhibitions that designers had themselves worked on, to expositions reported through the pages of journals such as *Architectural Review*, came together in the planning of the Festival of Britain. They were conveyed by hundreds of architects, artists and designers, congregating in Britain, who had come from all over Europe and beyond. How the Festival was planned and brought together is the subject of the next chapter.

3

'A CONSTELLATION OF EVENTS'

The Festival is nation-wide. All through the summer, and all through the land, its spirit will be finding expression in a variety of British sights and a great range of British sounds.

South Bank Exhibition Guide[1]

The Festival was planned to be a nationwide celebration spanning the United Kingdom. In fact, the map was only partially covered by the eight government exhibitions as half were held in London, one major exhibition was held in Scotland, one in Northern Ireland and none in Wales. Two travelling exhibitions toured to various sites: an exhibition aboard a series of lorries visited four English industrial cities while another aboard a decommissioned aircraft carrier visited ten cities around the coast, including Bristol, Dundee and Birkenhead. Beyond these official events, sponsored by the government, hundreds of committees of local people worked across the country to organize events. Meanwhile, Barry engaged a number of organizations to arrange events within the exhibitions and beyond. The Council of Industrial Design were responsible for choosing a series of industrially designed products for display across the exhibition sites; the Arts Council arranged a large national arts festival held all over the country, everywhere from large purpose-built theatres to church halls; and the Central Office of Information and British Film Institute collaborated on a Festival film season. Two special councils were formed to advise on Science and Technology and on Architecture, Town Planning and Building Research.

'The church', or rather the established Church of England was considered by the Festival Office to play an important part in the festivities. Gerald Barry invited the Archbishop of Canterbury, Geoffrey Fisher, to bring together a religious response to the Festival. This included limited representation of other Christian denominations and of Judaism.[2] A church committee organized exhibitions and services, and St John's at Waterloo was designated 'Festival church', a building that stood as a symbol of resistance, its crypt continuing to be a meeting place despite having been bombed. The National Book League came forward to ensure books were included in the Festival exhibition displays and arranged 80 or so exhibitions of books up and down the country, including a major one at the Victoria and Albert Museum.

As well as official events, Festival organizers were optimistic that people up and down the country, moved to respond to the occasion, would produce unofficial ones and a meeting of local authority leaders was held in London to inspire this. 'On that day the seed was sown from which the harvest is to be reaped this summer,' Barry wrote later, in typically pastoral language.[3] *Evening News* cartoonist Lee (1901–75) captured the mood within local authorities, where efforts had been focused for many years on making do with little resources. Lee drew a council chamber with banners on one side advertising National Savings schemes and on the other advertising the Festival, and the Mayor announcing, 'It's a dead heat between the National Savers and the Festival Spenders. I votes we tax for it!'[4] The 'calculated' grand gestures of the Festival would, it was hoped, elicit something of the opposite: responses that were unplanned or spontaneous.[5] The Festival Office selected the village of Trowell in Nottinghamshire as 'Festival Village', to provide a model for local activity across Britain. Trowell was no chocolate box village. It was a centre of local industry, which fitted with the Festival Office's intention to show Britain as a living country, not a museum. Trowell villagers had set about improving gardens and building a new children's playground in the name of the Festival and it was hoped that others would follow suit.[6] Barry considered privately, however, that they had made a mistake in its choice, perhaps because it was in fact too ordinary. 'This was an unfortunate, indeed a rather thoughtless choice; but we must see it through now,' he wrote in his diary.[7]

This fantasy of a public spontaneously celebrating the festivities was mocked in John Moore's 1951 novel *The Dance and Skylark*. Written as Festival preparations were taking place in villages across Britain, Moore's jocular fictional account exposed the level of planning and bureaucracy that was needed even for small-scale village events. This complexity hardly allowed for the 'spontaneous' overflow of enthusiasm of the Whitehall officials' rhetoric. Following a small English village preparing for the Festival, the novel set the frivolous balloon-filled jamboree that the village committee was planning against the poverty, industrial unrest and agricultural hardship experienced by workers in the surrounding areas, some of whom were being called off their other production work to produce decorations for the festivities. While the planning is underway, posters appear around the village saying 'WE DON'T WANT FESTIVALS WE WANT HOUSES, WORK AND WAGES.'[8] Although jovial in tone, Moore had highlighted a serious point: that this six-month Festival with its lengthy planning period would not simply co-exist with other important national activities such as food and fuel production, manufacturing and re-armament. Instead, people up and down the country were being called to postpone their ordinary work to prepare for festivities. Cartoonist Lee also captured the mood, drawing a scene in a village hall with a builder belligerently sitting up on a rafter and a local dignitary scolding 'Fie upon you, Mr Gummidge! Risking the postponement of Little Maudlin's great Festival effort by striking for beer money, of all things!'[9]

A major justification for the Festival was that it benefited the whole nation, and for this to be true people across Britain must take part. Novelist Evelyn Waugh, from the outset a Festival sceptic, remained convinced that the Festival had been imposed. He wrote,

> In 1951, to celebrate the opening of a happier decade, the government decreed a Festival. Monstrous constructions appeared on the south bank of the Thames, the foundation stone was solemnly laid for a National Theatre, but there was little popular exuberance among the straitened people and dollar-bearing tourists curtailed their visits and sped to the countries of the Continent where, however precarious their condition, they ordered things better.[10]

He was not alone in considering the Festival a ludicrous imposition. Artist and novelist Wyndham Lewis's *Rotting Hill*, written in Festival year, began with a vitriolic attack on the Festival, which he saw as a simple extension of the Attlee government's policy of tax and spend. 'Naturally everyone was dazed,' he started:

> But into this situation burst a handful of jubilant socialists, voted into power, with an overwhelming majority, on the Labour ticket. They were in no way dismayed by the national situation; they proceeded to

extract by huge taxation, direct and indirect, the colossal capital needed to stage a honeymoon for the liberated manual-working mass. This of course gave no one any time to despair at the disappearance of national prosperity ... To symbolize the extraordinary paradox the capital city burst into festivities all along the south bank of the Thames; there was whoopee at Battersea, there was the thunder of orchestras in a new national concert-hall, a thousand peep-shows, culminating in a Dome of Discovery lower down the river.[11]

The deep-seated opposition to the Festival expressed by Lewis came from both left and right. Those on the left focused on the leeching of precious resources away from the work of rebuilding homes and public services; those on the right railed against what many saw merely as propaganda for Attlee's particular brand of socialism.

Many local people did respond enthusiastically. Events were organized in villages, towns and cities up and down the country. There was to be a pageant at East Grinstead, the villagers of Abingdon in Oxfordshire produced a book of poetry, while industrial exhibitions were mounted at Tyneside and Luton. Bedfordshire County Council designed new village signs emblazoned with the Festival emblem. There were to be flower shows, cricket weeks, fetes and dances, whist drives, brass band contests, gymkhanas and sheepdog trials, all in the name of the Festival. All were things that might have happened anyway, but in Festival year they were over-branded with the Festival emblem and included in Festival listings. Magazines produced popular samplers with a pattern of the Festival map, which were enthusiastically bought and sewn. Festival ties and biro pens in the shape of the Skylon were snapped up across the country. The enduring pastoralism of the British national imagination was reflected in songs written for the Festival. The Arts Council commissioned poet Cecil Day-Lewis to write 'Song for a Festival', which became tantamount to a declaration of love for the island of Britain. '*Dear land, dear land, our roots are deep in you: May your sons, may your sons grow tall and true!*' Meanwhile the popular song 'The Festival of Britain This Grand Old Land of Mine' continued in this anthropomorphic vein, praising the land for nurturing a great nation.[12]

The nationwide festivities were to be structured around a story and all exhibitions were to be about the relationship between 'The Land and People of Britain'. 'The Land' was described as 'scenery, climate and resources', and each exhibition focused on how these have 'nurtured and challenged and stimulated the people', providing a strong link between national topography and British national character.[13] This theme of land and people uniting the nationwide Festival also made the whole of Britain and its people notionally a part of the exhibition itself.

> Many times before, nations or cities have organized exhibitions of industrial skill and progress … Behind the Festival of Britain lies a broader and bolder plan; for the idea is that in 1951 the land of Britain, and the people of Britain, will be open to view, demonstrating our achievements and our way of life.

Emphasizing the way these exhibitions inverted the structure of previous world's fairs on one site, the leaflet went on:

> The Exhibition of 1851 was confined to London. The Festival of Britain 1951 will be spread over the whole of the United Kingdom, and every locality will be encouraged to participate and add its own spontaneous and individual activity to the national events.[14]

The Great Exhibition of 1851 had been a comparative exhibition, allowing the produce of many nations to be shown side-by-side in a single building, the Crystal Palace at London's Hyde Park. 1951 marked the emergence of a new type of exhibition that turned the world's fair paradigm on its head. Eschewing the practice of gathering all exhibits from across the world in one place, the Festival instead assembled one country – Britain – into a single narrative of achievements for the world to observe, without reference to British colonies or Commonwealth. Being spread out, the focus could shift from the produce of many nations to abstracted notions about national characteristics found in British land and people. Festival organizers could follow through an idea that this was not a trade show simply focused on attracting buyers, but rather an act of philanthropy, a warm invitation extended to the world to join a party.

A NEW PICTURESQUE

The Festival of Britain events, spread out across the four nations, focused on reconciling 'land and people' in order to create a new sense of place after the disfigurement caused by wartime preparation and blitzing. Through their experiments at the Festival, this 'brief' or 'magical' city, designers would develop a pattern-book, a visual language that would have an impact on the look of reconstruction more generally.[15]

An important area of experimentation for Festival architects engaged with reconstructing the place of Britain after blitzing and industrial scarring was with methods for incorporating open space around buildings. This had also become a key focus for public authorities, the most significant commissioners of new buildings and landscapes just after the war. Local authority architects were developing ideas about how landscaping, in all its permutations from parks and common land to hard-paved areas, should appropriately be included in rebuilt urban areas. Principles of landscaping associated with the eighteenth-century Picturesque, developed and shaped on private country estates, again became operative in the design of Festival exhibition sites and, in turn, in the postwar reconstruction of British cities and of New Towns. These ideas were so influential in the design of the Festival of Britain that it is important to trace here how this Picturesque revival had come about.

Manifestations of Picturesque can be detected in English poetry, painting and thought from as early as the 1660s, when antiquaries and poets were beginning to show an appreciation of the impact of ancient ruins in the landscape. Despite the scattered formulation of these ideas, however, their original formalization into a written programme is most usually attributed to debates between two men: art collector and writer Richard Payne Knight (1751–1824) and writer and rural improver Uvedale Price (1747–1829). Both were landowners of neighbouring Herefordshire estates, and had been deeply influenced by their Grand Tour travels to France, Rome, Florence and beyond. In 1794, Knight published *The Landscape: A Didactic Poem* in which he extolled the virtues of rough and 'picturesque beauty' of natural landscapes that he had seen in paintings by Dutch and Flemish artists and by Claude Lorrain. In his poem, Knight set the English landscape in a wide political and national context, making an implicit comment on the impact of the Industrial Revolution, French Revolution and Whig politics, and using the landscape as a metaphor through which he sought to define English democracy. Published in the same year, Uvedale Price's *Essay on the Picturesque* celebrated the local and the diverse within the landscape. His essay put up a defence against what he saw as the uniform planning practices of gardeners such as Capability Brown. The essay set out to present ideas that could be adopted by others in their treatment of land in their control.

The interest shown in the look of the landscape by theoreticians of the Picturesque such as Knight, Price and Horace Walpole derived from their position as landowners.[16] The publication in 1927 of *The Picturesque* by the architectural historian, author and gardener Christopher Hussey reintroduced Picturesque planning for debate in the twentieth century. Hussey would describe the book as 'a pioneering venture in the field of visual romanticism', seeing in the principles 'a practical aesthetic for gardeners, tourists and sketchers'.[17] Hussey's interest in promoting and reviving the Picturesque was in line with his belief in the need for a revived squirearchy as a way of safeguarding the future preservation of the countryside. His focus was on how formations of Picturesque had been used on country estates and their potential for reuse within rural landscaping schemes.

From the 1940s, when the idea of a 1951 Festival was being mooted, the potential applications of the English Picturesque were rethought. This was the result of growing dissatisfaction with the long-term impact of the Industrial Revolution on the topography of Britain and unhappiness at the immediate impact of the Second World War on the landscape. Destruction had been wreaked by enemy bombing. War had also taken its toll through the impact of newly installed technologies and industries, new roads and the attendant need to fell trees in previously rural areas. In the aftermath of these changes, the possibilities of the Picturesque were rethought in two significant ways. Where it had only been considered in relation to rural schemes, Picturesque became discussed as applicable to urban conditions and where it had originated as the preoccupation of a group of land-owning aristocrats; ideas associated with the Picturesque became a plausible instrument for public authorities engaged in reconstruction schemes. Improving the look of Britain through a rigorous attention to the aesthetic impact of their work, thereby returning beauty to blitzed or notionally ugly and scarred places, was believed to have a beneficial effect on national morale.

One reason why the Picturesque, which might otherwise have merely been seen as an arcane anachronism, is likely to have gained such wide acceptance in official circles after the Second World War in part arose from the wider exercise of historical re-evaluation that was under way at the time. Commentators as diverse as writer John Gloag, architectural historian Ralph Dutton and architect Ralph Tubbs were united in their admiration for building and landscaping of the eighteenth century. The eighteenth century was eulogized as a golden age before the 'factoriculture' associated with the age of mass industrialization of the nineteenth century, the era before a 'decay of taste' and 'meaningless' architectural forms associated with the Victorians and before the social breakdown of the nineteenth century. In the minds of the same commentators, the eighteenth century became 'the most agreeable society England has ever known'.[18]

The call for a twentieth-century urban Picturesque revival was spearheaded by the editors of influential journal *Architectural Review*. Their campaign had gained momentum under the editorship of Nikolaus Pevsner, J.M. Richards,

John Betjeman and Hubert de Cronin Hastings, amongst others. It was fought through historical features that ran from as early as the 1930s alongside contemporary building features.[19] These features discussed the contribution of eighteenth-century figures associated with the Picturesque such as Price and Knight, essayist William Temple, and places associated with its development, such as Chiswick House and Alexander Pope's grotto at Twickenham. H.F. Clark, later lead landscape consultant for the South Bank Exhibition, wrote regularly for the journal. His 1944 article entitled 'Lord Burlington's Bijou, or Sharawaggi at Chiswick' publicly endorsed the journal's campaign for Picturesque.[20] In addition, the magazine ran articles calling for the direct application of these ideas. Most explicitly, an anonymous article also published in 1944 (written by Hubert de Cronin Hastings) was entitled 'Exterior Furnishing or Sharawaggi: The art of making urban landscape' and exhorted architects and landscapers to take lessons from the Picturesque organization of domestic interiors. Picturesque, Hastings opined, was a national visual form, a 'philosophy', for which the English could claim sole credit and, after all, 'a national picture-making aptitude exists among us'.[21] Art historian Nikolaus Pevsner (1902–83) claimed in a 1944 article in the journal that the Picturesque was England's greatest contribution to European visual culture, calling for architects to reconsider its significance for contemporary design.[22] *Review* magazine continued to pursue its agenda based on this tendentious claim and by 1949 had become strongly convinced of the need for a Picturesque revival publishing an article entitled 'Townscape: A Plea for an English Visual Philosophy Founded on the True Rock of Sir Uvedale Price'. The subject of the look of new urban landscapes – or 'townscapes' – would be a recurrent theme in the magazine for the subsequent decade, explored in more depth in the pages following Gordon Cullen's 1949 'Townscape Casebook' in the *Review*. This 'Casebook' included the South Bank amongst a number of examples to illustrate concepts of 'Exposure' (the 'sense of release' felt when suddenly out in the open) and 'Ornament of Function' (the decoration of a scene with flags, colours and objects).[23] Holding up Picturesque as part of a national democratic tradition, *Review*'s editors wanted to see the design of modern Britain tempered by appropriate historic visual references. The journal, which was read by architects and designers alike, was extraordinarily influential on the generation who designed the Festival.

The eighteenth-century Picturesque in its formalized manifestations was an aesthetic developed and controlled by those who owned the land, rather than those who lived on it, worked on it or visited it. Their focus was on asserting control over and enhancing the inherent qualities of places that appeared uncultivated, predominately forming areas of private country estates.

By contrast with these manifestations of private Picturesque, the twentieth-century or new Picturesque concerned the development of a practical aesthetic for reconstructing places predominantly in public ownership across Britain. Its proponents tried to reconcile, in visual form, the self-image of Britain as a rural nation, with a landscape that had dramatically been transformed by modern roads, buildings, industry and war.[24]

Like eighteenth century manifestations, the twentieth-century new Picturesque operated both in the realm of rhetoric and as an applied aesthetic. On a rhetorical level it was linked by its twentieth-century proponents with claims to an indigenous national visual culture, with the existence of a *'genius loci'* or character of place, and a Whiggish tradition of linking democratic politics with the land, as loosely evoked by critics such as Pevsner, thereby situating it as appropriately British and suited to the current conditions of a postwar social democracy. In its aesthetic application, it was promoted for its potential to create eye-pleasing arrangements of buildings in open space, its potential for visual variety and for creating ensembles, mapping onto the word it derived from: *pittoresco*, or painterly.

Town planner and architect Patrick Abercrombie (1879–1957) was pivotal to this refocus on visual planning, providing a regional planning context in which the adoption of new Picturesque ideas could be debated. Abercrombie's preference, expressed in his policy pronouncements, for constructing small-scale communities that combined aspects of town and country, reflected turn-of-the-century thinking about connections between social and spatial form that had been explored by pioneering Scottish planner Patrick Geddes (1854–1932). Abercrombie's interventions in planning debates from the interwar period onwards were highly influential. They included proposing creating a green belt to limit development around London, putting forward the idea of postwar New Towns, and requiring that towns drew up a blueprint for future development. These blueprints provided an occasion on which towns and cities across Britain had to rethink their environments on a significant scale, and a context for reconsidering approaches to visual planning and the English tradition of Picturesque. The influential writings of Lewis Mumford were also key to the reception of Picturesque revival. His 1938 *The Culture of Cities* had considered cities as developed forms of social relationship and how planning should nurture this relationship, ideas he developed in wartime proposals for regional planning, nature-friendly modernism and for schemes that put women and children first. The Picturesque was taken up by public planners in search of a way of expressing British national values, who saw in it a way of linking national visual culture with a distinctive British brand of politics.

During the second half of the 1940s – the period when planning started on the Festival – a new Picturesque started to inform a number of government reports, local schemes and the work of agencies, all united in their role in reconstruction work. Where these ideas had previously been attached to an English tradition of Picturesque, through the control of a government with financial and legislative responsibilities for reconstruction across England, Wales, Scotland and Northern Ireland, these ideas were rethought for application across the four nations. Guidelines setting out policy on new public housing, for example, strongly advocated use of a reconfigured Picturesque as providing an appropriate look across the country. Eighteenth century landscaping dicta were echoed in HMSO *Government Housing Manuals* of 1949 and 1953, where the housing schemes cited as models emphasized dominant green space and buildings set into the contours of the land. Advice in the 1949 *Manual*, which covered both urban and rural schemes, focused on the importance of vistas into and out of building groups. It instructed that 'In urban areas the town dweller needs the visual relaxation that can be given by the sight of grass and trees' and 'Where estates border open country or a park, the layout should allow the country or park to be viewed from within the housing area,' ensuring that attention was paid to housing ensembles, as well as to individual elements.[25]

Beyond the design of new housing, this preference for pictorial values in British public reconstruction was also debated in the emerging profession of landscape architecture. A key exponent of this debate was landscape designer Brenda Colvin, who worked on many industrial landscaping schemes and explored the idea of 'locating' beauty in order to 'use' it in her 1947 book *Land and Landscape*. Describing the book as 'an examination of the latent causes of beauty', Colvin called for a strongly attuned philosophical aesthetic based on the sense of sight and not reliant on a sense of tradition. This urge to create 'new beauty' and to challenge 'ugliness' was not simply a wish to reverse modernization. Instead, Colvin suggested that people should learn a new 'discipline' of looking that would allow them to see modern public utilities as beautiful, stating,

> Viewing objectively, judged by the eye alone, certain windmills and certain transmission towers in certain positions are beautiful: but the eye is influenced by mental associations and memories.[27]

This appreciation of new technology within the texture of the landscape was key to the new Picturesque, which was mobilized in order to reconcile people and new structures in the landscape, supplying power, water or other collective needs. The Festival of Britain, particularly Glasgow's Heavy Industry Exhibition, would become an important showcase for technology within the landscape.

In the context of the Attlee government's nationalization programme, and fierce Parliamentary clashes over this reform programme that had become a feature of the government from 1945, Colvin's ideas marked a significant shift toward the acceptance of a permanently changed landscape, following the restructuring of national industries. In *Land and Landscape* Colvin had also stated that 'Our power-stations, oil refineries, factories and water-works must take their place, in time, with the pyramids, castles and temples of the past.'[27] For Colvin, where 'beauty' had previously been associated with the countryside and had been understood to have connotations of private ownership, seen in the follies and landscapes of private country estates, it should now be rethought and relocated in a land dominated by new public housing estates, power stations, pylons and roads. Landscape designers and architects open to these ideas would have a pivotal role in designing the South Bank site and in this context the Festival's focus on the British 'land and people' had a particularly strong resonance. While the relationship between land and people was the subject of displays, it was also part of the sites themselves, allowing people to be immersed in these temporary landscapes.

STRIKES AND SHORTAGES

Severe material shortages experienced nationwide also had an impact on the building of the Festival. A plethora of raw materials were in short supply. The Festival Office called upon architects and designers to make the temporary exhibition spaces from unrestricted materials wherever possible. John Ratcliff, Construction Controller at the South Bank, later recalled, however, that due to adverse weather conditions leading up to the Festival most buildings ended up being constructed of more durable materials.[28] All non-ferrous metals, rubber, sulphur and coal were in various states of short supply. For several years steel production had been maintained and increased by importing large quantities of steel scrap from Western Germany but the flow was drying up and the British steel industry started to face severe problems with meeting demands. Festival architects started designing with the understanding that there would be virtually no steel available, although it was decontrolled half way through the planning period. There were significant supply problems for timber and wood pulp, too, with consumption severely restricted throughout Europe, but especially in Britain, which was a chief

3.1 WORK IN PROGRESS
(Above) Archaeologist with 'find' made during
preparation for the South Bank Exhibition in August
1949;
(Below, left) Henry Hull, a labourer at the South Bank;
(Below, right) workers drilling gusset plates onto the
roof of the Dome.

3.2 PAINTING IN PROGRESS
(Above) Graham Sutherland working on his painting *The Origins of the Land* for the Land pavilion, South Bank in March 1951;
(Below) Kempster and Evans at work on their mural *Research at Sea* in the Dome of Discovery in April 1951.

European importer, something that got worse as Festival planning continued, meaning that original estimates for softwoods had to be halved.[29]

Strikes were held regularly at both the South Bank and Battersea during the building period. 250 builders working on the Royal Festival Hall came out on unofficial strike in December 1949 in protest at the dismissal of carpenters and labourers said to be too incompetent to share bonuses and there was general unhappiness about working conditions. Mural painter Barry Evans later recalled the terrible discomfort of working inside the Dome, which was dark, damp and very cold. He said 'the lighting was minimal ... and a "Valor" stove for heating the wax emulsion we were using as a medium was not enough to heat us ... The noise was deafening. Right behind us was a pneumatic drill. Forklift trucks, girders crashing, workers shouting above the noise'.[30] Misha Black had vivid memories of the unlikely wonder of the Festival in construction: this 'magical city', as he described it, built on an industrial wasteland, dogged by strikes and bad weather. He remembered all the construction workers having a candle-lit meal on trestle tables in the Dome of Discovery (the pavilions were not electrified until just before opening). All were in sombre mood until one threw the plate he had been eating off into the air and a thousand men started spinning paper plates, 'dome shapes spinning in the Dome'.[31]

4

'ALL THROUGH THE LAND'

Exhibiting the Land and People of Britain

Amid the calculated displays, the exhibitions and the processions, concerts and pageants, spontaneous expressions of citizenship will flower in the smallest communities as in the greatest.

Basil Taylor, *The Official Book of the Festival of Britain*, 1951

The Festival of Britain opened on Thursday 3 May 1951. It had taken just three years to plan and build, an extraordinary achievement in the light of bad weather and material shortages. A service of dedication at St Paul's Cathedral attended by 300 people marked the opening. Processing from Buckingham Palace, the Royal Family arrived to fanfares.[1] Dignitaries of the Church were in attendance, and the Dean of St Paul's prayed 'Let us give thanks today for the blessings granted to us since the Great Exhibition, one hundred years ago.' Immediately after, King George VI stepped out onto the west steps of St Paul's to speak to the crowds, words that were broadcast across the country, to – in Gerald Barry's words – 'housewives working at the sink, men at the bench, the sick in hospital, children at school'.[2] The Festival of Britain was to be a 'visible sign of national achievement and confidence', he explained, but 'though the nation has made a splendid effort towards recovery, new efforts have fallen upon it and dark clouds still overhang it'. 'In this Festival', he concluded, 'we look back with pride and forward with resolution.' Church bells rang out around the country. That evening the King attended the opening concert at the Royal Festival Hall, during which several dignitaries missed half the performance, having got stuck in the lift.[3] Outside a chain of bonfires were lit across the country as the focus for local singsongs and gatherings.[4] Bell-ringing and bonfires had a particular resonance both as picturesque local traditions and as symbols of national endurance: bells had been pealed throughout Britain to signal victory at the end of the Second World War, and chains of bonfires lit along the coast to defy the Spanish Armada.

The King opened the South Bank Exhibition the next morning. Rain fell on the crowds, including Prime Minister Clement Attlee and Winston Churchill who took shelter under the Dome of Discovery. Important visitors and dignitaries stood solemnly, hats off, as a 350-piece massed band played the *National Anthem*. Author Harold Nicolson recorded the occasion briefly in his diary. 'Viti and I go to the South Bank Exhibition', he noted,

> We are entranced from the first moment. It is rather a nuisance that we keep on running into the King and Queen, but nonetheless we enjoy it uproariously. It is the most intelligent exhibition I have ever visited. I have never seen people so cheered up or amused, in spite of a fine drizzle of rain.[5]

For those designers who had done a 'ghoster', working all night to make finishing touches, the opening was an extraordinary moment. Most stood on the edges of the ceremony, wearing yesterday's clothes, unwashed and sleep-deprived.

George VI had been at opening ceremonies of other major exhibitions: the Wembley Empire Exhibition in 1924 and the Glasgow Empire Exhibition in 1938. This would be his last. By the time of the Festival of Britain, the King's health was in severe decline and he would be too ill to open the Belfast Festival exhibition a few weeks later. 'Pomp in Reduced Circumstances' ran the headline in US *Life* magazine above a story about the Festival's opening. It hailed the pageant-filled Royal opening as peculiarly English and praised the 'glittering, ultramodern buildings and striking displays' as a symptom of an optimism that had been dispelled by 'less sunny days of continued austerity and political turmoil'.[6] For the *Life* journalist, the rain that accompanied the opening was emblematic of the subdued public mood. *The Times* carried the lukewarm headline 'So Far so Good at Festival', reporting that a rodent exterminator had had to be brought in to kill hordes of rats, that parts of the exhibition were still incomplete and some of the displays not yet working.[7] Various exhibition cases, which still stood empty on the first day, were covered with paper until the Festival closed.[8]

TOURING THE SOUTH BANK

Most visitors to the South Bank entered through the Station Gate. Once through the turnstiles, they stood in the exhibition site's largest open space, the concourse, facing the Thames straight ahead, with long views to the Dome and Skylon. Ralph Tubbs' vast Dome of Discovery stood, as he described, to 'contrast the visual solidarity of a series of sweeping horizontal galleries of reinforced concrete with the extraordinary lightness of the vast aluminium saucer dome which spans out and beyond all the galleries and which is supported on very light tubular steel struts.'[9] It was built to contain a complex display about pioneering Britons but was to become the most celebrated temporary pavilion at the South Bank.Next to the Dome, on the riverfront, stood the towering Skylon, designed by Hidalgo Moya (1920–94) and Philip Powell (1921–2003) in their recently established architectural studio in Westminster, with help from structural engineer Felix Samuely (1902–59). As Powell later explained, it was Moya who had conceived of the idea in response to the competition for a vertical feature, while he had dreamt up an alternative scheme for a tall tower with Mondrianesque coloured panels floating over it. Moya's idea was clearly the stronger, so they entered that.[10] The Skylon was to become the other great Festival icon.

The two-part structure of 'Land and People' was useful: it allowed South Bank designers to make a virtue of the newly built Thames-side industrial site, divided halfway through by a railway embankment. Upstream – to the left – was the 'Land of Britain' (overseen by Misha Black), downstream – to the right – 'The People of Britain' (overseen by Hugh Casson). Guides and signposts bid visitors to follow the circulation route, to enter the upstream 'Land of Britain' by walking beneath a blue concave aluminium cone, the portico signalling the start of that section (designed by Jim Cadbury-Brown). The South Bank's circulation route invited visitors to start from the moment when the earth was formed, following through to the moment that its products – be they of the soil, minerals found underground, or water – were used to produce power, and finally becoming objects used in everyday life.[11]

Buildings were set over many levels, with steps and walkways taking visitors up and down, to gaze over constantly changing views. There was much incident: fountains played and ducks bathed, helium balloons were set off into the sky above with tickets attached for lucky passers-by, and people stopped to catch their breath while watching cascading water sculptures. Some ate Cornish pasties while perching on one of the many chairs scattered about the site, resting in open-air cafés in the shade of a coloured umbrella, or gazed out across the Thames at the magnificent views towards the Houses of Parliament, Waterloo Bridge and St Paul's. The South Bank was crowded in places with densely planted shrubs and trees, dotted with concrete planters holding jauntily coloured flowers.

In the buildings, architects used geological samples brought from other parts of Britain in the buildings, landscaping and paving, alongside the concrete, brick and new materials also used. Royal Festival Hall, designed by Robert Matthew and Leslie Martin with Peter Moro of LCC's Architects' Office, made much use of geological samples. The Hall's large external columns were faced with Derbyshire fossil marble known as 'Derbydene', a polished variety of carboniferous limestone composed mainly of fossil debris. The columns exposed 'occasional corals and brachiopods embedded in a matrix of comminuted fragments and lime mud', carefully left in to hint at its origins. This direct link with the land was even more evident when the quarry source of this 'prehistoric slab, with interest close-to' ran out and a section at the top of the building could not be covered.[12] This detail was picked up on the front cover of *Architectural Review* for June 1951, which showed a close-up of the fossilized limestone used at the Royal Festival Hall with a caption: 'The Cover shows the genius loci of the Royal Festival Hall as it manifested itself to Gordon Cullen while he was examining the Derbyshire marble walls of the foyer.'[13]

The South Bank's walkways used a wide variety of igneous, metamorphic and sedimentary rocks displaying textures, structures and fossils hinting towards their origin and evolution including ash layers from Ordovician volcanoes, a Devonian coral reef and Jurassic scampi burrows.[14] The LCC also used Cornish granite to build the new river wall at the South Bank, laid by a Cornish mason. In January 1950, while the South Bank was still under construction, Richard Dimbleby broadcast for the BBC from the site, interviewing an LCC Engineer about this. He observed, 'This recognition of the harmony between the national character and its natural environment form the basis of the layout of the Exhibition.'[15]

At the South Bank visitors walked through a succession of pavilions devoted to the theme of 'the land', all by different architects: The Land of Britain, The Natural Scene, The Country and The Minerals of the Island. While being told about the land in the exhibitions' content, visitors to the site were invited to enact their relationship with the land through their exposure to the site itself, and landscaped areas recreated the geological structures of Britain.

The landscaping of the South Bank richly referenced the land of Britain, using British plant species and geological samples transported from around the country. The design of the South Bank landscape was planned as part of

4.1 SOUTH BANK EXHIBITION LANDSCAPE
Preparatory sketches for planting schemes by H.F. Clark
and Maria Shephard.
(Above) Rock garden;
(Below) Setting for a rock pool in a country stream at
the base of the plaster tree in the Natural Scene.

the wider architectural scheme. H.F. (Frank) Clark (1902–71) was landscape consultant to the Festival Office for the whole site, assisted by Maria Shephard (1903–74). Peter Shepheard (1913–2002), Peter Youngman (1911–2005) and Jim Cadbury-Brown (1913–2009) worked to them. Landscape architect Peter Youngman described how he had recreated Westmoreland rock formations at the site, planting rock and stream gardens and rock abutments to the Origins of the Land pavilion, imaginatively signposting visitors away from their immediate surroundings to the land of Britain beyond. Like many others working on the Festival, Youngman had a fledgling career by the late 1940s. 'My training was in the world of rock gardens, which came in incredibly handy at the Festival' he explained. In order to complement the farming or geology themes of the buildings, Youngman was asked to landscape the surrounding spaces. 'I was given the greenery as counterpart with the obvious suggestion that this should be rural,' he explained. 'I wanted to give a feel of the geology externally with dry stonewalls and with the rockery. The dry stonewalls complemented the theme.'[16] Youngman was at the vanguard of the new profession of landscape architecture, using traditional craft skills to get the right look.

Youngman engaged rock garden and dry stonewalling specialists to build the section around the Origins of the Land and the Country pavilions. 'I knew quite a lot of rocky landscapes', he explained later. 'I liked hill walking in the Lake District and had lived in the Yorkshire Dales as a boy, so I had that as a background.' The job of building the walls went to someone 'good at drystone walling, sensitive at laying the walls with a much more underlying sense of the strata running through whereas some just stuck stone on the face of it.'

Architect Jim Cadbury-Brown was responsible for the design of The Origins of the Land pavilion and the landscaped area around it.[17] The building was designed in a 'heavy elemental style' in deliberate contrast to the many lighter buildings around it.[18] Cadbury-Brown's work at the South Bank allowed him to extend the internal display about geology seamlessly onto the exterior landscaping.[19] Recalling how he had designed a series of rock formations to cluster around the opening, he said 'The entrance [to the Land] looks like a bit of landscape – I think the stone came from Derbyshire, obtained by Costain, but they were lumps and I had wanted them more stratified, which would have been better … but one would have needed to go to a different mine to get stratified stone and it all had to be done relatively cheaply.' These displays were not intended to look entirely naturalistic: Yorkshire stone sat beside square-formed Forest of Dean stone and red sandstone – a geological impossibility. Instead they made strong, clear references to the British land beyond that visitors could clearly pick up on. They employed the materials that they represented – in this case a stony outcrop in the British landscape – to tell their own story. Cadbury-Brown recalled visitors on a day-trip to the South Bank becoming so convinced by the earth-strewn boulders that clustered around the mouth of his pavilion that some started picnicking on them, something that was firmly clamped down on by attendants fearing the display would be ruined.

The idea that a day out at the South Bank had much in common with a country ramble was borne out by an *Architectural Review* article explaining that at the Land of Britain pavilion visitors first, 'enter a sort of cave-mouth between rough stone walls set into a boulder-strewn hillside'. The 'mouth' of the Origins of the Land pavilion was designed by Cadbury-Brown to resemble the opening of a cave, giving the impression as visitors entered that they were plunged down deep underground. A succession of chambers depicted the geological evolution of the British Isles. In the first was Graham Sutherland's painted mural *The Origins of the Land*, which referenced primeval Britain through abstracted sculptural shapes showing sea life and a pterodactyl. Commissioned to set the scene as visitors entered, Sutherland's work presented an unsettling vision of primitive chaos in acid colours, rather than the more cosy and familiar elucidation of British origins that Cadbury-Brown had envisaged. 'Hopeless … it certainly didn't work,' he said later. 'Any rate, you walked round it, through it, past it.'[20]

After passing Sutherland's mural and going further inside the Land of Britain pavilion, there was a display designed by virtuoso animator, V. Rotter, who knew well how to bring dour subjects alive.[21] The story told in the pavilion spanned 400 million years of geological evolution, focusing consistently on the economic value of rocks created in the process. The centrepiece, designed to explain the geological origins of the land, was an animated 'topographical 3D map', which moved and changed – using 'Pepper's Ghost' illusionary techniques with plate glass and special lighting – to show 70 million years of geological evolution. Designed by Rotter with engineer K.G. Danielli, the display consisted of four elaborate relief maps

4.2 *SOUTH BANK EXHIBITION LANDSCAPE* (facing page)
(Above) Rocky outcrop and waterfall by The Country;
(Middle, left) Dry-stone wall and rocky outcrop at
entrance to The Land of Britain;
(Middle, centre and right) Landscaping by The Country;
(Bottom) Moat Garden by The Unicorn café with
Edward Mills's abacus screen in the distance, masking
Waterloo Bridge.

that moved in sequence using hydraulic pumps, film and a diorama. Moving between being flat and three-dimensional they aimed to illuminate how the same areas of land had changed over time. Danielli's complicated mechanism depended on compressing air within cavities of latex rubber, with four maps all mounted on carriages and turntables that turned in sequence through 90 degrees.[22]

Film was an important medium for telling this geological story inside the Land pavilion. A central pillar of 'rock' concealed a 16 mm projector showing a continuous film loop that was projected onto the surface of the maps. Films made for the section included *Fossils Which Come to Life*, *Land Fauna and Reptiles*, *Earth in Labour* and *Landscape Scenes*, which further developed the geological focus again providing an imaginative link with the wider geologies of Britain. At Glasgow there were parallels in 'Coal' where animated maps covered in engraved Perspex showed the surface geography when illuminated by general lighting, and the coalfields concealed beneath were revealed when edge lighting was switched on. A direct link between production and the geological make-up of the British land was also asserted in the Minerals of the Island, where an exhibit covered coal-mining methods from prehistoric times or 'Before History' to the present day and showed how developing mining technology had pierced through stratified layers of earth, rock and minerals.

After visiting the Land of Britain, this visual and spatial variety continued into the next pavilion on the circulation route, the Natural Scene, a building by architect Brian O'Rorke and display by graphic designer F.H.K. Henrion. A brightly lit space, it contrasted with the darkness of the last, dramatically rising in height and filled with the cries and whistles of birds. 'See the seals and eagles, the foxes and wild cats, of these still wild islands', explained visitor Dylan Thomas.[23] In the centre of the display was a massive, twisted

4.3 SOUTH BANK EXHIBITION LANDSCAPE (facing page)
(Above, left) The Country with farmer's wind-pump as a rotating model of sun and moon;
(Above, centre) Concrete flower pots and Ernest Race chairs in front of Dome;
(Above, right) The Unicorn café with planters;
(Middle, left) Lawns outside Homes and Gardens;
(Middle, right) Herbs set in paving outside Homes and Gardens;
(Bottom, left) Pool and Jacob Epstein's *Youth Advancing* outside Homes and Gardens;
(Bottom, right) Wall-mounted pots and planters outside Homes and Gardens designed by Maria Shephard.

plaster tree with an irregular woodland garden of leaves and wild flowers at its foot and pools of water.[24] Visitors looked to the base of the tree through a tank of live butterflies. The Natural Scene showed 'the wildlife of Britain and the variety and interdependence of our animals and plants', through vignettes of specific places in the British Isles such as 'South Devon and Dartmoor' or 'The Craven Limestone'. Henrion's designs were a masterful exercise in combining disparate media. Behind frames using wood appropriate to that region, he combined models showing cross-sections of the geology of the land that pivoted on an axis, with phototransparencies, cut-out models and real sample flora and fauna such as stuffed birds, butterflies, flowers and shells. Nearby there were also live birds that had been brought to the site. Displays described Britain's varied natural life showing that even London's urban metropolis – described by Dylan Thomas as 'the natural history of owled and cuckooed, ottered, unlikely London' – had a vibrant natural life. By showing it, Henrion reinforced ideas about particularity of place, the varied characteristics of local places across the country.

The Country was the next section visitors came to after the Natural Scene, displays also designed by Henrion. It traced 'how we have shaped our landscape' becoming 'one of the most efficiently farmed countrysides in the world'.[25] Mechanization and science were linked with the breeding of plants and livestock and the geological narrative continued, showing the wealth of the countryside as coming from the minerals lying underneath the surface. The Country was, on first inspection, a simple farm building looking out to a slice of countryside, with running water surrounded by a stream and dry stonewalls. But in the byre-like buildings tractors were mounted on stands of varying heights, surreal figures sculpted by F.E. McWilliam stood as allegories of the four seasons and a farmer's wind-pump became a rotating model of the sun and moon. 'See all the sculpted and woven loaves, in the shape of sheaves of wheat, in curls, plaits and whirls,' said Dylan Thomas, relishing such eclecticism. 'And men are thatching the roofs of cottages; and – what could be more natural? – the men are made of straw. And what a pleasure of baskets!

4.4 THE NATURAL SCENE (facing page)
(Above) Plaster tree in the centre of The Natural Scene, resembling a rock pool in a country stream with woodland flowers;
(Below) Display about The New Forest in The Natural Scene with introductory text, geological cross-section, samples of flora and fauna and a plant tank, with a photographic background framed on battens.
Display design: F.H.K. Henrion.

Trugs, creels, pottles and punnets, heppers, dorsers and mounds, wiskets and whiskets.'[26]

After leaving the Country building, the circulation route took visitors into the Minerals of the Island, again plunging them into a sequence of gloomy cave-like galleries. The geometric building was designed by Architects' Co-operative Partnership (ACP), the landscape surrounding it by Peter Youngman. Youngman explained it was based on 'the idea of a coal tip'. ACP had wanted it, he said, 'to be covered in grass, as a hillside'.[27] Youngman was faced with the problem of how to cover something with grass at this angle. 'In the end the Clerk of Works found a solution: he cut up pieces of peat turf that could be laid like bricks, so a timber structure had to be created on top of the concrete structure and the peat blocks could be stacked on top.' Internally, the Minerals pavilion linked the surface of the earth, with the riches that lay beneath, with those people that dig the riches out, and to the new products that these materials make. It showed recent advances in the technology of mining the earth for everything from coal, to salt, to sulphur. By demonstrating the contemporary dependence on the minerals found beneath the surface of the earth, the display aimed to show heavy industry as relevant to all people and directly linked to the land around them. Light and dark, space and scenery were modified both within and outside the buildings to give visual and emotional variety and the impression that they were actually in the landscape.

FESTIVAL PLANTING

Planting schemes were of special importance at the South Bank in order that the site became not only a landscape but a green landscape, fulfilling Barry's idea that it would really be 'alive' for the summer of 1951. At Harlow New Town, landscape consultant Sylvia Crowe had specifically chosen indigenous tree species such as oak, birch, holly and hawthorn for her planting schemes contemporary with the Festival. Such species were also the preference in Festival planting guidance. These species were, however, difficult to use at

4.5 THE COUNTRY (facing page)
(Above) Interior of the Country with agricultural machinery (Architect: Brian O'Rorke, Display design: F.H.K. Henrion);
(Below) Country Life section with rural crafts in the background (Display design: F.H.K. Henrion).

the South Bank where planting decisions had to be governed by practical considerations such as finding plants with shallow roots that could be moved and which would last the duration of the exhibition. Indigenous plants alone would not last from May to September so others had to be brought in. One dismayed MP asked why the Asian tropical species *zelcova acuminata* was being planted at the South Bank. He was told that the plant was of horticultural interest, a suitable shape and shallow-rooted, so easy to transplant.[28]

Planting across the South Bank took many different forms. Some was made to appear like the undergrowth around wild rivers or streams. Youngman designed a Moat Garden, a practical landscaping device aimed at controlling crowd flow, which appeared like a riverbed with large stones, shale and water, surrounded by bushes and plants. Snaking around one of the café areas, this stretch of water drew the eye into the immediate environment and away from the buildings just outside the site. On other parts of the South Bank planting was more manicured. Round the Homes and Gardens building lawns, wall-mounted stoneware planters and a sunken garden by Peter Shepheard dotted with kitchen herbs gave the impression of a lovingly tended domestic garden. Meanwhile, Gordon Cullen was commissioned to design a modest pocket garden with rubble stone walling on a terrace outside Homes and Gardens.

Tree replacement after their loss during wartime deforestation, to make way for roads and aerodromes, was a symbolic act of reconstruction. Landscape architect Peter Shepheard described his conviction that trees could be used in a process of reconstruction. 'There is hardly a town anywhere which has not some scar of industry or railway yard, gasworks or speculative building, which could be healed by the careful planting of the right trees in the right places.'[29] Using trees to 'heal' scars linked with a deep, quasi-spiritual belief in the capacity of elements from nature to cure the urban condition. This idea was followed through with great ambition. Semi-mature, 30 feet high trees were transplanted to the South Bank in the autumn of 1950.[30] A thicket of rhododendron from a Rothschild garden on the edge of the New Forest was lifted and brought to the site (its roots allowed for such transportation), providing a sheltered area without the need for a wall. Across Britain, tree planting was also a significant part of the Festival, drawing together villagers and townspeople in ceremonies to dedicate newly planted specimens. In Belfast, officers of the Belfast Battalion planted a hundred almond, cherry and plum trees. Underlying this activity was an idea of locating beauty and particularity of place, even in places that had been demolished and entirely rebuilt. Even where a *tabula rasa* existed as a result of total destruction, or there was deep industrial scarring, places could notionally be returned to their 'proper' form, an original form that identified the *genius loci*, a kind of prelapsarian state.

Festival planting, which brought greenery and countryside features to the South Bank, helped visitors link this urban exhibition site with the rural world beyond. It also provided a pattern book for showing how the country might be integrated with the city. 'The main beauty of [the South Bank Exhibition] was to show people that an urban site is just as much fun as a rural site,' landscape architect Peter Shepheard would later comment. He went on, 'built into the English mind is the idea that peace is in the country and, of course, much funnier ideas that "God made the country and man made the town", which of course is horribly untrue. We wanted to demonstrate that.'[31] Hugh Casson, who observed that London was 'a city of secret places, of unexpected country lanes and hidden gardens', did not, it seems, intend the Festival to be a halfway house between city and country, a form of suburbia, which many modernists professed to consider anathema. Cities were to be resolutely urban townscapes incorporating green space and visual variety in city square gardens and overgrown pathways running between terraced streets.[32]

FESTIVAL ARCHAEOLOGY

If the Festival was to be celebrated as a phoenix rising from the ashes, it helped to show the South Bank site itself had a deep history. The Presentation Panel had hoped that while the South Bank was undergoing deep excavation in preparation for the new exhibition, a significant archaeological discovery might be made on site.[33] Contractors were instructed to go beneath the foundations of Victorian industrial buildings during excavations into 'levels of potential archaeological interest' and told to liaise closely with the LCC's archaeological officer and the Festival's Director of Science, Ian Cox, if a discovery was made. These hopes were rewarded. A male human skeleton, 'possibly Roman', was found 12 feet below ground near Hungerford and Waterloo Bridges. Clay pipes, pottery, old jars and a neo-Gothic bust were also found. Some of these objects were displayed in a case at the Festival Office, Savoy Court. A contemporary press cutting said 'workmen have been asked to keep a close watch for signs of the unusual … Curiosity has … been aroused by the discovery of a bed of peat … still capable of making satisfactory fuel … Potsherds of the delftware produced by the Lambeth pottery works in the seventeenth and eighteenth century are being laid bare in considerable quantity. They appear to be fragments thrown away by the kiln operators after one glazing ... The watch for [Roman remains] is somewhat complicated by the extensive use of mechanical excavators.' The LCC held an exhibition just along the Thames at County Hall in 1951 called 'South Bank Past & Present', which they hoped would 'rekindle' interest in the area's history and character from Roman times onwards. Most objects came from existing collections, but the exhibition guide noted a Coade stone lion's head from the Festival site, a 'grindstone', 'traces of the kiln in which the product was fired and a number of moulds and casts of architectural ornament, parts of statues, etc.'[34]

In the People of Britain pavilion, archaeology was also the subject of displays. Items from archaeological collections provided the hard evidence to underpin these ideas: an archaeologist's trowel and Mesolithic flints, a bronze age skeleton and Beaker shards shown in a mocked-up dig, reproductions of iron age harness fittings, examples of Anglo-Saxon art and replicas of the treasure of Sutton Hoo. Archaeological societies rallied round to provide objects for the exhibition: the Somerset, Sussex and Wiltshire societies were particularly active in reproducing copies of their finds for the Festival in London, while the British Museum and Cambridge University's Museum of Archaeology also came forward to lend material. This was organized into themed displays such as 'A Man's Goods 1800 BC to 450 BC', which bought tools, weapons and domestic implements together with photographs showing how jewellery was worn or tools used. Artists were brought in to enliven the People of Britain displays. Illustrator Eric Fraser drew a panel bringing Roman Britain to life, while Morris Kestelman created a 'Stonehenge Setpiece', a model that ambitiously tried to evoke the original within the confined space. Archaeologist Jacquetta Hawkes (1910–96) acted as theme convenor for this section, which traced the evolution of the Britons. From Celts, Romans, Anglo-Saxons and Danes, the narrative made an imaginative link between these people and their land. Hawkes' ideas for the Festival were mirrored elsewhere in her prose, poetry, plays and film. Her popular geological fantasia *A Land*, which she worked on while contributing to the development of the Festival of Britain, was published in 1951. Fusing archaeology, literature and art, *A Land* explored Britain past and present, evoking 'an entity, the land of Britain'.[35] Using an unusual quasi-biographical treatment, which anthropomorphized the natural world, Hawkes traced the development of the land of Britain from the beginning of its creation as land, via the creation of species, up to the present day. Her strong sense of a physical connection with the land was expressed in her opening description of lying on a patch of grass in her back garden on a summer's night. Imagining the London Clay below, and the evolution of that clay, she wrote 'this hard ground presses my flesh against my bones and makes me agreeably conscious of my body'.[36]

In *A Land*, Hawkes linked the shape of the land of Britain and the people who lived there across millions of years – 'I see modern men enjoying a unity with trilobites.'[37] The geological narrative in *A Land* echoed that in The People of Britain pavilion, which described the development of a native people within the land. By adopting the longest evolutionary period for the British story and telling a version of Britain's geological past, without dates, Hawkes suggested what is now called 'Britain' was a pre-determined land mass. The disruption of the relationship between the land and people that had come about as a result of recent war, and longer-term industrial devastation, was then put in the context of a much longer, continuous history, where they were merely brief phases. Archaeology was not only an important part of the Festival's exhibition displays, it was also important to the message of renewal that drove the Festival. Having solid evidence from the ancient past of Britain's capacity for assimilation and renewal after invasion and hardship was crucial. It allowed the Festival, held in this period after the privations of the Second World War and when the country's international influence was on the wane, to tell a story about Britain triumphing in the face of adversity. Over thousands of years, so the message went, the British had stayed strong and true to themselves, a model democracy without parallel.

SCULPTURE AT THE SOUTH BANK

Hawkes' *A Land* was illustrated with drawings of abstracted stone figures by sculptor Henry Moore. Moore's work had also featured prominently among the sculptures set in the landscape of the South Bank exhibition. Although the fledgling Arts Council commissioned much of the painting and sculpture around the South Bank, Moore's bronze *Reclining Figure* was one of two works commissioned directly by the Festival Office. Moore had suggested that being near the Origins of the Land would be more enticing than being on the Fairway, and that his work must face south, but he did not have more of a role in siting the work than this.[38] The work was listed in the South Bank guide as 'set against the turf slope near the Country Pavilion', as if an intriguingly shaped boulder, stumbled upon by chance on a country walk.[39] This description did not suggest site specificity but rather a serendipitous coincidence. Indeed Moore's complex figurative abstraction created an uneasy juxtaposition against the landscaped pavers and dry-stone wall. A cartoon by Lee suggested how visually challenging *Reclining Figure* was considered.

4.6 SCULPTURE AT THE SOUTH BANK
Barbara Hepworth's *Contrapuntal Forms* with crowds,
beside the Dome of Discovery.

It depicted a cantankerous old man wiring up the Moore to the Skylon as
lightning conductor and declaring 'It's a million to one chance, they say
... but here's hoping!' Some sculptural works at the South Bank extended
ideas of physical embodiment in the land in a more straightforward way.
Mitzi Cunliffe's *Root Bodied Forth*, which sat on the viewing platform of
the Station Gate, symbolized the 'Origins of the Land and the People',

according to the South Bank Guide.[40] It consisted of two bodies entwined together, as if coming from the earth. Barry's diary recorded a visit to the works where Cunliffe's piece was being cast, having been tipped off that it might be a 'study in sodomy', which, he concluded, was 'anatomically impossible'.[41]

The River Thames played an important part in creating the South Bank's new Picturesque, running, as it did, past the South Bank and Battersea Pleasure Gardens, as well as near Lansbury. The Thames provided a visual backdrop against which the South Bank's activity could be played out. The river was a recurrent symbol through Festival films as diverse as Humphrey Jennings' *Family Portrait*, Basil Wright's *Waters of Time* and the Ealing Studios film *Pool of London* as a historical and literary symbol of national prosperity and the home of Shakespeare.[42] *The Islanders*, a massive relief sculpture by Austrian-British Siegfried Charoux (1896–1967), looked out towards the Thames from in front of Spence's Sea and Ships and reinforced a sense of rootedness. Its group of man, woman and child standing cartoon-like in their simplicity, dominated the river, underlining Britain's island status as a key element in national identity.[43]

The majority of sculptural works at the South Bank were based on the human figure, each expressing a different sense of being in the landscape. Daphne Hardy's expressionistic *Youth*, with its exaggerated elongated limbs, towering and naked in front of Manasseh's '51 Bar, suggested naïve vulnerability. Frank Dobson's *London Pride*, two Primitivist women cast in bronze, hinged on the association with the plant saxifrage, which was growing in a clump on their knees. Often known as 'London Pride', saxifrage was one of the few alpine plants that thrived on city air, so expressing a link between the subjects and their urban surroundings. Meanwhile, John Matthews' bronze female group set in a womb-like niche embedded in the wall of Homes and Gardens expressed a sense of peaceful homeliness. Barbara Hepworth had two commissions at the South Bank. The monumental *Contrapuntal Forms*, standing under the eaves of the Dome of Discovery, was sculpted from Irish blue limestone while *Turning Form* was a motor-driven kinetic sculpture; both expressed a sense of detachment from the immediate space around them. Lynn Chadwick's sheet metal and canvas tower mobile *Cypress* stood tall in a South Bank courtyard in a position where a tree might otherwise have stood. Spanish critic Rafael de Aburto, reporting a few months after the Festival in *Revista Nacional de Arquitectura* magazine, decried the Festival's sculpture as its most troubling contribution. His article ended with a valedictory poem, bidding farewell to monumental sculpture and hailing the Skylon as a technological substitute.[44]

'THE EXHIBITION AS LANDSCAPE'

In August 1951 *Architectural Review* proclaimed: 'the South Bank Exhibition may be regarded as the first modern townscape'. In a special Festival edition, its editors triumphantly declared the Festival of Britain's South Bank Exhibition layout 'represents that realization in urban terms of the principles of the Picturesque in which the future of town planning as a visual art assuredly lies' and that it had 'triumphantly demonstrated the vitality of contemporary British architecture and should have a worldwide influence'.[45] Anonymous articles addressed 'The Exhibition as Landscape' and 'The Exhibition as a Town Builder's Pattern Book'; while Editor J.M. Richards wrote about 'The Exhibition Buildings' and Assistant Editor Gordon Cullen's 'South Bank Translated' described how future planners might use principles from the exhibition in the permanent development of the area. They praised the way the buildings outside the boundaries of the exhibition had been visually connected with those inside, the way the exhibition's buildings linked old and new.

This Picturesque, which the *Review*'s editors claimed as the triumph of the Festival, appeared to be self-justification after years of campaigning. But it was indeed the professed intention of the Festival's designers – Hugh Casson in particular – to achieve such an impact. Casson had spoken out in favour of the Picturesque at a talk at the AA in November 1945 at which Pevsner had developed his theory of revived Picturesque.[46] And in a letter from Casson to H. de C. Hastings, one of the driving forces behind the *Review*'s Picturesque campaign, he declared 'I regard myself your creation.' Casson later recalled taking Hastings around the South Bank site, being delighted when he commented '... it was something like I had always wanted' and declaring '[Hastings] was my guru and certainly the guru of the South Bank Exhibition.'[47] Casson's close relationship with *Architectural Review* was to be cemented when, in 1954, he joined the journal's editorial board. However, Casson was perhaps more enamoured of these ideas than his colleagues. Gerald Barry, admirer of orthodox architectural modernism, would comment that 'The vogue for sharrawaggy (*sic*) – the natural reaction from a too-stark functionalism – can be overdone', referring to the enthusiasm sparked by *Architectural Review*'s campaign for Picturesque revival.[48]

Instructions Casson wrote for Festival landscape designers dictated 'The use of colour and plant forms should be in the spirit, though not necessarily in the manner of the 18th century landscape garden, which was designed to evoke emotion, and awaken dreams.'

Appropriate planting should, they were told, 'attract the eye and stimulate the senses'.[49] Eighteenth-century ideas of Picturesque were revived for use to transform the landscape of this public exhibition space on an ex-industrial site. Eye-pleasing arrangements of buildings in green space, experiments with visual variety and consciously created scenic ensembles were created that had hitherto been strongly associated with the design of the country estates of England. Speaking of the South Bank's design in 1951, Casson said, 'on purpose it did not have the symmetry and the repetitive grandeur of some other great cities and their exhibitions. It was planned intimately, like rooms opening one out of another.'[50] Festival designer Gordon Bowyer confirmed such Picturesque considerations were at the forefront of its designers' minds, recalling Casson walking around the South Bank site with landscape designer Peter Shepheard and expressing delight when some of the planning alignments had been lost, producing a pleasing irregularity.[51] Festival landscape architect Shepheard had a wider belief that the land had an intangible, but specific 'character'. 'The landscape architect is concerned with the existing site; with its *character* and the *genius loci*. Buildings also, and especially modern buildings, must, of course, fit the site and acknowledge its *character*; but landscape *is* the site,' he explained.[52]

The new Picturesque impact of the South Bank site was partially achieved through a kinetic relationship between displays and people: the action of visitors moving through the exhibition spaces, from dark and dim to brightly lit or natural light; from enclosed, narrow corridors to colossal, open inside and outside spaces. Even the Dome of Discovery, this icon of British modernism, this harbinger of the future, was part of the new Picturesque. It appeared at first to be a perfectly symmetrical disc but changed in view and proportions as visitors walked around it, with steps allowing for changes of level and vantage point.[53] The South Bank site's new Picturesque effect was also achieved by departing from Beaux Arts symmetry, which had been favoured in the layout of international exhibitions such as the 1867 and 1889 Paris Expositions. Casson and his team instead chose a design based on informal routes that meandered around the site. This aspect of the Festival of Britain owed a debt to the landscapes of the 1930 Stockholm Exhibition, but if the impact of irregular pathways was claimed as a key design achievement of the South Bank site, it was also made necessary by the site's small area.[54]

The revival of ideas associated with an English land-owning elite of two centuries earlier and their use at the Festival was certainly not met with universal adulation. While *Architectural Review* magazine and, to a lesser extent, its sister publication *Architects' Journal* were experimenting with the potential for a twentieth-century Picturesque, *Architectural Design* magazine (jointly edited by Monica Pidgeon and Barbara Randell from 1950) developed an antipathetic agenda. Writers such as E.A. Gutkind expressed their disappointment at this aspect of the Festival. Describing the use of vistas at the South Bank as 'empty ostentation' and tracing this back to the tradition of exhibition design pioneered in Paris by Haussmann, he dismissed the site as belonging to another age.[55] Gutkind was nevertheless strongly enthusiastic about the South Bank exhibition's innovative architecture, which pioneered a 'fourth dimension', he maintained, by combining time and space.

FESTIVAL COLOUR AND LIGHT

The South Bank's Picturesque worked both by day and by night. At dusk, the Festival site was designed to undergo a transformation using a combination of fountains, dancing, music and lighting to enable visitors to continue at the site after dusk. The moment when day became night would later frequently be recalled as a favourite memory. Floodlighting of Festival buildings and structures glimpsed across the Thames was designed to create a magical environment. The towering Skylon, which was lit from inside by hundreds of light bulbs, could be seen from afar, while Waterloo Bridge and buildings on the one and a quarter mile north bank stretch of the Thames known as the Victoria Embankment were lit up – the Houses of Parliament, Big Ben and Whitehall Court appearing when illuminated, according to one observer, like 'a fairy castle suspended in the sky'.[56] The lights that were set in the paving slabs of the site illuminated pathways so that visitors could walk, sit looking out at the view or dance to the strains of music penned for the Festival and played by Geraldo's Embassy Orchestra. Fairy lights in red and white set in trees were switched on, as were lights in the so-called Fountain Lakes, designed by Jim Cadbury-Brown, who had been inspired by a visit to see the fountains at Versailles and supported by Gerald Barry, who had visited Rome in 1950 to look at the fountains and floodlighting. Fire-making technology and gas flares were incorporated into them to make an additional mist. Artificial lily-pads with lights set into them, dotted about in ponds, were also turned on after dark to help navigate through the space and to allow the daytime Picturesque to continue into the evening.

After blackouts, nighttime bombardments, restrictions on electricity, regular power cuts and fuel shortages, the Festival's nighttime transformation was conceived of as an important part of the spectacle. 'How very different will be the London seen by night this Festival summer, when compared with the long nights of darkness that preceded it,' exclaimed an *Illustrated London News* journalist.[57] As well as bright floodlighting, which provided a vivid nighttime structure for the Festival, allowing visitors to see the extent of the site even after the pavilions were closed, strong colour was an extraordinarily important part of the Festival spectacle. This colour was carried through the open-air sites, as well as into displays and objects. The exhibition sites 'blazed with bright nursery colours' – carried though the signage, the blue and red umbrellas at the outdoor cafés, balloons released daily from the South Bank.[58] Colour was also carried in murals such as John Piper's prominent 50 feet wide *The Englishman's Home* with its collage of buildings painted in bands of yellows, reds and blues, eye-catching screens such as Edward Mills' molecular and ACP's tetrahedral one. These performed the practical purpose of shielding visitors from the grey desolation of the industrial wasteland remaining beyond the site. In this sense, colour performed a structural purpose, compensating for missing buildings and unwelcome empty spaces. But beyond this, colour had a strong symbolic value, signifying modernity, vitality and simple 'gaiety'. As Casson commented, 'the colours were as carefully considered as the forms of the buildings'.[59] The vivid colours associated with the Festival are almost universally remembered as being the most striking element of 1951, a sensory counterpoint to the extraordinary greyness of the time. They were another way of achieving visual variety through the exhibition sites.

One South Bank architect, Jim Cadbury-Brown, claimed that through the Festival he and other architects had been experimenting with creating identity of place. Colour, building and landscape design was all focused towards finding the elements that make up a place. Through these, he explained, 'you created a kind of identity with them'.[60] For Festival organizers and designers, this focus on the landscape and these experiments with identity of place did not signify naïve parochialism, engaged, as they were, with reconstructing urban modernity through some of its most formalized groupings. Instead they were setting the scene for people to reconnect with their damaged land, to help those who had lived through the deprivations of war to forget the horror of it all. They provided a glimpse of the time before war and industry had defaced the land, while showing a vision of an appealing future.[61] Exhibitions demonstrated the close link between the evolution of the geology of Britain and raw materials extracted for manufacture, where the geological wealth of the land became the cultural and social wealth of the people. By doing so they healed the perceived rift between Britain pre- and post-industrialization. While restating the possibilities of Picturesque as a way of reconstructing people's relationship with their land, Festival of Britain designers engaged with a wider reassessment of British history. The intricacies and complexities of designing the Festival *gestalt* – its landscaped, built, edited and designed environment – were all focused on the project of reconstituting national memory. Reconciling 'Land and People' was central to all the Festival exhibitions both at London's South Bank and beyond; from those exhibitions of books that focused on people within the topography of Britain, to farming and industry exhibitions; and to exhibitions of homes and their surrounding neighbourhoods. These themes, twinned and brought together in the Festival, relied on the idea that a rift had developed between land and people, which needed to be healed.

1. Sketch for Festival nationwide map by Eric Fraser.

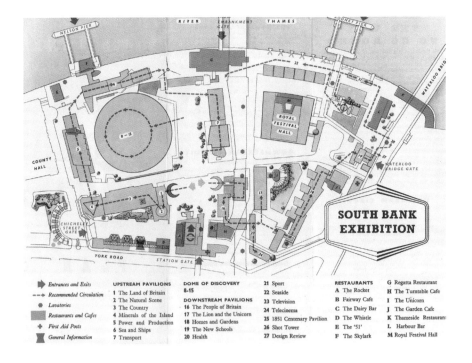

2. Plan of South Bank Exhibition.

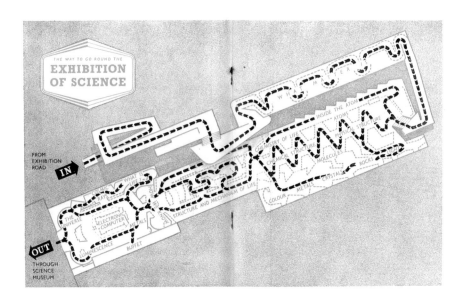

3. Plan of Exhibition of Science, South Kensington.

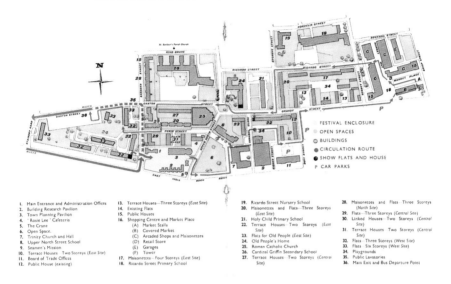

EXHIBITION OF ARCHITECTURE

FESTIVAL ENCLOSURE
P OPEN SPACES
BUILDINGS
CIRCULATION ROUTE
SHOW FLATS AND HOUSE
P CAR PARKS

4. Plan of Lansbury 'Live Architecture' Exhibition, Poplar.

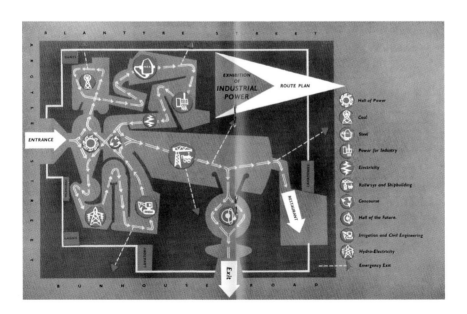

5. Plan of Exhibition of Industrial Power, Kelvin Hall, Glasgow.

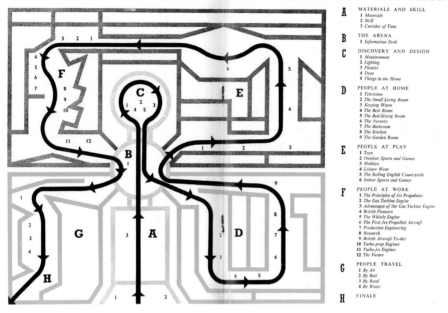

A MATERIALS AND SKILL
1 Materials
2 Skill
3 Corridor of Time

B THE ARENA
1 Information Desk

C DISCOVERY AND DESIGN
1 Measurement
2 Lighting
3 Plastics
4 Dyes
5 Things in the Home

D PEOPLE AT HOME
1 Television
2 The Small Living Room
3 Keeping Warm
4 The Best Room
5 The Bed-Sitting Room
6 The Nursery
7 The Bathroom
8 The Kitchen
9 The Garden Room

E PEOPLE AT PLAY
1 Toys
2 Outdoor Sports and Games
3 Hobbies
4 Leisure Wear
5 The Rolling English Countryside
6 Indoor Sports and Games

F PEOPLE AT WORK
1 The Principles of Jet Propulsion
2 The Gas Turbine Engine
3 Advantages of the Gas Turbine Engine
4 British Pioneers
5 The Whittle Engine
6 The First Jet-Propelled Aircraft
7 Production Engineering
8 Research
9 British Aircraft To-day
10 Turbo-prop Engines
11 Turbo-jet Engines
12 The Future

G PEOPLE TRAVEL
1 By Air
2 By Rail
3 By Road
4 By Water

H FINALE

6. Plan of Land Travelling Exhibition touring to Manchester, Leeds, Birmingham and Nottingham.

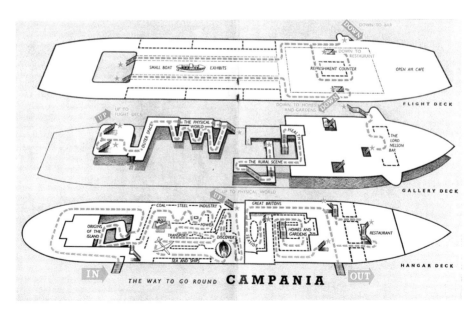

7. Plan of Sea Travelling Exhibition aboard HMS Campania.

FESTIVAL OF BRITAIN
PLEASURE GARDENS

FESTIVAL OF BRITAIN
SCIENCE EXHIBITION

FESTIVAL OF BRITAIN
ARCHITECTURE EXHIBITION

FESTIVAL OF BRITAIN
SOUTH BANK EXHIBITION

↑ ALTERNATIVE DIRECTIONAL SIGNS ↓

FESTIVAL OF BRITAIN
PLEASURE GARDENS

FESTIVAL OF BRITAIN
SCIENCE EXHIBITION

FESTIVAL OF BRITAIN
ARCHITECTURE EXHIBITION

FESTIVAL OF BRITAIN
SOUTH BANK EXHIBITION

8. Page from *Festival of Britain: The Use of Standardized Lettering in Street and Transport Signs*; laid out in Gill Bold Condensed.

9 and 10. Pages from *A Specimen of Display Letters designed for the Festival of Britain 1951*, designed for the Typography Panel of the Festival of Britain 1951 for distribution to architects and designers, particularly for the titling of buildings and laid out in Egyptian type cut by Figgins, Thorne and Austin, 1815–25.

It is hoped that architects and designers will make full use of the possibilities which these alphabets present for applied decoration and for three-dimensional use

It is hoped that architects and designers will make full use of the possibilities which these alphabets present for applied decoration and for three-dimensional use

11 and 12. Pages from *A Specimen of Display Letters designed for the Festival of Britain 1951*, designed for the Typography Panel of the Festival of Britain 1951 for distribution to architects and designers, offering the potential for applied decoration and for three-dimensional use.

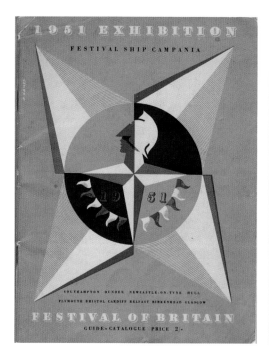

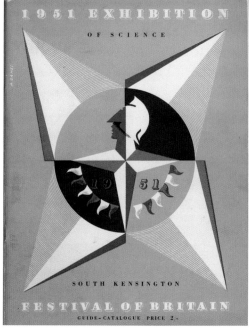

13, 14, 15 and 16. Festival Guide-Catalogue covers
designed by Abram Games and published by HMSO.

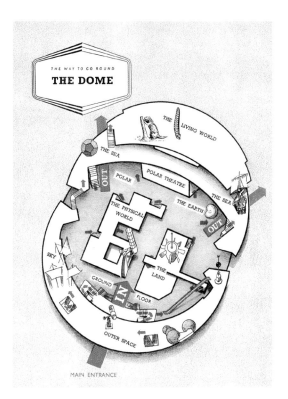

17. 'The Way to Go Round the Dome' (from the *South Bank Exhibition Guide*). Exhibition design by Design Research Unit inside Ralph Tubbs' Dome of Discovery.

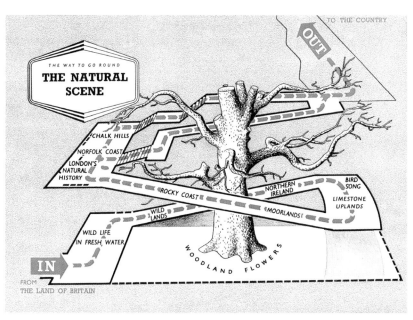

18. 'The Way to Go Round The Natural Scene' (from the *South Bank Exhibition Guide*). Exhibition design by F.H.K. Henrion inside Brian O'Rorke's building.

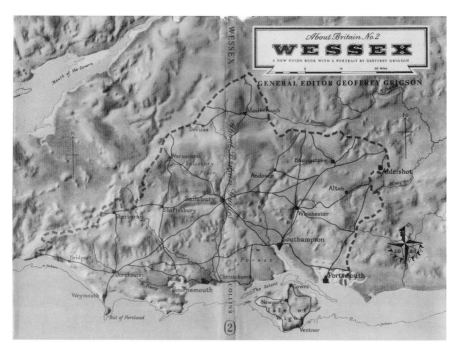

19. Cover of *About Britain Guide No. 2: Wessex.*

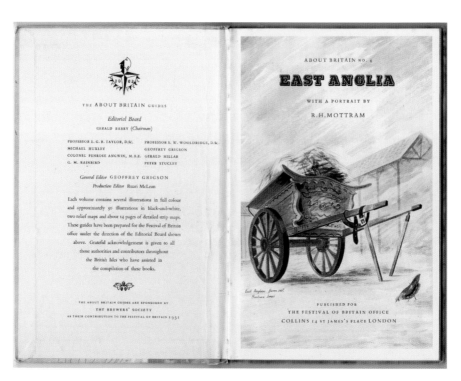

20. Inside cover of *About Britain Guide No. 4: East Anglia* with (Left) details of Editorial Board and (Right) frontispiece by Barbara Jones depicting an East Anglian farm cart.

21. Frontispiece by E.W. Fenton from *About Britain No. 3: Home Counties.*

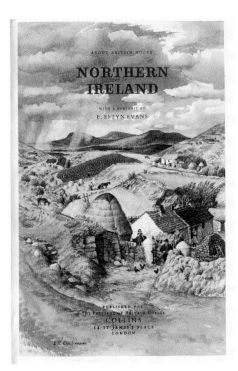

22. Frontispiece by Stanley Badmin from *About Britain No. 13: Northern Ireland.*

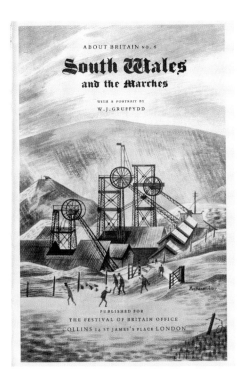

23. Frontispiece by Barbara Jones from *About Britain No. 6: South Wales and the Marches.*

24. Frontispiece by Kenneth Rowntree from *About Britain No. 2: Wessex.*

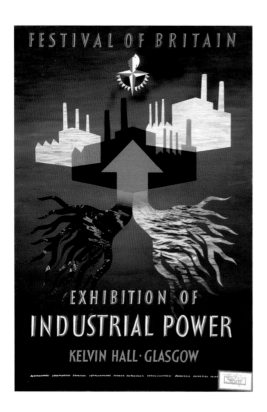

25. Sketch for poster for Exhibition of Industrial Power.

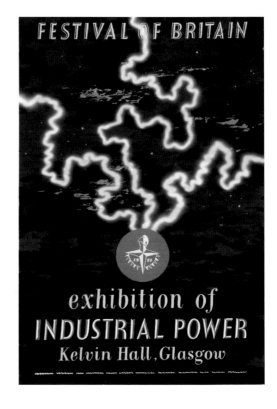

26. Sketch for poster for Exhibition of Industrial Power.

27. Poster for Ulster Farm and Factory Exhibition by L. Bramberg and W.M. de Majo.

28. Poster for Live Architecture Exhibition.

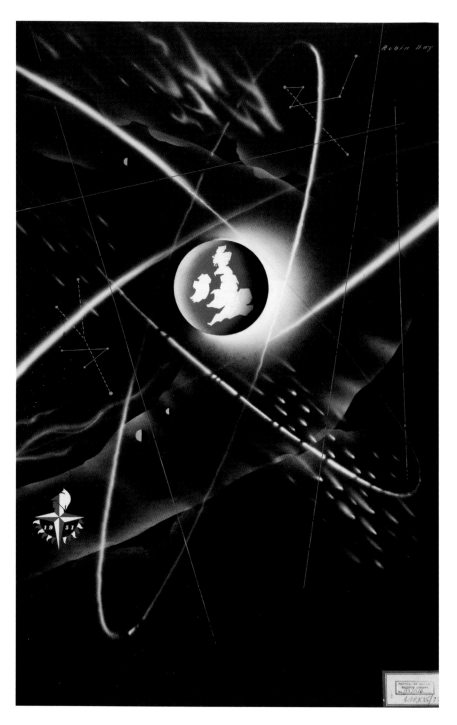

29. Sketch for poster for Science Exhibition by
Robin Day.

30. Festival of Britain advertising flyer showing the variety of activities happening around the country.

31. The Land of Britain pavilion with Architects' Co-operative Partnership's tetrahedral screen behind.

32. The Royal Festival Hall with Shot Tower to the left and Skylon to the right.

33. 'Bright nursery colours' at the South Bank: Edward Mills' abacus screen.

5

'SPONTANEOUS EXPRESSIONS OF CITIZENSHIP'

Exhibiting People at Work

Climb our heathered hills; scan our landscape; visit our towns and villages; mingle with us at our work and play.

Ulster Farm and Factory Exhibition Guide

The Festival had to be justified to Parliament and to the country. It was to be a source of fun and solace after grim years, the chance to put democracy on show to the world. But Gerald Barry thought it needed a more solid purpose too. The exhibitions must provide a pattern book for wider national reconstruction. Moreover, they should – in themselves – add to the national rebuilding programme, rather than diverting national resources from it. Ideas of productivity, of people actively making and doing things that would contribute to the greater good of the nation, were central to the Festival. These were the things that brought the people into contact with their land. Productivity was both a subject and object of the Festival: demonstrated through the Festival's exhibitions displays, as well as simply through showing people living and working in their country.

Showing off the work of industry was of particular significance to a country in the throes of reconstruction. The efficiency and improvement of national industries was a key focus of the Labour administration through its policies of nationalization, which focused in particular on coal, iron and steel following extreme shortages in the early years of the administration. This had been due to a terrible combination of shortages of skilled labour and adverse weather conditions, making work in heavy and agricultural industries extremely difficult.

Through the experience of war, many British people had come closer to the land through the need for each family to grow as much produce as possible to supplement meagre food rations. The farming industry was also in rapid change from the end of the Second World War. As food rationing continued, it was important that the national food production programme be as buoyant as possible by putting incentives in place for high yields.[1] The 1947 Agricultural Act ensured farmers were offered generous guaranteed prices for major agricultural products. New varieties of cereal were introduced and from the 1940s new pesticides were developed, as well as artificial fertilizers to further boost yields. Farming was also becoming increasingly mechanized, tractors almost universally replacing horses.

Working people were still at the time the numerically predominant group in British society.[2] If Barry was to achieve his desire of showing their contribution to the life of the nation, heavy industries and farming needed to be included in the Festival, linking different parts of the country where farming or mining for raw materials were characteristic sources of work. There were many advantages to making these a part of the Festival. Seeing things being produced showed Britain to be a living country. Productivity, whether visually appealing or not, was in the national interest so worthy of inclusion.

PRODUCTIVITY NOT PRODUCTS

There was also an ideological aspect to this focus on productivity, rather than trade. By putting the whole of Britain on show, people could have direct access to the means of production: the farms, factories and laboratories through which wealth was created. The active process of producing, of being productive, was distinguished from the end products that had been the major focus of the 1851 Great Exhibition of the Industry of All Nations. In a productive nation the people, the land and the means of production were linked. According to Director of Architecture Misha Black, writing shortly before the Festival, all international shows since 1851 had been on the same theme, '... the glory of the machine; the glory of capitalism; the glory of mass-production; the glory of human expansion measured in the terms of international capitalism'. Funded by a combination of private sponsorship and public funds, these exhibitions had glorified trade. But it was no longer enough to show the end products, Black asserted, 'The next great exhibition … must relate production to the needs of the people.'[3] Despite providing the starting-point for the Festival idea, 1851 was not an appealing model for Festival designers such as Black who saw the Great Exhibition underlining the hegemonic relationship between powerful producers and unwitting consumers.[4] Visitors to the Crystal Palace had been able to witness the end product of a complex industrial design process, the industry of all nations in a highly finessed state. The enormous, glass building where manufacturers could welcome the public to see their ornate final products laid out in bays underlined this. At the Festival, this relationship between producer and consumer was blurred. Visitors were invited to see people at work and play and to take part in the telling of a national 'autobiography'. It was unclear who was looking and who looked at, who was active or passive, who was telling and who being told.

Exhibitions of industrial products, machines and models of machines, had been held in England and France since the 1760s.[5] But it was the Great Exhibition at which the focus was on the products, rather than on the machinery and the processes by which they had come about. Moreover, it was 1851 when this produce was first displayed nation-by-nation, side-by-side. The qualities of the products shown at the Crystal Palace were strongly criticised by commentators a century later, most notably by Pevsner – in his Festival year study of 1851 exhibits – as 'bulging' and 'abominable'.[6] By focusing on productivity, the Festival avoided the singular preoccupation with 'good' or 'appropriate' design that had dominated exhibitions such as 'Britain Can Make It'.[7]

BUILDING AT SPEED

The building programme at the South Bank was intended to show the wonders of modern productivity. Pavilions would dazzle with their modernity, as they had a century earlier. The very evolution of the Crystal Palace as architectural space had, for contemporary onlookers, epitomised the wonder of the modern industrialized world. The Palace measured a monumental 1,851 feet in length, stood two storeys high and was the first structure to use iron and glass on such a scale (800,000 feet of glass). It was built with extraordinary speed: within 17 weeks, using pre-fabricated sections. This structure was to be much admired by architects for the next century; indeed, influential modernist architect Erich Mendelssohn had expressed his admiration for the Crystal Palace while visiting England in 1930.[8]

At the South Bank every building except the Royal Festival Hall was designed to be temporary. And, against the odds, buildings were built at great speed. 'Remember the stomach ulcers?' asked one Festival architect, recalling the pressurised conditions under which the buildings went up.[9] Robin Day (1915–2010), as furniture consultant to the LCC, designed all the Hall's seating from tip-up auditorium seats to restaurant furniture. The Hall was much admired for its acoustics and structure by many including modernist architect Le Corbusier, who praised its beauty. But some also loathed it. Eminent conductor Sir Thomas Beecham asked whether 'in 350 years, there has ever been erected on the soil of this grand old country a more repellent, a more ugly and more monstrous structure'.[10]

The Dome and Skylon became the Festival's great symbols. Their size and scale were significant in this. The Skylon was nearly 300 feet high and 70 feet high at the pylon. The name 'Skylon' was thought up by Margaret Sheppard Fidler, the wife of Crawley New Town's Architect, because it floated in the sky, and sounded similar to the new wonder material 'nylon' (it also clearly echoed the word 'Trylon', the icon of the 1939 New York World's Fair and had associations with 'pylon'). It did not serve any particular function, except to amaze, and its lack of visible structure became a popular metaphor for the state of the British economy (with 'no visible means of support'). The Dome, meanwhile, was the largest aluminium structure erected by 1951, and indeed the largest Dome, with a span of 365 feet (and height 97 feet). Producing a spectacle of scale was a common trope of world's fairs and international exhibitions, which for many decades had seen sites populated with gigantic experimental structures. At the 1889 Paris Exposition the world had been impressed by the 1,000 feet tall Eiffel Tower and 375 feet wide Machinery Pavilion, with its springing arches spanning a vault without any intermediate support, that came to dominate the skyline and iconography of the city from then onwards. At the 1938 Glasgow Empire Exhibition, Thomas S. Tait (1882–1952) had designed a 30 feet high 'Tower of Empire', which dominated the site; while the 1939 New York World's Fair showcased the Trylon, a 700 feet high triangular obelisk and the Perisphere a 200 feet wide globe. Misha Black writing in 1951 showed the Festival's designers were strongly conscious of scale, '[we decided] the main Exhibition structure – our Eiffel Tower, as it were – should be a saucer dome. This, of course, would have to be the largest Dome in the world.'[11]

The Dome and Skylon ensured the gigantic and spectacular were part of the Festival, as at previous international exhibitions. The buildings were signifiers of modernity asserted on a massive scale. Critic Reyner Banham, writing at the time, declared them 'proper symbols for the mid-point of the Technological Century', capturing this sense of their being giant forms of punctuation – the vertical Skylon as exclamation mark, the Dome as full-stop – which marked the middle of the twentieth century.[12] Elsewhere at the Festival, scale was also used symbolically. Tall 'vertical features' were part of the exhibitions at Belfast and Lansbury. At Belfast, de Majo designed a miniature 'Skylon', and a crane was installed at Lansbury with signage carried aloft, both adding height and visual variety.[13]

At the South Bank modern buildings housed displays showing off the wonders of the modern age, anchored in a narrative of past achievement and future possibility. H.J. Reifenberg and George Grenfell Baines's Power and Production building, which from the outside looked like a factory, housed working machinery. Basil Spence's building was a largely open steel structure built around frames, with a giant abstracted funnel protruding through the centre, gantries and hulls giving the sense of being in shipyard. These echoed forms in the Rotterdam Ahoy Exhibition of 1950, which had made use of water, forms of ships, rigging, derricks and light-weight steel platforms.[14] Architectural modernism was presented through building forms, and linked with ideas of progress and productivity, but these ideas of the present and projections into the future were not at war with the past. Inside the pavilions, British productivity through farming, industry and science were positioned to show their direct relationship with British scenery and natural resources. Heavy industry was located geographically, by showing its reliance on raw products brought out of the earth. At the same time, contemporary production was located temporally, by showing its evolution from the past.

Not all enjoyed their visit to the South Bank Exhibition. Architect Albert Richardson, vociferous critic of the Festival of Britain, was brought to the South Bank for lunch with a group of chartered surveyors. 'I had vowed not to go to the place,' he wrote in his diary. Leaving the restaurant at the Royal Festival Hall, Richardson wrote, 'I looked towards the crazy display with feelings of despair. Then I turned towards the Dome of Dishcovery and saw a seething mass of people. I asked a policeman to direct me to the nearest exit. He said make for the Waterloo Station Exit where the Garden is. I staggered to this Exit but could not find my car with Miss Logan so I staggered along to the County Hall and after waiting for half an hour I managed to secure a taxi. Thank God I said to myself when I reached No 31 Old Burlington Street.'[15]

FARMS, FACTORIES AND HEAVY INDUSTRY ON SHOW

Beyond the South Bank, exhibition sites and themes were chosen by Gerald Barry and Festival officials to show off the productivity of Britain and Northern Ireland more generally. Major Festival exhibitions were held in Scotland and Northern Ireland to show off the particular strengths and contribution of those places, expanding on issues raised at the South Bank. There was no major Festival exhibition in Wales. By mutual consent between the Festival Office and Welsh Festival Committee, the annual celebrations of Welsh culture and language, the Eisteddfodau, became their contribution to the Festival.

The Scottish Festival Committee chose Glasgow as site of an Exhibition of Heavy Industry, reflecting its importance as a major producer of coal, steel and 'power'. The show told 'the story of Britain's contribution to heavy engineering, of the machines and their inventors, the men who make them and the power which gives them life', positing a link between industries and those who ran them, an approach that fitted with the Festival's preference for linking people with the objects displayed.[16] Sir Thomas Johnston, Secretary of State for Scotland, was chairman of the Scottish Festival Committee, which directed the development of this exhibition. Johnston's crowning achievement had been the establishment of the North of Scotland Hydro-Electricity Board during the war with £100 million investment from central government. The Heavy Industry Exhibition, devoted to displays of iron, steel and hydroelectricity, was developed within an economic discourse around the reconstruction of Scottish traditional heavy industries. In addition to the Glasgow show, exhibitions of books were held in Edinburgh and Glasgow and a 'Living Traditions' Exhibition showing Scottish craft traditions was mounted at Edinburgh.

Castlereagh, a predominately Protestant industrial suburb of Belfast, became the site of a Farm and Factory Exhibition.[17] Developed by the Ministries of Agriculture and Commerce of the Government of Northern Ireland, it was sponsored by the provincial administration.[18] The core of Northern Ireland's wartime contribution had been heavy industry and food production; in armaments manufacture, ships and aircraft; and textiles for uniforms and equipment. Enormous productivity increases in Northern Ireland's farming had followed the 'Plough for Victory' campaign from 1939, where the existing 471,000 ploughed acres were almost doubled by 1943. In the late 1940s, the Northern Irish state was striving to create a secure future during a positive period of economic growth and the Korean War provided the state's traditional industries of shipbuilding and linen manufacture with the new lease of life it much needed. The Northern Ireland Festival Exhibition was intended to show the importance of hard work – 'This Exhibition is a Story of Endeavour' – and, moreover, to demonstrate the particularly impressive contribution the six counties were making to the process of postwar recovery.[19] 'Though Ulster's only a twentieth the size of the United Kingdom, it produces no less than a fourteenth of the agricultural output.'[20]

Northern Irish industry was set within the progress of a hundred years, focusing in particular on the progress of the previous thirty years from 1920, since the Northern Ireland legislature had started, devolved from but subordinate to the London Parliament. It championed its inhabitants' dual identities as British and Irish as a coherent whole.[21] Ulster's incorporation into the Festival of Britain's national whole was important politically, showing a unified nation, and providing a striking contrast with the Great Exhibition of a century before where Ireland had been largely excluded.[22] Dublin – by 1951 a part of the Irish Free State and partitioned from Ulster – had played host to several previous influential international exhibitions: the 1853 Dublin Great Industrial Exhibition, 1865 Dublin International Exhibition of Arts and Manufactures and 1907 Irish International Exhibition. But because of a perceived lack of local expertise in exhibition design, the government of Northern Ireland asked the London Festival Committee for ideas of suitable designers. This resulted in the appointment of émigré designer Willy de Majo, a celebrated Yugoslav-born product designer, who organized the exhibition long-distance from his home in London's Chelsea. L. Bramberg was Associate Designer, while Northern Irish architects Ferguson and McIlveen and Henry Lynch-Robinson built the exhibition's structures.

As well as exhibiting the contributions of Scotland and Northern Ireland to British life, located national identities were shown vying with notions of Britishness. The official line was that the ascendant quality of all Festival exhibitions should be to put 'Britishness' on show. Scottish architect Basil Spence designed the Glasgow Heavy Industry Exhibition, following a script written by journalist Alastair Borthwick, the show's organizer. The two had collaborated before on the 1938 Glasgow Empire Exhibition, Spence designing pavilions and Borthwick running the pressroom. Despite being based in Scotland, designed and conceived of by Scots and directed by a Scottish Festival Committee, their showcasing of specifically Scottish industry was negligible. In the *Daily Mail*'s Festival preview, Scottish Festival Chairman Thomas Johnston stated:

> It may be necessary at the outset to make it quite clear that the Exhibition of Industrial Power in Glasgow's huge Kelvin Hall <u>is not a Scottish show</u>. It is British to the core and British in its scope. Scottish patriotism has

been aroused merely to justify the confidence which the Festival of Britain authorities placed in the Exhibition organizers by choosing Glasgow as the venue for what is indisputably the largest Festival Exhibition outside London.[23]

Scottish architect Basil Spence had been more brilliant than usual in his exhibition designs because 'Scottish prestige is involved in the presentation of this great story of British achievements,' Johnston said. So implying that the desire to attract prestige in the name of 'Scottish' identity was a stronger driving force than the wish to boost perceptions of British achievement.

Discussions around the Belfast Exhibition differed significantly from those around Glasgow's. The Belfast show was not concerned with pointing to the greatness of the four nations, with Northern Ireland simply an element of a greater whole. Instead, exhibitions and guides – locally arranged and funded – sought to show Northern Ireland farms and factories as distinctive parts of the pattern of British industry and agriculture. Departing from the script of displaying Britishness alone, they instead offered an account of the indigenous linen and shipbuilding, woollens and cottons industries, 'the thrilling story of "Land and People", with a particular slant on Northern Ireland's industries, developments, achievements and craftsmanship', according to de Majo.[24] Underlining the particular role of Northern Ireland in the United Kingdom, they at the same time supported the idea that in temperament and culture the people of Northern Ireland were British.

Forms of Continental modernism clashed with references to Northern Irish cultural achievement. The show's graphics, structures and sculptures owed their origins to a loose interpretation of modernism as mediated by co-ordinating designer Willy de Majo. As at the South Bank's exhibitions, the show used bright colours, animations, photographs, models and scripts to describe the industries. Production statistics were illustrated pictorially and through flow-charts. Textiles and industrial materials were included in

5.1 GLASGOW EXHIBITION OF HEAVY INDUSTRY
(facing page)
(Above) Magnified version of Michael Ayrton's painting, The Four Elements, fitted into the bow of a ship, Shipbuilding section. Enlarged 600 times, Festival literature claimed it was 'the world's largest photograph';
(Below) Model of Loch Sloy Power Scheme displayed in the Hall of Hydro-Electricity (Display design: Arthur C. Braven).

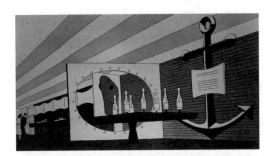

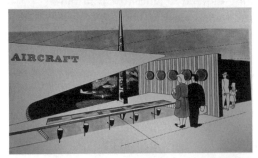

the displays and abstract patterns created a decorative quality from them. The most striking displays were of new industries: the manufacture of nylon and rayon. In the rayon section a cutout reel-shape showed fluorescent rayon yarn being latticed, the display activated by ultraviolet light. Nylon stockings were shown through a fan of cut out leg forms wearing glamorously highly coloured stockings. Veronica de Majo designed an outdoor mobile sculpture in primary colours that was heavily influenced by US sculptor Alexander Calder's kinetic works. Furniture designed by Ernest Race, also used at the South Bank, was dotted around the site. These were set stylistically against works such as John Knox's figurative sculpture 'The Gleaner', an allegory of thrift – a woman on bended knee, with the inscription 'Thrift is the gleaner behind all human effort' – and the local building style of the two farms on display.[25] The Exhibition was unlike anything many visitors had seen before with its modern buildings, displays that verged towards abstraction and surrealism and exotic European foods served in open-air cafés. Before the Festival of Britain, architecture inspired by European modernism had hardly penetrated the Province at all. 1951 was the first year that people of Northern Ireland were exposed to such buildings at the Farm and Factory Exhibition. Also, importantly, architectural modernism was shown through a small Festival show in a one-storey bombed-out building in Belfast itself. The show, organized by the Royal Society of Ulster Architects included a 'modern living room' and a series of photographs. It put open plan living on show for the first time.[26]

At the Farm and Factory Exhibition, Ulster's productivity was also the major focus. The Exhibition had not only to tell a story about industry and agriculture across Northern Ireland, but itself to be productive. Farming

5.2 ULSTER FARM AND FACTORY EXHIBITION
(facing page)
(Top) Preparatory sketch for Shipbuilding industry by
Willy de Majo;
(Second row down) Sketch for display of Aircraft
industry by Willy de Majo;
(Third row down, left) Introductory panel to Agriculture
section;
(Third row down, right) The Farm of the Future
(Architect: Henry Lynch-Robinson);
(Bottom, left) General view of open air part of
exhibition with John Knox's *The Gleaners* on left, main
exhibition building to right;
(Bottom, right) *The Gleaners* with the two farms in
background.

and industry were ideal vehicles for showing productivity and allowed the Festival's focus on land and the people to be adapted to the local situation, which was considered a fitting representation of the six counties. *Land of Ulster*, a specially made film screened as part of the Exhibition, gave 'a vivid impression of an Ulster farmer's daily life and of the distinctive features of farming in Northern Ireland' and contrasted traditional farmhouses with modern and well-equipped buildings.[27] It acted as celebration of both farming tradition and progress, highlighting the mix of indigenous with imported modern technologies.

Belfast's organizers tried to take a middle course between embracing technological modernism and tradition. A new model factory was built at Castlereagh for the Farm and Factory Exhibition, designed by R. Ferguson and S. McIlveen.[28] It was built with the idea that when the exhibition closed, the site would immediately become a working factory. Divided between a factory building and large open-air site, visitors entered the Exhibition through the main building. They saw machinery displayed alongside indigenous, non-mechanized techniques in the thirty sections focused on industry – from linen through to tabulating machinery – then on agriculture – from eggs through to food processing. Each industry was explained through graphics, photographs, models, mannequins and live demonstrations.

LIVE DEMONSTRATIONS AT THE FESTIVAL

The practice of giving live demonstrations, of bringing people in to exhibitions to demonstrate how to make or use things, forcing them to act out aspects of their culture or work on a continuous basis, had long been part of the spectacle of international exhibitions.[29] They might be brought in to demonstrate enduring craft traditions or to demonstrate how to operate machinery. Skilled practitioners were transferred from their usual sites of work, to make things by hand or demonstrate the use of machinery. In 1888, Glasgow's Great Exhibition had put imported 'exotic' people on display alongside working machinery in order to inspire local pride. At the 1904 St Louis World's Fair a factory manufacturing light bulbs had been situated in the Department of Manufactures, while the Department of Mines and Metallurgy had boasted a working anthracite coalmine.[30] Live demonstrations, particularly those of machinery in operation, had allowed the exhibitions symbolically to show a nation's prowess as industrial nation. They also brought an exhibition closer to real life, appearing more like an extension of reality, less like an artificial representation.

In the Festival, this trope of live exhibits also became part of the spectacle of productivity, enabling Britain to be shown, in the words of Gerald Barry, 'not merely as a museum of ancient buildings, but as a living country'.[31] Such demonstrations illustrated Britain's traditional means of production, its old craft techniques, and its modernised ones. At the South Bank Sport section skilled craftsmen demonstrated how to make sporting equipment: to whittle willow cricket bats and sew leather balls. At the Festival's 'Living Traditions' Exhibition in Edinburgh, craftsmen gave hand-weaving and sewing and other displays that were distinctively local – tapestry and tartan weaving, stone and woodcarving – and fishing tackle, pillow lace and pottery were made.[32] Meanwhile, mechanized sweet manufacturing processes were showcased at the South Bank's Power and Production.

Live exhibits could help tell a story about things that were self-evident, or hard to understand outside their working context, such as agricultural or industrial processes. Those who gave these live displays were not actors but skilled working people, displaced into a different context in which they reproduced their daily work while on public show. In the light of the severe labour shortages affecting Britain at the time of the Festival, it is perhaps anomalous that people should have been removed from their real work of reconstruction to demonstrate their 'work' in this way. But the practice signals the seriousness with which the Festival was perceived as a tool for boosting public morale and as a context for demonstrating that significant strides were being made towards reconstruction: through visible and conspicuous displays of what were usually hidden processes.

Live demonstrations allowed visitors to see first-hand techniques and processes that they could otherwise only read about or see in photographs. At Belfast a handloom was displayed next to a modern power loom, without privileging the mechanised. When the Queen and Princess Margaret visited the Exhibition opening, leaving an ailing King at home, the Northern Ireland press chose to picture her with Robert Foye, a Lurgan handloom weaver, and celebrated his ability to turn out 'four finished articles every day', rather than picturing her watching modern weaving machines in action.[33] Although contemporary accounts saw the handloom industry in decline by 1951, as described by Estyn Evans in a book of that year, the display was presented as a significant local tradition, indicating deep reserves of indigenous skill, and the fruits of Foye's loom sold in the Exhibition's shop.[34]

At Belfast, various goods were produced on site to demonstrate this dynamic of making in action. Inside the factory building, Festival cigarettes were produced as part of the 'Story of the Tobacco and Cigarette Industry

in Ulster' section, with packaging by co-ordinating designer Willy de Majo and bearing the Britannia emblem.[35] By selling such items, manufactured on site, the exhibition tried to sustain the idea of a series of 'real', working industries on show, rather than mere reconstructions. A number of industrial processes were demonstrated including production of nylon clothing, and rope and stoppers for mineral water bottles in a section dedicated to the Aerated and Mineral Waters Industry in Belfast. Agricultural productivity was also showcased. An August press release from the Farm and Factory site announced 23 weaned pigs and four calves, born on the exhibition's opening day, were now thriving.[36] The pigs were going to market; the cows had yielded a thousand gallons of milk, sold to a local dairy. This simulation of a farm producing real yields was considered by the exhibition's designers to show real farming in action. But it was an elaborate game of make-believe. The exhibitions could not accurately recreate productivity or make real profits, being far from economically viable beyond the subsidised world of the exhibition. The Festival cigarettes made at Castlereagh made a significant loss for the tobacco manufacturers, who demanded that their losses be defrayed by the Festival's organizers.[37]

Live demonstrators at other sites also lost out financially from Festival work. A blacksmith was invited to recreate his forge at the South Bank's Country pavilion. Thomas Haywood, who ran the Falcon Works at Coulsdon in Surrey, was brought to the site to make wrought iron lanterns, fire baskets, chestnut roasters, boot scrapers and wind vanes. He later wrote angrily to designer F.H.K. Henrion about his experience, having been forced to carry out live demonstrations continuously for the long opening hours. Worse, he had had to turn down lucrative work leading to significant financial loss and had received no compensation for this disruption, while being removed from important reconstruction work, leading him to feel frustrated and exploited.[38]

5.3 LIVE DEMONSTRATIONS (facing page)
(Above) Display of the Post Office Underground Railway
at Transport, South Bank Exhibition (Architects and
designers: Arcon);
(Below, left) Miners working on a 'Samson' loader,
which loads up to four tons a minute on to trucks or
a conveyer at Hall of Coal, Heavy Industry Exhibition
(Display design: Hulme Chadwick);
(Below right) Two blacksmiths from Edinburgh at work
in the Hall of Steel, Heavy Industry Exhibition (Display
design: Albert Smith).

'MINGLE WITH US AT OUR WORK'

The Festival was a celebration, but not always light-hearted and never escapist. Visitors had, after all, been invited to 'climb our heathered hills; scan our landscape; visit our towns and villages; mingle with us at our work and play'.[39] This was not about departing from ordinary life into Elysian abandonment, it was a party dominated by the Protestant work ethic. Exhibition designers faced with exhibiting subjects from science or industry recognized they had a hard task to draw crowds. 'Festivals imply festivities' commented Glasgow organizer Alastair Borthwick, 'and it is beyond dispute that there are few objects which inspire joie de vivre to a less extent than boilers and gas turbines'.[40] Basil Spence tried hard to keep the focus of visitors to Glasgow by employing spectacular techniques to show arcane technical processes such as extrusion in a hydraulic display. Some of this machinery, Spence and Borthwick hoped, might even be considered appealing in its own right. 'A giant turbine assembly is an extremely beautiful thing, and could stand on its own as a centrepiece without embellishment,' Borthwick wrote.[41] At Glasgow, tons of water crashed around visitors entering 'Hydro-Electricity', which highlighted recent Scottish innovations in the development of this source of power. The atom bomb was illustrated in the final 'Hall of the Future', with one million volts of electricity shooting with a loud bang up to the ceiling, making visitors jump with surprise. The visceral quality of these exhibitions, which appealed to the senses and emotions of their visitors, was used to compensate for worthy subject matter. Despite this, only a quarter of a million visited the Glasgow show, compared with the anticipated 1.5 million.

The Glasgow exhibition not only brought visitors into contact with the processes of industry but also with the origins and evolution of industrial materials. These were presented in situ and described through an evolutionary story. The 'Coal Swamp' at Kelvin Hall set out a spectacular story of the evolution of coal from the swamps to the coalmines and visitors were treated to a spectacular version of geological history. Walking around a huge model of the sun, which was 'blindingly' bright and hot, they found themselves in a 200 million year-old coal swamp. They heard 'the sound of trees crashing down into the primaeval mud – the beginning of coal'.[42] For its organizers, industry was an ideal subject through which to draw out the link between the characteristics of the land of Britain and the people who lived in it.

On entering the Glasgow Exhibition, visitors were first confronted with a coal cliff, the vast wall of sculpted figures by Thomas Whalen (1903–75). Whalen's sculpture illustrated the sun god creating the figure of a man – on

the right side as visitors entered – going through the evolutionary process
to become a miner, shown on the left. The striking, pantheistic imagery
mediated references to the Greek Parthenon's figure of the River God with
neo-Celtic decoration, which Scotland's *SMT Magazine* claimed was Whalen's
main inspiration.[43] Leith-born Whalen, a shipwright during the First World
War, was likely to have seen English painter Stanley Spencer (1891–1959)'s
epic *Men of the Clyde* series painted at a shipyard in Port Glasgow between 1940
and 1946. In Spencer's works the daily toil of shipyard workers took on epic
proportions. Whalen's work, like Spencer's and contemporaries affiliated to
AIA, was suffused by a socialist realism that glorified the struggle of work and
workers. Not all exhibition critics were impressed. The conspicuous dourness
of Thomas Whalen's coal cliff and of the Heavy Industry Exhibition in general
was the subject of 'Festive Sculpture?', a short article in *Architects' Journal*:

> The expression of a blind, toiling leisureless life can be seen in Whalen's
> work. It may portray the Ideal Man, gloriously muscle-bound, but why
> the mechanical rigidity of his stance? Why the grotesque grip on his
> diminutive coal-pick? Should we not have less high seriousness, in this
> Festival year, and more joyful love of life?[44]

Festivals should surely be marked by levity, the journalist believed, and this
fell short.

If Festival visitors were entreated to mingle with working Britons, they were
also invited to mingle with Britons at play. Architects Eric Brown and Peter
Chamberlin's South Bank Seaside section, which lined the bunting-strewn
Thames, showed the pleasure of seaside holidays. Period peepshows, funny
hats and mock-ups of Victorian boarding houses and bow-fronted Regency
facades were all part of it. But it was not all about Punch and Judy and end
of pier shows: the seaside was a working place where people made their
livelihoods in bustling ports or protected Britain's coastline from invasion.
The make-up of the land of Britain was also scrutinized on the coast, 'the
fluvial landscape' transformed into 'seascape', the sand, rocks and plant-life
that made up the coast.[45]

With its focus on productivity, the Festival could present a time spectrum
linking past invention, exploration and breakthrough to modernity, modernism
and future prosperity. By demonstrating the close interdependence between
urban and rural production in sustaining the wealth and livelihood of the
entire nation, these exhibitions went towards correcting a prevailing idea
that the Industrial Revolution had succeeded in making Britain a wealthy
country at the expense of the beauty of the countryside.[46] A photograph

in the *Official Book of the Festival of Britain*, the main souvenir guide to the festivities, juxtaposed a solitary man using a manual plough and horses beside another aerial photograph showing a large modern power station with two imposing cooling towers and two elegant chimneys.[47] Both photographs set the particular industries within the context of rolling countryside stretching beyond them, linking Britain's productive capacity with its beauty. Both traditional and modern techniques were valid, both considered representative of a contemporary Britain.

Showing historic traditions and modern utilities as of integral national importance, both embedded in the landscape, was also a strategy of the popular weekly magazine *Picture Post*. In the *Post*, people living in picturesque villages were shown side-by-side with the residents of urban streets, without preference. Similarly, at Glasgow's Hall of Hydroelectricity, images of the Loch Sloy Dam, which had only just opened in 1951, were shown as integrally beautiful architectural structures that did justice to their spectacular Highland setting and as a crucial means by which to produce electrical energy to serve local people, twinning beauty with productivity. One display tackled the issue of the aesthetic impact of these hydroelectric power stations directly. Under the heading 'Beauty or Blot?' the display demonstrated the lengths to which architects had gone in merging their structures into the landscape of the Highlands, arguing the structures should be regarded as beautiful. Parallel arguments were taking place in *Architectural Review*, which devoted two special editions to the look of structures of power generation on their settings. In a 1947 article Mark Hartland Thomas called for a 'revolution' in people's attitude to gasworks. 'There is no logical reason why [they] should not be a thing of great beauty, an asset to any landscape'. Hartland Thomas, Chief Industrial Designer for COID (co-ordinating their Festival contribution), and a MARS member, strongly echoed landscape architect Brenda Colvin's statements about the beauty of new industrial structures in her book *Land and Landscape*, published the same year.[48]

At Belfast, displays showed modern farming methods evolving from historic ones, in an attempt to make modern methods appeal to farmers. Leaving Belfast's main exhibition building and going into the landscaped grounds, visitors came to two farms. Both farms were designed by Northern Ireland architect Henry Lynch-Robinson (1920–84). Lynch-Robinson's recreation of an '1851 farmstead' was a one-room white-washed farmhouse 'with authentic furniture and equipment, and display of old farm implements and vehicles', a one-storey, thatched building consisting of a kitchen, bedroom and byre each with earthen floors; its interior was complete with 'authentic' implements and furniture that visitors were free to touch. There were no acting inhabitants of the farmhouse – either human or animal – and visitors were encouraged to sit around the hearth of an open turf-burning kitchen fire, furnished with traditional pot-oven, three-legged pots, griddle, turf-fork, tongs and hand-bellows, and to sit on three-legged stools (or 'creepies').

The picturesque presentation of the 1851 farmstead was heavily influenced by Emyr Estyn Evans (1905–89). Evans was an influential historical geographer. From the 1940s, using field studies, Evans had tried to write what he called Northern Ireland's 'unrecorded history', linking climate, soil, land-use and social life in books such as *Irish Heritage*.[49] As a member of the Northern Ireland Festival Committee Evans gave recommendations on setting up a traditional peasant house of a type detailed in his studies.[50] Evans' writings about how the character of the people of Northern Ireland reflected the characteristics of the land they lived in were strongly politicized. He used the geology of the land to underpin his unionist sympathies, showing how the geology of the north of the island was more akin to that of Scotland and northern England than to the Republic. Indeed, the choice of 1851 as the date of the old farmhouse, just after the devastation of the Great Famine, a choice that was certainly endorsed by Evans, is another indication that notions of indigenous culture were more important in the Festival than historical sensibility.

Letters written by exhibition visitors to the *Belfast Telegraph* suggested the 'authentic' 1851 farm was a picturesque fiction. Writing to the paper's editor, one reader complained:

> To begin with, it is not a farm-house at all, but more like a labourer's cottage of 100 years ago. Certainly, no prosperous farmer would have lived in the poverty-stricken hovel shown at Castlereagh. It is a thousand pities that those responsible for the Farm and Factory Exhibition have made such a misrepresentation of rural Ulster.[51]

Evans used a rhetoric of the soil to describe the character of local people, and rejected non-indigenous manifestations of modernity.[52] His old farm reflected his wider aversion to modern farming methods and a preference for asserting dying Irish rural traditions, even if it meant accepting the poverty, hardship, discomfort and inefficiency that went with it. Evans was not alone in using imagery of the soil to characterize the people of Northern Ireland. One BBC Festival broadcaster declared:

> The background of all of the North of Ireland people is the land. The population – even in Belfast – is not very far removed from the soil and they've all got farming in their blood.[53]

Because of the predominance of farming in Ulster, the people of this part of the United Kingdom were also more closely bonded to the soil, he said.

Leaving the 1851 Farm, Belfast Festival visitors walked on an axis to the 'Farm of the Future', described as a 'working farm, with stock, farm house and modern equipment', and presented as a 'real' working farm, a fiction sustained through the herd kept on site that produced milk served in the Exhibition's café. Where, by the mid-1950s the word 'future' would take on a science-fiction connotation in the context of Peter and Alison Smithson's 'House of the Future' displayed at the 1956 Ideal Home Exhibition, the futurism of the Belfast Farm of the Future was well within reach of the present. However, the *Belfast Telegraph* reported the building under the heading 'Ultra Modern Ulster Farm' as 'one of the Exhibition's most controversial features'.[54] Designed to show the potential for development using new technology, the steel-framed farmhouse and its surrounding buildings were painted in festive colours, which formed a conspicuous contrast to the 1851 building. The white buildings had details picked out in purple, doors painted orange and a bright duck-egg green. Fully electrified, with an intercom system for communicating with other areas of the farm, inside were a fitted kitchen-dining room and a first-floor balcony from which the imagined farmer and his wife would get a full view of their farm. During the exhibition, the balcony provided visitors with a vantage point to look out over the site and to the farm buildings, complete with modern farming machinery.

Although initially appearing very different, due to the technological modernism and bright colours, structurally both belonged to a tradition of Ulster architecture. The modern farm used familiar local materials such as a tarred plinth that ran round the walls and whitewashed outer walls for all the buildings, and had an open space underneath which, Lynch-Robinson maintained, could be used to keep both animals and a car – mingling features from the earlier farms where animals were kept in the main building with features associated with orthodox modernist houses such as Le Corbusier's Villa Savoie designed with parking spaces beneath. Commenting on the Farm's design in *Architectural Review*, Lynch-Robinson said 'though planned to save time and labour the building belongs to a native agricultural tradition'.[55] He had applied common principles to both farm buildings. The Farm of the Future existed for the didactic purpose of reconciling farmers with the possibilities of modern farming methods, to 'teach farmers new habits'.[56] This was not a simple attempt to discredit tradition in order to promote modernity. Both were embraced. The old farm was referent towards Irish traditional culture and the new farm towards Irish agricultural modernity, showing technological modernization as compatible with social continuity.[57]

Journalist William Holt's BBC broadcast from the exhibition demonstrated a similar approach, appreciating the old while applauding the new. He was 'moved' by the delight with which visitors, especially older ones, responded to the 1851 farmhouse, its look, and the smell of the peat fire:

> There was a peace and restfulness and unhurried air and dignity about that old place, with its slow ticking clock ... The stillness ... almost seemed to speak. The animals have gone, like the old folk, but what a haunting memory they've left behind.

And he was impressed by the efficiency of the Farm of the Future:

> The farm buildings are laid out in a way that shows the time saving devices, and it shows what can be done by power and machinery to make work easier for the farmer ... All this, of course, leads to increased power and the farmer and his family can shape and enjoy their leisure.[58]

While Holt himself tried to tread a middle way, appreciating old and new, his report highlighted the more ambivalent responses of exhibition visitors. He recorded a 'young woman from Dungannon' criticising the interior design of the new farm, first, for allowing limited space for meals, and, second, for forcing living and eating to take place in the same space. Three other farmers also had unfavourable reactions to the modern farm. Meanwhile, a Londonderry-based farmer's daughter was impressed with the new farm and its labour-saving gadgets and dismissed the old farmhouse, the burden of work it would have given housewives and its lack of hygiene, animals sharing the house with humans.

Belfast was not the only Festival site where new farms were exhibited: the Welsh Dolhendre Rural Farming Scheme was an opportunity for government to showcase continuity between their ownership of a piece of land and the private ownership that had preceded it. Festival exhibitions at Lansbury, Dolhendre and in the New Towns were a golden opportunity to assert the government, in its various guises, as good landlord. Dolhendre in North Wales – the only significant Festival event in Wales – was an improved farm buildings scheme, a modest 'rural reconstruction scheme'. It had four elements: first, the replanting of 119 acres of woodland; second, the preparation, draining and fencing of a 318-acre area of afforestation; third, the erection of four houses; and last, the replacement of decrepit trees. Forming part of the Glanllyn Estate, previously part of the extensive Wynnstay Estate of prominent Welsh landowner Sir Watkin Williams-Wynn (the richest family in Wales of the eighteenth century), the success of the Dolhendre Scheme was ideologically important to the government. In 1946 the land had been transferred to the government in lieu of Death Duties, and as the largest agricultural unit in public ownership, the government had the opportunity through the Scheme to show their skill as public rural landowners.[59] The Scheme focused on modernising an area of land and restoring to working use keepers' and farmers' cottages, which had become derelict in private ownership. Glanrafon Cottage was illustrated in the exhibition's catalogue before and after reconstruction: before, with a tiny first floor plan including pantry, parlour, kitchen, scullery, stables and kennels and, after, with a modern larder, kitchen and inside bathroom. Stables and kennels had become storage and more extensive outhouses. These buildings, which remained fundamentally the same two-storey stone cottages set in a 'pleasant wooded vale', had been conspicuously improved and modernized. Modern cultures of farming and land management were shown in Festival exhibitions as on a continuum from, not a rupture with, the past.

Attlee's Labour administration was perhaps surprisingly sympathetic towards the landed gentry, evident through various tax concessions during the early post war years. Given the administration's aspiration towards land nationalization, private landowners were generally thought to have provided a good inheritance to public authorities – having ensured land was not broken up. Public authorities could therefore continue farming and urban social practice within the ideologically palatable context of public ownership. At the Festival the merits of public landownership were espoused through exhibited model farms and housing.

In London, LCC planners made a direct link between LCC as major landowner, working within a new system of democratic accountability, and an erstwhile land owning generation, projecting historical continuity into the new, British welfare state system. Speaking at the 1951 meeting of CIAM about the LCC's work at Lansbury, Arthur Ling, LCC coordinating planner, asserted that they saw themselves taking on the mantle of eighteenth-century private landowners. While not supporting the architectural methods of their forebears, Ling said they nevertheless owed them a debt for the prevailing system of 'large-scale ownership of land', which, 'allowed architects and planners to produce works of unquestioned merit'.[60] Influential planner William Holford echoed this in an article on Lansbury, stating the LCC were taking over from landowners, and that their creation of neighbourhoods was 'Taking the place of the old autocratic edicts for town planning of the estate management policies of the great landlords … and giving meaning to patronage of the arts in this century'.[61]

FESTIVAL SCIENCE AND TECHNOLOGY

If Britain was going to be shown at work, science and technology needed to play a major part in the Festival. The wonders of science were shown in many parts of the Festival, Britain's greatness showcased through displays of discovery and innovation.

At South Kensington, the Festival Exhibition of Science was held in a newly built wing of London's Science Museum. Visitors approached the entrance past Brian Peake's massive hexagonal partition: aluminium units based on the carbon atom. Once inside they navigated through many sections within a continuous space devoted to demonstrating the straightforward idea that 'Science means knowledge' and that 'the fabric of modern life' had grown from the application of scientific discoveries. Scientific discovery was rooted in the everyday. The exhibition was organized by some of the country's most influential 'men of science', as the catalogue described them.[62] Key to the organization of the Festival's Science Exhibition was Polish émigré scientist Jacob Bronowski, who wrote the exhibition catalogue and uniting captions, steering its conceptual framework. As Scientific Deputy to the British Chiefs of Staff Mission to Japan in 1945 Bronowski had written the extremely influential report, *The Effects of the Atomic Bombs at Hiroshima and Nagasaki*. Bronowski's *The Common Sense of Science*, a philosophical discussion of the potential of science to benefit nations and, at the same time, to be used for malign purposes by its politicians, was produced in the same year as his work on the Festival.[63]

Other scientists advising on the Science Exhibition were also working simultaneously on internationally significant projects. One of the Festival's Science panel, Sir Wallace Akers, was key to secret atomic development in Britain. As Executive Manager of ICI, he was involved early on in secret informal co-operation between the company and the government on the project to prepare an atomic bomb. In 1941 he was the 'chief protagonist' in a bid by ICI to take over the entire nuclear project and to run it on behalf of the Ministry of Aircraft Production.[64] Though this takeover attempt was rejected, he was nevertheless selected to become the director of the atomic project from 1941 as Director of Atomic Research at Tube Alloys. Another member of the Festival's science committee, Sir Edward Appleton, was from 1941 also a member of the committee of the War Cabinet that advised the government that manufacture of an atomic bomb was feasible. Festival Science Committee member Sir Ben Lockspeiser was in 1946 appointed Chief Scientist of the Ministry of Supply. In this role he masterminded British research into problems of nuclear physics, supersonic flight and guided weapons.[65] These eminent scientists were being invited to take roles in the Festival due to their prominent roles elsewhere in government where they were engaged in discussions of a more covert type, developing Britain's Cold War armoury.

The Festival's Exhibition of Science, its organizers claimed, provided unfettered access to Britain's ongoing scientific programme. 'Here is the modern world for all to see, built transparently from the clear ideas of science,' Bronowski's commentary stated.[66] The message of this exhibition, as elsewhere, was that visitors were seeing things in real time, unedited, as they were. Live demonstrations were again used to reinforce this message of transparency.

But the substantial sections on atoms did not on the whole hint at dangers or raise fearful imagery. 'Everything is made of atoms', Basil Taylor explained in the *Official Book of the Festival*.[67] The Science Exhibition covered atomic structure through a series of factual models and diagrams, recounting the splitting of the atom as a historical event without hinting at its darker implications as the moment at which total annihilation became a possibility. In a similar vein, Laurence Scarf's painted mural of 'Nuclear Physics Laboratory, Harwell' for the Physical World section of the Dome of Discovery was a rather clinical depiction of a working lab showing radiochemical experiments underway and a ventilation plant, all within a controlled environment. Although nuclear testing was not carried out by the US or UK until the year after the Festival of Britain, news of the bombing of Nagasaki and Hiroshima in August 1945, following the first US testing of a nuclear bomb detonated at the Trinity site in July the same year, had sent a shock-wave through the British public and the atomic threat was a regular focus for contemporary newspaper articles. The catalogue to the Festival's Glasgow Heavy Industry exhibition, which contained an atomic display in the final hall, mused on whether atomic energy would be used for good or evil. The near absence of other discussion of the nuclear bomb in the manifold technological descriptions of the Festival reflected the absence of parliamentary debate during these crucial years in the development of this technology.[68]

This rather upbeat presentation of atomic science was mirrored earlier in the 'The Atom Train', an exhibition for the Atomic Scientists Association, which toured the country for several months in 1947. Designed to popularize the subject of atomic energy and carried in two railway coaches, the exhibition, which was designed by Peter Moro and Robin Day, dealt with the theoretical and practical sides of atomic energy, while the benefits derived from atomic energy, labelled 'The Brighter Side', were introduced by a mural by Gordon Bowyer (later designer of South Bank Sport displays). This was a rather different approach to atomic material from right-wing newspaper *The Daily*

Express's 1947 Atomic Age exhibition, which carried a photograph of the mushroom cloud on its exhibition guide cover, an indication of its general tone. It was also very different from the Atomic Energy Exhibition held in Copenhagen in 1949 (which had impressed James Holland and Alastair Borthwick during pre-Festival reconnaissance). The Copenhagen exhibition had tackled the pros and cons of atomic power in a straightforward manner, addressing the nature and behaviour of the atom, the 'story' of atomic research, the atomic bomb and the effect of possible atomic warfare, peaceful uses of atomic discoveries, finishing on a 'one world' plea against taking the potential threat lightly.[69] Even advertisements published in the Festival Science exhibition's catalogue were more frank in their description of the ultimate uses to which technology might be put. One Festival advertisement for Leland Instruments Ltd. asked 'does your problem concern the time in flight of an atomic missile?'[70]

The story of the land and people, which united all the content of the Festival, also underpinned scientific displays. In the Dome of Discovery the underlying message was that through scientific discovery British people had been given greater access to explore their land, both above and below ground and, indeed, to circumnavigate the world. Displays of scientific instruments were used to show how people could know their own local environment more deeply, to tap into particularity of place through knowing more about the make up of local geologies and the complexion of local weather patterns. It was not enough to describe how different locales experienced specific climates and weathers in the Exhibition; weather-recording equipment must be demonstrated too. Instruments for capturing local weather conditions were demonstrated at the South Bank site. A Meteorological Office was set up at the South Bank and 'Dome' weather charts sold as souvenirs at 1d. per copy.[71] Hydrogen-filled balloons were also released daily from the South Bank, with the idea that their travel would be governed by weather conditions and advice on this was issued by the Meteorological Office. The evolution of science was closely linked with the development of the land. At the Science Exhibition, the earth's core was explained as being made up of chemicals and the scenery in which people lived, described as 'often little more than rock and water'.[72] A Petrology section explored the way that fossil fuels developed underground in order to support human life today, as a means by which people propelled themselves across the land.

Technological futurism was shown from a firmly anchored present. The South Bank's Shot Tower had been fitted with a radar beacon and large reflector, similar to those used for the supervision of harbours and ferries, from which signals were received from a small area of the River Thames

5.4 THE DOME OF DISCOVERY
(Above) Dome at night;
(Bottom, left) Interior of Dome with escalator to right,
looking towards Outer Space display;
(Bottom, right) Directional sign designed by DRU for
Dome interior.

between Lambeth and Blackfriars. These were displayed on a radar map on a cathode-ray tube. Radar technology had developed rapidly in Britain during the 1940s so this was a perfect subject to show off. Being the only remaining element of the industrial site the Shot Tower carried a sense of historical specificity into the newly-built site, described in the catalogue as a 'beacon for the Festival'. Visitors could transmit messages to the moon and see them returning from within the Dome of Discovery while surrounded by photographs and maps of the moon, again reinforcing a sense of locatedness. People could also send telegraphs – writing them out, sending a message and seeing it received and printed out as a souvenir.

Displays of science at the Festival showed visitors that past discovery had implications for the present, while the present pointed to the future. The impact that the work of scientists of the past such as Faraday, Newton and Rutherford had had on contemporary life was a major focus. Architects Powell and Moya had initially been commissioned to design a centre where ideas of gravity would have been explored, which was to be known as Newton-Einstein House, based near to the Science Exhibition at South Kensington. Felix Samuely (who had collaborated with Powell and Moya on the Skylon) was to be consulting engineer while the company Hazlehurst were to be consulting mechanical and electrical engineers.[73] Various designs were drawn up, the building was to have a hexagonal roof and an upper bowl housing a mock putting green and pond surrounded by a cycle track, a lower bowl with a room for experiments in gravity and a skittle alley. In the end money ran out and the scheme was scrapped.

The Festival showed that new technology could also potentially take humans in uncomfortable directions, to discover things that might alarm: computers and robots, which might take over from people and rockets that might bring them into contact with unknown life forms. With the wartime development of technologies that allowed the skies to be searched for invaders, people's imaginations were running rampant: what other alien objects or life forms might also be present there? Unidentified flying objects – usually described as wingless missiles travelling at great speed – were first reported after the war in Sweden in the summer of 1946; the first report of a 'flying saucer' came from the United States in June 1947, soon prompting many reported sightings in Britain too. By 1950, the press were reporting so many British sightings, some of them by experienced RAF officers, that the Ministry of Defence was prompted to set up its 'Flying Saucer' Working Party, which operated in secret. Its final report, produced in secret in 1951, concluded all UFO sightings could be explained as misidentifications of ordinary objects or phenomena, optical illusions, psychological delusions or hoaxes, and

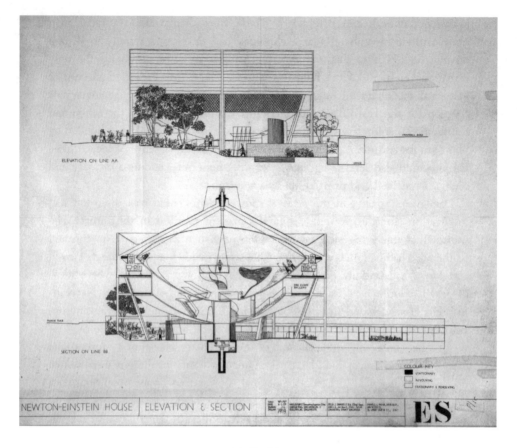

5.5 NEWTON-EINSTEIN HOUSE
Sketch elevation and section of Newton-Einstein House,
a scheme that never came to fruition, designed by
Powell & Moya with Samuely and Hazlehurst, drawn
March 1950.

recommended that any further investigation take place if material evidence
became available.[74]

For the Land Traveller Exhibition, Richard Levin designed an 'ectoplat',
a 6 feet wide translucent flying saucer made of a new type of plastic, which
suggested the possibilities for future travel. Elsewhere at the Land Traveller,
Manfred Reiss painted a mural depicting space rockets and space ships,
flying saucers and astronauts ominously encircling the moon. In the Science
Exhibition a Nimrod Computer made by Ferranti demonstrated the way
machines could add up. Visitors were invited to take on the machine in a
game of the card matching game Nim, with the idea that they would be

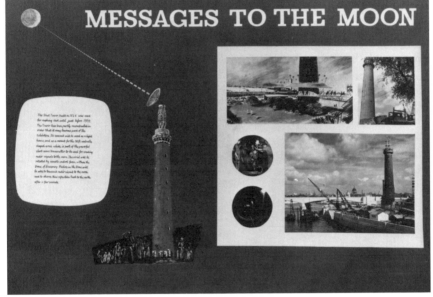

5.6 TECHNOLOGY AT THE FESTIVAL
(Above, left) The computer, Exhibition of Science;
(Above, right) Visitors wearing polarising goggles while
watching the stereoscopic Technicolor film 'Royal River'
at the Telecinema, South Bank, May 1951;
(Below) Detail of display inside the Shot Tower,
South Bank about sending 'Messages to the moon'.

very unlikely to win. The unnerving moral was that machines could beat
people. Simple robots were also shown actively moving around autonomously,
without human help.

The way Festival buildings were photographed and drawn reflected the
contemporary fascination with outer space and the unknown. The Dome
appeared in some photographs, particularly at night, like the flying saucers

that were already starting to grip the national imagination. The futurism of the Dome and Skylon as buildings – and depictions of these buildings in drawings and photographs – was rooted in this imagined other world and in anxieties about the developing Cold War. Displays inside the Dome of Discovery also played with some of this futuristic imagery, inspired by new technologies which allowed man to probe further into space and the unknown than ever before. Eerily dimly lit, the Dome's platforms – reached by an enormous escalator – housed displays designed by eight teams from DRU, overseen by Misha Black, devoted to British discovery and exploration, through sections like 'Earth', 'Sea' and 'Outer Space'. The space rocket-like Skylon so excited the editors of *The Eagle* magazine, first published in 1950, that they devoted a colour centre-spread to a cross-section drawing of it. The imagery of the South Bank site would also become the imagery of comic-book character Dan Dare's world.

6

'AN ESSENTIAL INGREDIENT OF DEMOCRACY'

Exhibiting the English Language

... the building of the rainbow bridge that should connect the prose in us with the passion ...

E.M. Forster, *Howard's End*

The English language was subject and object of the Festival of Britain. Identified as the instrument for asserting a singular, cohesive British identity, discussions of English language became a focus in many of the exhibitions and displays. As object, the English language was one of the integral media through which ideas were communicated in the Festival, through text in the exhibitions and around the sites, Festival guides, catalogues and leaflets, guidebooks, topographical studies and works of literature. By showing and describing the British character and their way of life as conditioned by their surroundings, the English language became a way of elaborating further the British people's relationship with their land.

English language was displayed in the Festival as a key element of the British 'story'. It was shown as a profound contribution to world civilization and to the democratic principle, originating in and from the people and traditions of the three nations of Britain and Northern Ireland, and one of their most important 'exports'. In *The Projection of England*, Stephen Tallents had argued the English language provided an opportunity for Britain to make money out of education and communication.[1] Beyond this, the reciprocal, identity-giving relationship between the British people and their language was central to Gerald Barry's idea of the Festival of Britain. Within the Festival events displays of English language and literature fulfilled a number of duties. Exposure to important works of literature and to exemplary use of the language could subtly influence and 'improve' British people. These works of language and literature, 'the vehicle by means of which many of the most potent and subtle ingredients of the British character and British habits of thought are conveyed, and have influenced the minds of other peoples', also put the nation's people on show, providing the key to their character and habits.[2]

Ex-editor Gerald Barry also believed in the importance of use of language, declaring 'I hope we shall be able to achieve a decent standard of English usage in our Exhibition notices and Festival programmes – plain English and plain lettering.' [3] Barry was not isolated in arguing for the capacity of the English language to morally improve those exposed to it. In the decades directly leading up to the Festival, a clear correlation was made between readership, use of language and moral standards. Writer and poet Cecil Day-Lewis asked in a wartime *Picture Post* article 'Do we read better books in wartime?' He concluded that people's reading habits had 'improved' due to the 'spiritual' and 'emotional' conditions provided by war, something he welcomed.[4] Earlier in the century, organizations such as the Society of Pure English had refused to acknowledge varieties of English. Eric Partridge's 1940 tract on the pitfalls of slang, for example, argued that poor language was synonymous with moral and spiritual decline.[5] In 1946 George Orwell echoed this, asserting that cultural decline was linked to declining standards of language and vice-versa, and that people needed to fight against 'bad English' lest the nation deteriorate further.[6]

The English language as an instrument for cohesion was an idea present in Winston Churchill's writings. Churchill believed there to be a crucial link between peoples sharing a common language. His four-volume *A History of the English-Speaking Peoples* was first published five years after the Festival of Britain, a project he had begun in the 1930s. Tracing the history of Britain from the Roman Conquest of 55 BC to the beginning of the First World War, Churchill determined his definition of 'English-speaking peoples' as being of one of the following types: those who lived on the land-mass of Britain, those who were part of its Commonwealth of Nations, united under 'the Crown', or else people of the United States of America who had originally been ruled by 'the Crown', but had broken away. For Churchill, through their use of a common language, they were a cohesive group to be united by a single historical account.

Gerald Barry sympathized with such ideas. Explaining the importance of the displays of English language at the Festival of Britain, Barry demonstrated his belief that language was the most important way of transmitting peaceful, democratic ideas. 'In fulfilling this purpose, the English language is itself perhaps our most persuasive missionary.'[7] Barry's focus, having previously been editor of a national newspaper, was not only on speaking to foreign visitors but also to a home audience. The English language could function as a force for cohesion for the British people themselves within the Festival, being integral to national political culture, the key vehicle for 'freedom of expression and of interchange in knowledge and ideas'. He saw these as the privileges of democracy, alluding to non-democratic states where freedom of expression was not a given.[8]

LANGUAGE SHOWING 'DIVERSITY WITHIN UNITY'

Central to Barry's Festival was the idea of the language showing British 'diversity within unity' which he claimed as 'an essential ingredient of our democracy'.[9] But despite this averred support for the diversity of British local traditions and cultures within the Festival, variations of the local, regional or national languages of the four nations were only shown to a very limited extent as a valid part of a multitudinous British identity. Difference was tolerated only where it pointed to unity. Festival competitions held to promote Celtic and Gaelic were sponsored not by the Festival Office run by Barry, but by the Arts Council in Wales and Scotland. A limited number of Festival guides were bilingual in Welsh and English. The guide to the Dolhendre Rural Scheme was sponsored by the Welsh Festival Committee and printed not by the publishers of the main guides, His Majesty's Stationery Office (HMSO), but by the Welsh company, Cambrian News. By mutual consent between the Festival Office and Welsh Festival Committee the major annual celebrations of Welsh culture and language, the Eisteddfodau, remained independent from the Festival. Limited attempts were made to display regional or local languages or accents in the Festival elsewhere. At the Live Architecture Exhibition in London's Poplar, caricatured cockney rhyming slang was the basis for naming the 'Rosie Lee Café', while the South Bank's Lion and Unicorn pavilion offered a tiny section about linguistic diversity, highlighting cockney.

Radio broadcasts, which Gerald Barry described as 'one of the most potent vehicles for expressing the national life and spirit', marked the start and end of the Festival.[10] The BBC arranged a complete series of radio programmes for the Festival of Britain, including Home Service broadcasts from the opening ceremonies at St Paul's and the Royal Festival Hall, royal visits to Festival sites, concert and opera performances, and outside broadcasts from a number of nationwide exhibitions. The BBC's Light Programme broadcast a programme about listeners visiting the two Festival Travelling Exhibitions, while the BBC's Third Programme transmitted plays, concerts and talks. Special broadcasts were made from Scotland, Wales and Northern Ireland, as well as in England's 'North Region' and 'West Region'.[11] For the Festival's office, radio was another way of linking 'the centre with the outposts and the outposts with the centre: a State event one day, a village ceremony the next …', thereby allowing them to achieve more nationwide coverage and to bring to people's imaginations places large and small.[12]

BBC broadcasts from Festival sites were characterized by a standard voice, the BBC presenter summarising and overseeing events, contrasting with voices of local interviewees.[13] Journalist and design commentator Geoffrey Boumphrey broadcast a regular 'Festival Notebook' for the Home Service from sites around the country characterized by high-handed generalizations such as 'Ulstermen don't seem to have the inventive genius highly developed: planning, organizing and hard work are more their keynote.'[14] William Holt broadcast for the BBC's General Overseas Service from the Castlereagh Farm and Factory site. He referred to a civil servant from Belfast deferentially as 'Miss Agnes Bruce', while two Ulster farmers were referred to simply as 'sunburned sisters from a farm at Portadown', their faltering speech contrasting with Holt's authoritative confidence, as did their preference for the older style of farm.[15] The voice of the Festival Office was also a standard voice, the imagined voice of the nation. Written guides, catalogues and advertising materials for the Festival, as well as numerous articles written by Gerald Barry and colleagues in the Festival Office, made authoritative declarations on behalf of the nation. They declared 'The Festival is … one united act of national reassessment' and 'Britain is at home to the world', confidently suggesting everyone was participating. The Office's imagined vantage point was a centralising one, as if seeing from above and surveying the four nations.[16] Other voices were almost indecipherable within the Festival's literatures.

English was the *lingua franca* for all the peoples contributing across the four nations whose first languages might be Welsh or Gaelic, or in the case of the many émigrés living in Britain after the war, a number of other languages. Many of those employed to work on the Festival and to tell its 'story', were émigrés – designers Misha Black, F.H.K. Henrion and Willy de Majo, to name only three. Perhaps it was easier for the conceit of a singular Festival 'story' to be sustained by people with an outsider's perspective than by those who represented a fraction of its multiple national traditions.[17] All who worked on the Festival were co-opted into telling a single story about Britain and events focused on presenting what the English language, as a carrier of wider meanings about the nation and democracy, had achieved. The new 'story' that could potentially have been told in 1951 – of the important contribution made by the wartime influx of émigrés, speaking a diverse range of languages and adhering to other religions – was edited out.[18]

LETTERING IN THE DESIGNED ENVIRONMENT

The role of words and lettering in exhibition and shop-window displays, their incorporation onto packaging and into planning schemes, was the subject of much interest in post war trade journals, manuals and amongst product designers.[19] The postwar Labour Party was itself aware of the impact of typography and lettering. It had been casting around for a new look after the Second World War when in 1948 the Party commissioned typographer Michael Middleton to write *Soldiers of Lead: An introduction to layout and typography for use in the Labour Party*. This declared that Labour could win if they thought harder about how to unify their look.[20]

Beyond packaging and developing a corporate look, there was a growing awareness of the impact of lettering in the landscape. Graphic designer Milner Gray was commissioned to create all the symbols for the Festival exhibitions and, with Robin Day, created signage for the South Bank site. Gray had, by 1951, created brand identities for Ilford Ltd and Courage & Co. Ltd, work undertaken by his consultancy DRU. He had also participated in planning research in the early 1940s into the way that street lettering could be included in wider planning schemes.[21] Led by planner W.G. Holford and Sir Stephen Tallents, the research focused on creating standards for legibility, materials and siting of signage and on respecting the architectural and civic character of a locality by allowing for variation within reason.[22] The work looked towards finding accurate ways of reflecting the character of a place within the formal qualities of text, while simultaneously reflecting the values of contemporary design. Such ideas were in the spirit of the *Architectural Review*'s campaign for a Twentieth-Century Picturesque. Through a collage of photographs and illustrations the magazine would set out examples of 'successful' townscapes. These included incidents of where street signs, shop signs and advertising billboards were in or out of keeping with the 'spirit' of the area. 'Townscape', an article of December 1949, used an illustration by Gordon Cullen to demonstrate where painted advertisements fitted well within their environment. It depicted an

6.1 FESTIVAL SIGNAGE AT THE SOUTH BANK
(Above, left) Sign designed by Robin Day and Milner Gray;
(Above, right) The Left Luggage office at the South Bank with symbols designed by Milner Gray;
(Below) Symbols designed by Milner Gray.

end-of-terrace house plastered with magazine and cigarette advertisements, suggesting such written advertisements could have a significant impact on the environment – either positive or negative – depending on where they were situated.[23]

Early in the development of the Festival the PR team, led by Paul Wright, commissioned lettering to be used in Festival marketing and publicity. Many criticized this bitterly as insufficient, full of inconsistencies and 'a rather typical advertising agency job'.[24] It was agreed that it should be replaced. In pursuit of a unified look for all of the Festival's signing and text – in particular the 'titling of buildings' – the Typography Panel was set up to advise on this aspect of the exhibitions. Graphic designer Charles Hasler (1908–92), Chairman of the Panel, later explained the panel had wanted to achieve a look that was 'British in feeling', that designs had been inspired by early nineteenth-century type specimen books.[25] The Festival's official script, designed by Philip Boydell working with Ernest Ingham was a modernized version of 'Egyptian' slab serif lettering, using variations of Roman and Italic script, based on 'Egyptian' types re-cut in the nineteenth century by Figgins, Thorne and Austin between 1815 and 1825.[26] 'A Specimen of Display Letters Designed for the Festival of Britain, 1951' was written by Hasler as a guide for Festival designers. The guidelines added yet another layer to the already restricted and circumscribed nature of designing a section. They were to be attended to alongside the thematic script dictating the 'story' designers were given.[27] At the South Bank, lettering was chosen that lay flat against buildings and did not project in three-dimensions from the surface to which it was applied – although it was designed as if in three-dimensions. This was favoured because it was considered universal enough to fit every Festival context. At the Festival, the decorative styling of the text was intended by the alphabet's designers to contrast with the minimal decoration of the signage, litterbins and buildings to which it was applied.[28] In fact, many of the direction signs were sober in character, adopting a condensed sans serif. One influence for such lettering was Gordon Cullen's cut-out metal lettering in Thorne Shaded, used to notable effect as the nameplate above the front elevation of Tecton's Finsbury Health Centre (built 1935–8). Cullen was co-opted to the Typography Panel to act as liaison between the group and architects and designers working on Festival sections.

Another influence for such typographic styling came through the work of graphic designer Robert Harling (1910–2008).[29] While *The Penrose Annual* and Herbert Spencer's *Typographica* covered international graphic arts contemporary with the Festival, Harling explored historical typefaces and notions of indigenous fonts in the journals he edited. The covers of his magazine, *Typography* (published 1936–9), were decorated with large Victorian letters in strong colours. During the same period, Harling re-drew nineteenth-century typefaces and created new ones for Stephenson Black foundry that were Victorian and decorative in character, such as Playbill, Tea Chest, Keyboard and Chisel. Lavishly illustrated in colour plates and focusing almost exclusively on British graphic design, his magazine the *Alphabet and Image* (published 1946–8) set out, according to an editorial, to 'reproduce only the work of artists of these islands'.[30] All articles took exclusively British subjects, contemporary and historical, and explored historical typefaces. The January 1948 issue, for example, focused on so-called 'artistic' Victorian printing, the type designs of Eric Gill, pre-Raphaelite drawings and architectural drawings by Hugh Casson. There were strong parallels between the almost exclusively British focus and admiration of historic typefaces in *Alphabet and Image* and the graphic style favoured by the Festival's Typography Panel, whose modernism was tempered and blended with a taste for the historic and the indigenous.

The writings of lettering historian Nicolete Gray (1911–97) were extraordinarily influential on the generation of Festival designers and may have been another impetus for the Festival's typographic styling. Gray's book *XIXth Century Ornamented Types and Title Pages* (1938) was written at a time when Victorian printing was unfashionable and neglected. She enthusiastically rediscovered it and her book played a major role in reviving interest in 'English Vernacular', the native originality of script and decoration expressed in carved tombstones and painted pub signs. Gray would look back at lettering used on the South Bank, commenting that 'unfortunately' it had been two-dimensional, rather than using 'architectural letters' that might have fitted with the buildings rather better, but that this did still provide a positive demonstration of how space could be created between a letter and its background.[31] Pevsner had responded to criticisms of two-dimensional Festival lettering. He had praised the lettering schemes for the way they had contrasted with the buildings around them. The distinct difference between the florid Victorian, 'over-robust' Festival lettering and the experimental modernism of the buildings with 'transparency of glass, slim and vigorous steel struts, and thin aluminium lattice work' as background to the lettering was, he thought, integral to their design. The contrast was, for Pevsner, its ingenuity, and an important and central aspect of the Picturesque presentation of the Festival that he had argued for elsewhere. Pevsner remarked,

> The result is effects of different textures, or geometrical patterns, the criss–cross of the lamella roof of the Lion and Unicorn Pavilion, the tiled side strips of the Festival Hall, the balcony and balcony railing arrangements of flats, the walls of flint, rubble, and so on contrasted with their smoothly plastered neighbours at the South Bank. It all witnesses a rediscovery of variety and contrast, qualities for which the great art of landscaping in the English eighteenth century was famous all the world over (...) Now it is in relation to this that lettering at the Exhibition must be understood.

Aside from lettering, Pevsner also saw Picturesque in the way paintings and sculptures had been laid out at the South Bank, as well as in 'minor elements of external furnishings' such as,

... the ponds with rocks and pebbles, the lights, the wastebaskets, the signposts, the variety of pavements, the planters that serve to guide and barricade visitors' access, and the enormous variety of wall surfaces.[32]

Such thoughts were also in the minds of Festival designers. The visual variety favoured on the South Bank site followed through from the architecture and landscaping into the lettering and section design. Key to this was blending the modern with the historic. Signs demarcated Festival sections in 'Grotesques, Romans, Italics, shaded, condensed [and] extended' lettering. Lettering as part of a designed environment including buildings and landscapes played a significant role in creating distinctive places and an 'appropriate' identity of place.[33]

Lettering was also designed to be made of the very thing it described. In Henrion's Country section, 'The Modern Hen' section was marked by a sign spelt out in eggs and in his Natural Scene Perspex letters – which he worked on with the young Terence Conran (who was working across the South Bank site on various jobs as assistant to architect Dennis Lennon) – spelt out the title of each section and carried samples of them. The sign for 'Trees' carried twigs, leaves and pinecones and 'Rural Crafts' carried horse shoes, nails and scissors. These looked very good for a few weeks until the juices of rotting animals started to seep out, making a stench, and had to be taken away. Meanwhile, textile designer Jacqueline Groag made a sign for 'The Living World' section of the Dome of Discovery made from threaded bones. Elsewhere, Gordon and Ursula Bowyer spelt the word 'sport' letter-by-letter in Egyptian font across one side of their stands of the Sport pavilion, to be seen from far off. Enormous black and white text, to be used on the walls of exhibitions, were blown up through a photographic process and applied like wallpaper, colour-washed if necessary.[34]

Lettering was part of the built environment of the Festival. Lettering was also part of the published Festival. HMSO published the massive array of Festival literature. Written guides were produced to accompany each event explaining who was involved, how to circulate and what the displays were about, mediating visitor's immediate visual experience with ideas that were paralleled and extended in written form. Detailed catalogues to objects on display gave the name and provenance of items. These guides and catalogues, along with leaflets advertising events and maps giving directions to sites, were another vehicle by which the Festival's 'story' was communicated to visitors. Around 3.5 million guides were bought by the almost 13 million visitors to nationwide Festival events.[35]

6.2 FESTIVAL LETTERING

(Above) Lettering in eggs for the 'Modern Hen', the Livestock section of The Country designed by F.H.K. Henrion;

(Below, left) Jacqueline Groag entrance sign to the 'Living World', made of threaded bones in the Dome of Discovery;

(Below, right) Perspex direction sign in the Natural Scene incorporating bark, leaves and twigs designed by F.H.K. Henrion.

The guides followed a shared format. With a coloured jacket designed by Abram Games, with his emblem at the centre, they told visitors how to go round, and introduced the overall idea of the exhibition, including maps and script about each part. Some of the catalogues were attributed to an author, making them more than an accompanying reference text, a book to be read in its own right. Ian Cox wrote South Bank and *HMS Campania* guides, for example. Although setting out maps of sites and introducing themes, they did not explain the content of a section or refer to the exhibits and display techniques. Nor were the accompanying photographs taken from exhibitions themselves, but from official sources or photo libraries, illustrating the subject of the section more widely. By partially referencing the events, these catalogues existed independently, as portable content to be taken away from exhibitions. Gerald Barry – the consummate editor – pored over the final proofs of the Guides himself. He was not always happy with the final result. After a meeting about the Festival souvenir guide, he wrote in his diary, 'I don't like it. Quite well written, but the drawings are thin & spindly & the layout old-fashioned. Why must they have chosen Perpetua for the headings, with that mannered, rather ugly upper case?'[36] Perpetua remained amongst a hotchpotch of fonts used in the final versions of the Guides and Catalogues. Despite this these popular souvenirs proved infinitely more durable than other exhibits that were lost or broken up after closure. For some who never got to visit an exhibition, reading a catalogue was an experience of the Festival. 'Thick, high quality paper and filled with exotic designs and optimism which, in a slum street in Halifax, seemed magical' wrote architect Michael Hales many years later. The catalogue 'was one of the things that gave me the notion that I might be an architect when I grew up; and that the world "out there" might be as hopeful and imaginative as the catalogue was a delight to have and to hold.'[37] Through these Festival guides, the event would continue to exist long after the exhibitions had been destroyed.

The representation of the Festival in maps that defined or confined the celebrations spatially followed through the idea that 'Festival' was coterminous with the physical boundaries of the four nations. Maps were used in many ways: to show sections of the exhibitions, the full site of one exhibition, exhibition sites across a city, or sites mapped across Britain. In the Festival, the mapped central view, giving a single cohesive viewpoint and rationale was in tension with the peripheral one.[38] Visitors were invited to have a multiple perspective that enabled them to conceive of a spatially bound Festival whole, while also participating in particular events.[39] Maps on Festival advance information leaflets evoked a spirit of adventure; some were even drawn to pastiche maps from the age of exploration with scrolls, regal coronets and sea creatures (see, for example, image 1.1). Made as navigational devices, to be carried by visitors travelling between sites, maps gave visitors an overview of the events they took part in, while being immersed in one section.[40]

THE FESTIVAL *ABOUT BRITAIN GUIDES*

Beyond catalogues and guides many other books were published for the Festival, a large number of them taking topographical themes. Thirteen Festival *About Britain Guides* mapped out areas of Britain, offering routes for exploration. Initially they were to be accompanied by *About Britain* coach tours, dividing the country into 13 'districts', which exposed visitors to the scenery, monuments, buildings and people of Britain. Tours and *Guides* were planned so the Festival Office could boost the limited number of events they had arranged outside London. The tours were abandoned on grounds of expense and practicality but the series of guidebooks that had been planned to accompany them were still published by Collins in the hope that visitors would find a way of undertaking independent journeys by car, coach or bicycle.[41]

Gerald Barry was chairman of the *Guides'* editorial board, with the prolific poet and topographical writer Geoffrey Grigson (1905–85) as General Editor. Also on the editorial board were geography professors E.G.R. Taylor and S.W. Wooldridge, and *The Geographical Magazine* founder-editor Michael Huxley. The dust-wrapper of each book bore a map of the region featured within. A series of 'expert locals' were invited to write the 13 guides, those who had written other topographical studies of Britain such as W.G. Hoskins and E. Estyn Evans and were interested principally in the geology, wildlife or local industries of those places.[42] Eminent artist-illustrators were invited to contribute topographical drawings. Barbara Jones and Kenneth Rowntree, among others, produced title pages showing local features or an imagined scene that evoked the putative qualities of the area. The title page of *The Lowlands of Scotland* guide, for example, was a watercolour by Joan Hassall. The ruin of Kelso Abbey framed an imaginary coalmine in the distance, evoking the Scottish Lowlands by showing polarities present within local scenery: majestic scenery, historic buildings and recent signs of industrial productivity.

In the interwar period, with the increase in car ownership, the perceived space of rural leisure had been transformed. British countryside and local cultural traditions were presented through a resurgence of topographical books that set out to help car owners explore the whole country.[43] These surveys focused on showing the scenic and cultural traditions of local areas of Britain.

Series such as Odham's *Britain Illustrated* and Batsford's *The Face of Britain* ran to many editions. Batsford's series had shown unbroken stretches of landscape, sustaining the belief that Britain's landscape continued to be largely rural and untainted by the built punctuation of modernity. Faber & Faber's *Shell Guides*, edited by writer John Betjeman and painter John Piper, were published from the 1930s until the late 1980s. Written by invited authors – artists Paul and John Nash, travel writer Robert Byron, writer Peter Quennell and planner Thomas Sharp, among others – they covered Britain county-by-county. Mainly, though not exclusively, they focused on its historic buildings, landscapes and sites of local interest. Where similar books had offered itineraries for visiting places, this series, which focused on the visual qualities of places, professed to offer more general but authentic, 'impressions' of the places from people who lived in them. After the war the *Guides* reappeared in 1951, including maps and illustrated indexes featuring black and white images of interesting architectural details visitors might spot on a trip.[44]

This British hunger for publications exploring local histories and traditions was more profound, simply, than a hobby for a weekend away. It pointed to a deep-rooted, wistful belief in a threatened British way of life and the search to reconcile the past with the present. The preoccupation with preserving dying British rural traditions and the countryside, which characterized many topographical studies, gained an even more acute significance after the Second World War.

The *About Britain Guides* aimed to update people's idea of how Britain looked. While they showed areas continuing their ancient rural traditions, they simultaneously made a virtue of industrial structures such as power stations and hydroelectric dams, enhancing the land. A photograph of the Loch Sloy dam under construction, its monumental stone structure magnificently bridging the gap within a Highland valley, was shown in one guide. This full-page image was shown beside another of an impressively bleak Caledonian landscape where the text under the dam stated '- one of the projects giving new hope to the Highlanders -' and ran continuously into the text of the Highland scene that said ' – who cannot live by the superb scenery', underlining the need for modern structures in the landscape, as had sections of Glasgow's Heavy Industry exhibition. Images of people working in mines and factories, or taking time off after their shifts, were chosen. In *Lakes to Tyneside*, a section about Durham and the Norman shrine of St Cuthbert featured a photograph of 'a housewife in the colliery district of Newcastle hanging out her washing in the street', overshadowed by derelict-looking warehouse buildings, rather than the historic shrine or Cathedral.[45] A full page photograph of a sixteenth-century timbered Tudor building in Cheshire

Distilling and the other small local industries of the Highland zone cannot solve the Problem. But perhaps it can be solved by the production of power in this land of lochs and high rainfall. Here is Loch Sloy Dam, one of the projects giving new hope to the Highlanders –

– who cannot live by the superb scenery of a Caledonia which is 'stern and wild, meet nurse for a poetic child.' The peaks of Arran, although so far south, with their Gaelic names of Cir Mhor and Caisteal Abhail, typify the beauty and bleakness of the Highland landscape.

In the 16th century, when Little Moreton Hall was built near Congleton on the eastern edge of the Cheshire plain, it was an essay in architectural modernism and virtuosity. There are few or no better examples in all England of a timbered Tudor building.

But modern Cheshire is industrial as well as rural, and the industries have their own notions of architecture. Oil-refining is one of these industries. Hence these spherical storage tanks and a concrete cooling tower 340 feet high, at Ellesmere Port on the Manchester Ship Canal.

appeared beside a full page photograph of spherical oil storage tanks and concrete cooling tower, mirroring the formal qualities of the Tudor house with its central brick chimney. Both were labelled regional architecture and shown as equally valid representations of the county.

Production Designer on the *About Britain Guides* was typographer Ruari McLean (1917–2006). McLean had worked from 1945–6 designing Penguin books with modernist typographer Jan Tschichold and would go on to write several seminal books about typography.[46] McLean chose to illustrate Britain with the work of photographers closely identified with the various regions, such as Scottish landscape photographers Robert Moyes Adam and J. Allan Cash for the two Scottish guides.[47] Shell and Odhams guides had not attempted to show the English people, focusing instead on histories associated with local landscapes and buildings. The *About Britain Guides*, meanwhile, showed what was exceptional as well as what was ordinary. British people and the British land were shown supposedly as they were. Poor living-conditions and unfamiliar modern structures such as pylons and cooling-towers were included so these things might become part of the re-assembled image of Britain. This was less akin to a tradition of topographical books and more like the visual presentation of *Picture Post* magazine to which McLean acted as freelance design consultant while working on the *Guides*. Like the *Post*, the *About Britain Guides* focused as much on explaining people's everyday life as on the grand historical narratives associated with places.

Barry, Chairman of the Guides' editorial board, was strongly in sympathy with this attempt to update people's knowledge. 'Everybody knows that Britain is a land of lovely scenery and a famous past,' he wrote. 'We're a bit tired of the everlasting pictures of the British way of life showing Beefeaters at the Tower of London, Chelsea Pensioners, and Cathedrals by moonlight. We've new things to show – new industries, new inventions, new techniques, new discoveries – yes, and new freedoms as well, though this may surprise you to hear.'[48] The central theme of the Festival – the land and the people of Britain – was not to be an anachronistic showcasing

6.3 ABOUT BRITAIN *GUIDES* (facing page)
(Above) The newly opened Loch Sloy Dam shown beside a photograph of the Highland landscape. A caption emphasized both as key to Highland life; (Below) A sixteenth-century timbered, Tudor building in Cheshire appeared beside oil storage tanks and a concrete cooling tower, which mirrored the formal qualities of the Tudor House with its brick chimney.

of British culture, but it was also about showing things as they were. While everyday British life in its unedited normality may have been of interest to British people, books aimed at foreign tourists gave a more limited picture. Ruth McKenney and Richard Bransten's *Here's England* produced for Festival visitors contained a chronology of major events in English history, a resumé of English architectural terms and a guide only to what was seen as either historically or aesthetically distinguished.[49]

In the *Guides*, aerial photographs enabled buildings and towns to be seen in a wider context beside natural and geological features. McLean drew heavily on the stock of the Aerofilms agency.[50] In one *Guide* an Aerofilms photograph of the port of Newhaven seen set within the context of the town and countryside beyond was juxtaposed beside a horizontal photograph of Lewes Castle with chalk cliffs behind it. It made a visual link between the chalky walls of this dominating man-made structure and the land that had produced its building materials, and was accompanied by text explaining that the castle guarded the 'gap in the Downs to which Newhaven leads'. This double vision – both vertical and horizontal views of Britain – was a recurrent trope in the Festival's written and exhibited presentation. It offered readers, or visitors, the opportunity simultaneously to experience Britain from a single point on the ground and also from an authoritative, elevated point above it, as powerful and all seeing. Text, map, itineraries and objects were, as in the exhibitions, presented in relay in the *Guides*, as one of their production team later commented: 'Around Mr McLean's desk were the *About Britain* series of pocket touring guides. They combined text and illustrations to complement each other rather than stating the same thing twice.'[51] Government officials, architects and designers wanting to project a vision of continuity, a modern Britain being preserved, shaped this presentation.

The *About Britain Guides* were aimed towards showing how British land and people were inextricably connected across time and space, a subject also of the Festival exhibitions, presenting a striking imaginative Picturesque. They extended the idea that people were a direct product of the geology, climate and landscape, be it rural, industrial or urban. Conversely, they also suggested national 'genius' could be traced, very specifically, back to particular topographies. Photographs and drawings captured people enjoying the land: walking, hunting, gardening and rambling; people working the land or working while surrounded by their landscape; people were absent but left their trace on the landscape through farming, walls, roads and factories. The *Guides* created a correlation between local and national heroism; heroes could be 'explained' by being traced back to the particular places that had bred and nurtured them, and at the same time these places were posited in this manner, and extended, by the 'heroes' that were associated with them. In *West Country*, 'Devonians' – Drake, Gilbert, Hawkins, Raleigh and Arctic explorer John Davis – were traced back to their specific local origins in the county.

As elsewhere in Festival exhibitions, geology was an integral element of the story of each locality in the *About Britain Guides*, key to understanding a place. Echoing this interest, architect Clough Williams-Ellis described the variety of historic building styles across the country in relation to the geology of the land in which they were situated. In addition to carrying an 'ordinary road map' with surface features, height above sea-level, the sort of land, whether moor of forest, down or arable, 'It is helpful to have a geological map also, giving the actual bones of the country on which all else ultimately depends (...) a key to the structure of Britain's body'.[52] Visitors could not really understand the country without knowing what lay beneath the surface, he believed.

The presentation of the country in the *About Britain Guides* was paralleled in representations of Britain's topographies in films of the same period. For Gerald Barry, films were 'a vehicle or instrument for expressing directly on the screen many aspects of the Festival's theme'. This was particularly true of documentary films, which were able to show activities, particularly industrial, scientific or artistic ones, that were less easy to show in exhibitions. The Festival film *Family Portrait* drew upon rhetoric of land and people. Directed and written by Surrealist filmmaker Humphrey Jennings (1907–50), the film set out 'a screen version of the Festival's central theme – the Land and the People of Britain'.[53] Jennings was interested in how industrialization had impacted upon national topographies, pursuing the theme of land and people in both the film's narrative and its visual content.[54] People were imaginatively linked with their environment. In one passage the camera moved from shots of mountains downwards, as if panning underground, to a coalmine where a miner was hard at work. The narrator declared 'Diversity of nature in this small space, the variety of landscape, local variation of soil and climate, the jumble of coal and rock underground: all somehow match the diversity of the people'.

Jennings' feeling for the contemporary British landscape was more conflicted than that in the Festival's topographical guides. Jennings sought out beauty and ingenuity within the new landscape, being exhilarated by the courage with which people had fought the war but appalled at the scars inflicted on people and their land by the conflict. Through *Family Portrait* he expressed nostalgia and regret for an erstwhile world before the Industrial Revolution and sought reconciliation with the contemporary world. A written film transcript for *Family Portrait* included as subtitle the quote from E.M. Forster's *Howards End* '... the rainbow bridge that connects the prose in us with the passion ...', suggesting his concern for bringing together practical and imaginative instincts.[55] Jennings' focus was not limited to ideas about how past and present intersected but was also on the sharp division between city and countryside and on people's relationship with the land. Any disruption of this was a cause for concern.[56] In *Family Portrait* these conflicts were linked more widely to the British national character. 'How to reconcile the farm and the factory?' Jennings' narrator asked. 'We are helped, saved perhaps by our paradoxes. We need innovation and like tradition, we like sitting quiet at home and like pageantry, celebrating heritage but acknowledge times have changed.' Rural traditions and modern industry were both valuable, but hard to reconcile. On screen Jennings' surreal juxtapositions underlined this. A cricket team played on the green at the Oval cricket ground in south London, flanked by vast gasometers in the background. Miners drilling underground or iron-smelting in progress were accompanied by classical music and a lyrical voice-over, not the ear-splitting sound of underground drilling or the loud clank of iron. As the narrator explained 'something like a quarter of the family live right on top of coal', the viewer was shown portraits of scientist James Watt and engineer John Wilkinson, who had invented 'a new kind of poetry and a new kind of prose', distancing the viewer from the immediate subject and drawing them into his wider philosophical musings on reconciliation: of science and art, poetry and prose, town and country, farm and factory, muddle and orderliness, industry and post industrialization, and of practical and imaginative 'gifts'. Every time the countryside was pictured, it was twinned with a narrative reference that was historical or literary, rather than focusing on the factual or documentary. A camera shot of Beachy Head linked with the Armada and Drake, docked boats unloading on the Thames at Bankside with Shakespeare.

The *About Britain Guides* had tried to show Britain contemporaneously, in its various guises, from historic monuments, to local factories and producers, to modern housing and grimy factory-scapes. Jennings' film set out his musings on how forms of pastoral and poetic Britishness might be reconciled with damaged or defective Britishness, without resolution. In an article about films in the Festival, Barry described Jennings' contribution as 'a poet's creation, precise yet elusive'.[57] In his private diary of January 1951, after an *in memoriam* screening following Jennings' accidental death in 1950, Barry noted:

> *Fires were Started*, first-rate, *Listen to Britain* (the sounds of Britain) very fine. All were moving (partly no doubt war emotions remembered),

until we came to *Family Portrait*, which definitely is not. Very competent, perhaps over-intellectual for the screen; Basil Wright says 'too much packed into the space'.

Family Portrait did not attempt to reconcile versions of Britishness as the Festival did elsewhere, which may explain Barry's criticism of it.[58]

The topographical photographs of Bill Brandt (1904–83) are a counterpoint to the visual language of the Festival's *About Britain Guides* and of Jennings' *Family Portrait*. Brandt's photographic series *Literary Britain*, produced in 1951, stood as publisher Cassell and Co's Festival contribution. Brandt had studied with Surrealist photographer Man Ray in Paris in 1929, returning to London in 1931. This close relationship with the Surrealist movement is something Brandt shared with Humphrey Jennings, who was co-organizer of the celebrated London International Surrealist Exhibition, held at the Burlington Galleries in 1936. In the late 1930s Brandt had made a striking series of social records that contrasted the lives of rich and poor, including *The English at Home* (1936) and *A Night in London* (1938). Brandt's war service was as photographer for the Ministry of Information, recording conditions in London in the Blitz, turning, after the war, to taking photographs of the British landscape. Rather than explaining a place through providing significant details of history, geology or productivity, as in the *About Britain Guides*, Brandt sought to locate or reveal the mood and emotion of places through his photographs alone. He was influenced in this by his contemporaries in the Continental Surrealist movement, whose attitudes to landscape were often determined by its powers of association. Hungarian-born French painter and photographer Brassaï (1899–1984)'s landscape photographs, for example, were overtly erotic. In his photograph *Ciel Postiche*, which appeared facing Brandt's pictures of the Scilly Isles in the journal *Minotaure 6* of December 1934, a female nude in the foreground mirrored the hills on the skyline beyond. Brandt's own photographs signalled this sense that being in the landscape was an act of embodiment, akin to being in an intimate maternal embrace. In the collection brought together as *Literary Britain*, Brandt pictured sites all over the country, where famous British writers had lived, worked or stayed, and in doing so Brandt sought to locate the 'spirit' or *genius loci* which had nurtured such greatness, using 'atmosphere to induce emotion'.[59] Unpopulated scenes were related directly with the characters they had nurtured: Blake's Cottage at Felpham and the Bronte's home at the Parsonage, Haworth, for example. Thomas Hardy was represented by photographs of the mysterious, primeval sites of Stonehenge and Avebury Circle under brooding skies, suggesting imminent rainfall or submersion under snow. Unlike the wordy Festival exhibitions and publications, *Literary Britain* was sparing with words. It sought to evoke an atmosphere of the writer's well-known works by summoning a viewer's fragmented memories of them, to evoke powerful feelings about the land of Britain. By eliding British history with British fiction, Brandt underlined the fact that places were formed in people's imaginations as much from fictional evocation as from factual accounts.

The motif of chalk figures in the British landscape operated in *The About Britain Guides*, Brandt's photographs and Jennings' *Family Portrait*. In the *About Britain* guide to the Home Counties, the mysterious chalk figure carved into the Sussex Downs, the Long Man of Wilmington, was both photographed and described. The angle at which the photograph was taken – from above, by the picture library Aerofilms – gave readers a bird's eye view of the figure, in the context of the rolling hills in which he stood. The *Guide*'s written descriptions revealed the Long Man as an indicator of past myths and poetic heritage, quoting patriot Rudyard Kipling's poem about the Long Man in his 1902 poem 'Sussex':

> I will go out against the sun
> Where the rolled scarp retires,
> And the Long Man of Wilmington
> Looks naked toward the shires

The Long Man was used here to allude to national myths and to indicate a literary heritage of which to be proud, but at the same time by showing the figure carved into the hillside from above, in rolling farmland, the make-up of the land became a focus: the chalk from which it was carved pointed to the specific geological processes that underpinned the place and provided the context for the productivity for the land, with fields of crops surrounding the striking figure.

In the film *Family Portrait* where the Long Man was an important motif, the figure performed a different role, providing an imaginative link between the past and the present, sandwiched in Jennings' film between discussions of modern scientific farming technology, an evocation of Kipling's poem, and a discussion about how to reconcile farming with technology. Jennings included various long views of the Long Man, most taken from across the fields, but shot from ground level so that he towered mysteriously above, acting in the film as a symbol of what was ultimately unfathomable. As scientific and technological progress was being made, Jennings indicated that much remained unknowable. Panning over the Long Man, a farmer and scientist deep in conversation striding towards it, Jennings' narrator asked

'Can you really treat John Barleycorn as you do the blades of a turbine?' casting the contemporary farmer as John Barleycorn, a figure from Neolithic mythology that had folkloric associations with the Long Man. In this myth, Barleycorn as the barley-god was buried each harvest time to ensure fertility for the following year's crops. His evocation of the story suggested a rupture between the two needed to be healed, pointing to the possibility of reconciliation. Brandt's *Literary Britain* did not include an image of the Long Man, but did capture other Neolithic sites: Avebury and Stonehenge stones and a photograph of 'The White Horse, near Bratton, Wiltshire, 1951', a grainy black and white abstraction of the figure, taken sideways, from close-to. Brandt had no interest in pointing to the geological features of the land for their own sake or in pointing to the fecundity of the land to make a point about productivity. Instead, Brandt took the horse out of context, its scale and scope were forgotten and its mysterious, abstracted qualities became paramount.

The topographical studies that were offered as a part of the Festival in the *About Britain Guides* tried to do a number of things: to show the interesting history and diversity of the British Isles, from small isolated communities to large, well-connected ones; to show there was no compromise to be made between maintaining the beauty of the land of Britain and, at the same time, existing as a modern, technologically advanced nation, equipped to meet the needs of its population through public utilities; and lastly, to show how high yields from the land did not rule out simultaneous use of traditional methods. These ideas were represented in the *Guides* as of a piece. Jennings' Festival film, by contrast, pointed without resolution to the problematic and potentially conflicting relationship between technological advancement and traditionalism, between rural and urban relationships, between artists and scientists, between – in his words – 'members of a family' with widely differing opinions. Bill Brandt, meanwhile, was not concerned with resolving conflicting images of Britishness, of supporting the reconstruction of the economy or of morale postwar, but rather with locating a more magical, evocative landscape, beyond historical specificity. Despite their differences, each representation relied heavily on their viewer's ability to draw on literary knowledge.

EXHIBITIONS OF BOOKS

While the Festival produced books, it also exhibited them as objects in their own right, part of the 'story' of land and people. Numerous Festival book exhibitions were held around the country. Herbert Morrison had spoken in support of their inclusion in the celebrations, seeing books as an important vehicle for representing British culture.[60] 'Books are more truly representative of the life of a nation than anything else can be,' claimed the National Book League, who were responsible for overseeing the Festival book exhibitions, 'Machinery, textiles and even paintings cannot rival books in this regard'.[61] The League's claim to 'representativeness' justified exhibiting books in a Festival that had many more visually arresting and innovative exhibits on display. The League were invited to arrange book exhibitions for the Festival in 1949, working with the Council of Industrial Design, who were responsible for the design of the book exhibitions. They oversaw around 80 book exhibitions across Britain, and directly organized three: at the V&A in London, the Mitchell Library in Glasgow and the Signet Library in Edinburgh.

Prior to 1951 many major exhibitions had included book displays. At the Great Exhibition of 1851 there had been a small display of British religious tracts that put this form of manufacture on show. Several international exhibitions since had shown book cover design and typography to promote or explain the publishing industry or to illuminate the intellectual life of a nation. Exhibitions had been shown in connection with book fairs in Leipzig and Frankfurt for centuries, while the 1928 Pressa Exhibition in Cologne had focused exclusively on exhibiting press and publications, the work of regional printers of newspapers and books and included type foundries and historical sections on the newspaper and the art of the book, providing a context in which German publishers could define themselves in a sensitive time for international politics.[62] The 1930 Stockholm Exhibition had included areas devoted to books, bindings and the graphics industry, a field where rapid technological change was in process. The books section focused, principally, on Swedish graphic style such as the font Futura, cut in 1927, which, although designed by German typographer Paul Renner, came to be closely associated with Swedish modernism.[63] A few years later, the 1937 Paris International Exhibition of Arts and Crafts in Modern Life again saw books displayed to illuminate French culture. In the 'Salon de la Pensée' ('Expression of Ideas Salon') and 'Salon de l'Ecrivain ('Writers' Salon'), portraits and manuscripts of famous authors were exhibited, accompanied by radio and phonograph recordings of their voices. The exhibition also included a section with 20 libraries containing an astonishing 20,000 volumes, covering a multitude of subjects from science and fine art to industrial enterprise and manual labour.[64] The books were not presented in glass stands as objects but as 'instruments of labour', to be read by visitors who used the room as they would any other library. The room of Printing and Paper put the subject of production itself on show.[65] The British Pavilion at Paris in 1937 also included a display of books, printing and illustration, with an innovative stand by graphic designer Ashley Havinden in the shape of a series of giant free-standing open books with inset shelves for display and explanatory texts above and below. The focus was on the design and presentation of the books, rather than on their content. Five years before the Festival, the V&A's 'Britain Can Make It' show had included a section on 'Books and Printing', with the overriding aim of putting the production of the publishing industry on display through exhibiting 200 books.

At the Festival's Power and Production pavilion, book production was one of six groups of British industries chosen for exhibition alongside woodworking, rubber and plastics, glass, textiles and pottery. In the vast hall designed by architects George Grenfell Baines and H.J. Reifenberg, visitors could cluster around or look down from the balcony on the spectacle of papermaking in action. East London papermaker Charles Skipper operated a 'Fast Three' single-colour offset printing press, alongside an enormous Axminster carpet weaving machine and a wafer-biscuit maker. Visitors could watch a live demonstration of hand papermaking and see recent examples of lithography and book illustration, leaflets and catalogues, invitations and greeting cards, and a limited number of book jackets and bookbindings. All these displays showcased technological developments.

The eighty or so book exhibitions held across Britain and Northern Ireland under the Festival banner had a different focus, closely related to the National Book League agenda.[66] The League declared their aim 'To foster the love of books and to inculcate wise habits of reading' and 'to bring to more and more people the joys and consolations that belong to books'.[67] Its agenda had a strongly moralising tone, guiding readers on how and what to read. Lionel McColvin's *How to Use Books* (1947) and Norman Birkett's *The Use and Abuse of Reading* (1951) argued that books had the potential to both benefit and damage the reader. The dogmatic and self-reflexive nature of its books-about-books was carried into *Readers' Guides*, which, alongside books about sport and hobbies, included guidance on how to read the work of British writers and the significance of *The Bible in English Life*. The League were directed by the Festival Office to present exhibitions in 'the dramatic terms which are to be employed elsewhere', an onerous responsibility considering the unpromising materials available to the exhibitions' designers: books chosen for their cultural significance, not for their bindings or graphic prowess, and to be set in museum display cases.[68]

6.4 FESTIVAL OF BRITAIN EXHIBITION OF BOOKS
Victoria and Albert Museum, display design: Hulme
Chadwick.

The largest Festival book exhibition was held at London's Victoria and Albert Museum.[69] Hulme Chadwick was designer, with the contribution of a paper sculpture by Warner Cooke, display typography by David Caplan and mural paintings by Ivor Fox. Despite the limitations of space and materials, *The Bookseller* enthused that Chadwick had 'produced a vivid and dramatic setting which certainly stands up to comparison with the much more elaborate jeux d'esprit on the South Bank'.[70] He used coloured aisles of exhibits decorated with lemon, blue and grey muslin sweeping up to a transparent ceiling on which brightly coloured letters of the alphabet glittered 'like stars'. Writer J.B. Priestley, whose own works featured, echoed this enthusiasm. As a rule, he found no joy in staring at books in glass cases but the Victoria and Albert Museum's show was 'gay, ingenious and enticing'.[71] Paradoxically, the professed intention of this 'visual presentation of five centuries of history' was not conceived, ultimately, to be visual but to work in the realm of the imagination, expressing abstract facets of 'the British temperament or way of life'. Visitors should feel emotional at the sight of Caxton's 500-year-old Chaucer manuscript, based on its significance to British culture. The emphasis was on contributing to the 'story' of the intellectual and imaginative life of the British people, eliciting a response to the books that it was hoped would last beyond the exhibition hall, resonating with people's thoughts and habits.

The 'Aisles of History', as the 14 sections of the V&A Book Exhibition were named (using a pompous Churchillian phrase unrelated to the a-historical thematic display adopted), set out to cover every aspect of British life. The starting point was a section devoted to 'The Bible' and the end one on 'The Artist' by way of 'The Children's Corner', 'The Sportsman', 'The Countryman', 'The Londoner' and 'The Thinker'. 'National Songs' included the score to *Rule Britannia* and the *National Anthem*'s first appearance in print. The exhibition's emphasis was on 'creative works', not works of reference or 'expository, critical or informative literature', which, it was acknowledged, were widely read by the public. Instead, texts such as William Beveridge's *Social Insurance and Allied Services* were displayed in 'The Free Citizen', illustrating 'freedom from insecurity' and providing an associative context for discussion of welfare state planning, one of many triumphant 'moments' signified by the hundreds of displayed books. No translations were shown, with the exception of the Bible, a decision justified by the argument that it was 'the foundation of British thought and the British way of life' and because 'the language of the Bible has echoed and re-echoed down our aisles of history', thereby appropriating the Bible as British in order to make it the intellectual focus, indeed axis, of the whole show.[72] Christianity was asserted as central to British identity in the Festival. 'Britain is a Christian community' proclaimed the main souvenir Festival book.[73] Barry believed the Festival would demonstrate 'the steadiness and Christian faith of our people', important largely because of Christianity's impact on the English language.[74] Speaking to a meeting of churches in 1951, Barry identified Britain's past as 'a Christian past' and Christianity as 'one of the main motive powers of our speech', giving Britain 'its proudest literary heritage and indeed its "vulgar tongue": the Bible and the Book of Common Prayer'.[75]

In Scotland, twin book exhibitions were mounted at Edinburgh's Signet Library and Glasgow's Mitchell Library. Both were designed by architect R.C. Carvell, the former focusing on eighteenth-century Scottish books, the latter on twentieth-century Scottish ones. The choice of these cities as host underlined an already existing bias: Edinburgh as the historic seat of intellectuals and Glasgow as the site of production. Glasgow had been the scene of an important turn-of-the century publishing revival that had taken root as early as 1809 when the publishing house later known as Blackie &

Son Ltd was founded, producing many books of great importance, including works of reference such as maps, dictionaries and gazeteers. By displaying literature, both exhibitions aimed to reflect national life, the Edinburgh show to be a 'history lesson', exposing the 'miracle' of eighteenth-century Scotland in the world of thought, and the Glasgow show to demonstrate the Scottish revival of the previous 50 years. Many book exhibitions were held elsewhere in towns and villages up and down the country, around half centred on touring collections displayed under themes such as 'British Country Life' and 'Women of Britain'.[76]

Books were also displayed in many other parts of the Festival. The furnished rooms of the South Bank's Homes and Gardens included 2,000 books in rooms 'ranging from those suitable for the nursery or the kitchen to those which might be found in a young City man's bed-sitting-room'.[77] The Pantechnicon, Power and Production and New Schools all displayed books that reflected the subjects on show. Russell and Goodden's popular Lion and Unicorn pavilion – dedicated to showing the British character – included a first-floor gallery aimed towards putting 'British People's native genius' on display, devoted to 'The English Language'. As at the V&A book show, English language started from the English translation of the Bible, 'the great beacon for the language' and its successive versions claimed as key to language; 'out of it came a resonance and a radiance which has suffused all our later literature and speech', again making a single exception in the English language bias of Festival books. An explicit link was made at the Lion and Unicorn between the language of Britain, the British character and 'the instinct of liberty' that the people of the island enjoyed.[78] At the heart of the presentation was a contradiction that remained unaddressed between the stated British 'instinct of liberty' and the history of Britain controlling and colonising large parts of the world, which had been the basis of national prosperity for over a hundred years. In the same way, the Lion and Unicorn's displays of the English language proudly asserted the homespun nature of the language, which was now, the exhibition claimed, spoken by 250 million people. Why this should be the case was at no point discussed.[79] Similarly, the V&A Book Exhibition's 'Venturer' section focused on Elizabethan travel narratives based on an idea of going and coming back, thereby avoiding the uncomfortable subject of when adventuring had become synonymous with settling, annexing or colonising.

In Festival book exhibitions each item was displayed in a glass case, unavailable for reading. Rare books were loaned from eminent named collections. Only two were not first editions; none were offered for sale. In this connoisseurial context books were intended to inspire awe and reverence. Visitors entering the exhibition were flanked by two cases of

Bibles, the earliest a manuscript of a 'Wycliffite' Bible, the latest some press proofs of the Revised Version of the Bible. Elsewhere, displayed books assumed the status of historical or religious relics. The provenance attached to them made them rare and inalienable, rather than mass-produced things to be read, shared and circulated. A copy of Scott's *Peveril of the Peak* lent by King George VI displayed a note stating that Queen Victoria had read it to the Prince Consort on his deathbed. The Festival book exhibitions and all of the books they contained existed to provide references to what was thought to amount to a greater meaning: what it meant to be British. No social criticism was perceptible within the exhibition but simply expressed 'a particular facet of the British temperament or way of life'.[80] All the books that contributed to the atmosphere of reverence created by the darkened room and cathedral-like aisles were intended to define and delineate elements of the land and people and its historical moments, to encourage its visitors towards the conclusion that Britain had – and would in future – go from strength to strength.

What motivated this interest in including books in so much of the Festival? During and after the Second World War there was an enormous increase in reading across the whole British population. During the War, readership increased dramatically amongst the British working classes as a direct result of people's wartime experiences, including the restriction in hobbies and expansion in secondary and further education to include works of fiction previously thought only to be available to the middle classes.[81] In Cecil Day-Lewis's 1944 *Picture Post* article on reading habits he noted, with satisfaction, the increased numbers of factory workers reading 'really tough, solid, advanced' technical books. 'A friend of mine, who has had a lot to do with factories during the last years' he wrote, 'estimates that there must be somewhere between one and two million factory workers who are reading such books, or possess the very high intellectual calibre necessary for reading them'.[82] Day-Lewis's observation that technical books were particularly popular among working-class readers was confirmed in statistical research carried out by Mass Observation in 1952. A survey of reading habits for a London library service showed that after works of fiction, scientific and technical books were the most regularly borrowed.[83]

Despite the increasing interest in technical books, a decision was made in the Festival that no reference books or manuals would be displayed. This was probably because such books were not considered the central reading focus of the predominantly middle-class target audience of this exhibition and because such manuals – although an increasingly key feature of national reading – may have highlighted an aspect of British intellectual life that was considered debased or discredited, being associated with manual skills rather than the stuff of the intellect and the imagination.

The Festival's rather exclusive approach to book selection formed a sharp contrast with books selected for that year's Ideal Home Exhibition. For the first time the 1951 Ideal Home Exhibition had a separate books section. Aiming to show literature 'on every topic of interest to the home lover', the Ideal Home included modern fiction, books on travel, adventure, biography, science, philosophy and religion, as well as a section devoted to instructional literature on every outdoor and indoor hobby from gardening to home handicrafts, music, the graphic arts and theatre.[84] Advertised in the *Times Literary Supplement* as 'A Unique Literary Occasion', the inclusion of 4,000 books was a proud part of the 1951 Ideal Home Exhibition, arranged 'With the hope that in many men and women it will create, or re-create, a desire to embark upon adventures of ideas and voyages of discovery in creative activity'.

The Ideal Home books exhibition was not the pretext for some light, literary entertainment, however, but part of a moral campaign. By encouraging reading, the exhibition aimed to 'do something constructive to counteract the drift towards mental and emotional passivity which modern man's increasing dependence on mechanical entertainment encourages'. In other words, ordinary men and women needed to be saved from the passivity that came from watching television and going to the cinema. Televisions were not widely owned in Britain in Festival year but cinema going was still very popular.[85] Ideal Home Exhibition organizers feared these forms of mechanical entertainment would precipitate moral decline. This fear was not evident in the organizers' planning for the Festival, where TV and film were important mechanisms for putting the cultural life of Britain on display. At the South Bank, neighbouring Telecinema and Television buildings designed by Wells Coates (1895–1958) explored these forms and their recent history. The BBC television service had only recently launched and TVs were an enormous novelty to Festival visitors. A social scientist carrying out research at the South Bank noted 'The television sets were often the cause of traffic jams'.[86]

While Festival books had been locked away in cases, Ideal Home Exhibition books were 'laid flat for easy examination', and any book that was displayed was also on sale. The Ideal Home's book show was a roaring success while the Festival's ones each had pitifully low numbers of visitors.[87] Despite these very low visitor numbers to the Festival book exhibitions by comparison with other parts of the Festival (such as the South Bank, which attracted 8.2 million), the presentation of the English language was central to the events considered, as it was among the Festival organizers, a central component of British civilization. Language was both the subject of the exhibitions, in Book Exhibitions and sections on English, and the medium and matter that made up these events: the design of the exhibition displays and accompanying literature. The overwhelming logocentricity of the exhibitions was an integral part of their visual and spatial experience. The Festival's book exhibitions attempted to remove people from the immediate concerns of the market place, instead presenting Britain in the form of a series of books pointing to an abstracted literary universe.

'FROM THE PLANNING OF THE KITCHEN TO THE PLANNING OF THE NATION'

Exhibiting Homes and Neighbourhoods

The key to homemaking is use of space.
Sign in Homes and Gardens, South Bank Exhibition

By the end of the Second World War, three million homes had been destroyed. How to rebuild Britain's homes and the areas around them was a key issue at the 1945 election.

Shortages of materials had led Housing Minister Aneurin Bevan to exercise tight controls on private developers, stipulating only one private house could be built for every four local authority ones. Despite this, people still had to wait up to eight years for council housing in the early days of Labour's term in office. Poor quality housing, with paltry minimum space allocation and a lack of indoor washing facilities, made the situation even more desperate. By 1949 many British families remained homeless or living in temporary pre-fabricated homes that had hastily been built to replace damaged ones. Building new housing to a 'human scale', with ample space and with modern, indoor washing facilities, was a key government policy. How new homes should look and how to deal with this problem of limited space was also central to Festival presentation of homes.[1] The wider Festival's focus on creating identity of place in the aftermath of the ravages of war and industry was also seen as key to creating good homes.

The problem of lack of space was addressed through government guidance on planning densities, suitable dimensions for new housing and suggested maximum numbers for spatial dimensions. The 1944 Dudley Report on *The Design of Dwellings* and resulting 1944 government *Housing Manual* had increased minimum spatial standards set out two decades earlier.[2] Aneurin Bevan revised these standards again in the 1949 *Housing Manual*, offering varying standards depending on whether the housing was to be occupied by families, old people, or people living alone.

Planners were pivotal in debates about giving people space. Planning a new Britain must, they believed, take place on every scale, 'from the planning of the kitchen to the planning of the nation' wrote planners Gilbert and Elizabeth Glen McAllister. Emphasis in all planning should be on 'space for living'.[3] The issue of limited space or 'congestion', as planner F.J. Osborn described it, pointed to wider issues about the condition of living in cities.[4] Cities needed to offer 'appropriate' conditions in order for human life to thrive. This included providing enough light and room inside the home to allow current inhabitants as well as new additions to the family happily to co-exist, and space in the environment outside and beyond the home for community relations to bloom. Enhanced awareness of what residents might actually want – instead of what they were perceived to need – resulted from increasing consultation in planning, public involvement on housing committees and the development of market surveys from the interwar period onwards. Planners such as Max Lock in his 1939 study of Ocean Street, Stepney, in East London had pioneered participative planning, considering the preferences of slum dwellers. Where interviewers had concluded that residents preferred houses to the flats the LCC were initially planning to provide, they produced alternative duplex units of two-storey flats inside low-rise flatted estates, for example.[5] Housing reformer Elizabeth Denby had sought tenants' opinions on housing early in the 1930s, while in the 1940s organizations such as the Women's Co-operative Guild sought the views of women in order to influence housing policy.[6]

The publication of the 1942 Beveridge Report on *Social Insurance and Allied Services*, the blueprint for a national welfare state, had also resulted in legislation and a refocus within government policy on British home life. The Report set out the idea of comprehensive public protection for all individuals and for the family 'from the cradle to the grave', against sickness, poverty, unemployment and poor living conditions by provision of minimal social services including free medical aid, improved housing and family allowances.[7] It was motivated by anxiety about declining birth rates, and the need to refocus on building families in order to improve the situation, locating wives firmly within the home in order to provide for their families. Such anxieties were echoed in the 1944 Dudley Report, which focused on producing ideal family environments, consulting women as housewives and mothers on how these new homes should be designed, concluding that improved conditions would be important in promoting 'family life', and in encouraging families to grow. While the family was seen as of key importance to the British government as the basis for sustaining the population and so the life of the nation, families were also seen as ideal receptacles for receiving and carrying out government policy.

The urge to make home, regardless of barriers of limited space or limited housing, gripped the postwar British imagination.[8] It was fuelled by the dislocation and displacement that many had experienced as a result of the Second World War. Graham Greene's 1949 short story, 'The Destructors', vividly illustrated this. In Greene's story a gang of boys set out wantonly to destroy the 200-year-old home of an old man that they have taken against for no reason, so that it could never again be a 'home'.[9] The longing for a settled place of home was also strongly evoked in postwar advertising, not least in the adverts that appeared in the Festival of Britain's many guides. One, for the malted hot drink Horlicks, pictured two empty wicker chairs in the garden outside a house. An accompanying caption read,

> In another half minute, John and Elizabeth will be seated in these two chairs, relaxing at last after a strenuous day. This has been their home ever since they were married. All their dreams, their hopes, their fears, are enshrined here: here, for them, is the axis of the world.[10]

Numerous other Festival advertisements celebrated home and home-making, often showing women and children taking delight in whichever product, whether Imperial Leather soap, processed peas, Carr's biscuits, Maclean toothpaste, Cow & Gate baby food or Creda cookers. Ingersoll locks were there to help you secure your home, and Crompton light bulbs to light it. Domestic conventions that continued from the interwar period – women in the home and men at work – were being re-established.[11]

Festival exhibitions of homes and neighbourhoods were not simply about showing off 'good' design and shaming 'bad', but about inviting visitors to imagine houses as homes and housing homely. Houses were divided into sections to show how areas of the home might be re-imagined for use in light of restricted space. The impact people could have on improving spaces through solving problems encountered in the home was the focus. In preparatory discussions for the Festival, designers argued the recognition of this issue of space was peculiarly British, so suited to the national focus of the exhibitions. This was justified, first, through the claim that Britons were conscious of living on an island and, second, because Britain was claimed to be 'the only country with an over-crowding standard'.[12] With this idea that British people were particularly conscious of space, came other beliefs about the British having a monopoly on home and domesticity. In a paper setting out the logic for including homes and gardens among the contributions to British civilization on display at London's South Bank, the Festival organizers made the startlingly superior assertion that 'the English have led the world in making a "home" and there are still many countries who have no word for it.'[13] Such chauvinism had been mocked a decade earlier by writer and *Architectural Review* Editor Osbert Lancaster in the 1939 preface to his survey of interior style, *Homes Sweet Homes*. 'The poor benighted foreigner, so we are frequently and authoritatively informed, *has no word for home,*' wrote Lancaster. 'And although one may occasionally wonder why, in that case the sentimental German spends so much time singing about his *Heimat* and his *Heimsland*, it is not for us to question what has long since become an article of national faith.'[14] Lancaster's jovial remarks underlined a widespread belief that 'home' was peculiar to the British, something created from a particular elision of national characteristics and conditions.

'A FAMILY PARTY'

If home was explored in the Festival's exhibitions, so was the notion of 'family'. The Festival's Chairman Lord Ismay claimed the family focus was particularly suited to this British celebration, declaring 'British life is based upon the family' and thus suggesting it was not central to that of other nations.[15] In Festival guidebooks and in exhibitions themselves the family was presented as the most important 'unit', underpinning life in Britain and, as such, worthy of display as part of a specifically British achievement. A separate section on 'The Family' had originally been planned, linking sections on Origins of the People and Homes and Gardens at the South Bank. Its inclusion was justified as a specific national achievement, 'The strongest reason of all for this Family section is that it is a British triumph which has never really been properly told.'[16]

The wider metaphor of the nation as a family was much repeated in the Festival. It allowed organizers to gloss over problems, rifts and inequalities between different people and parts of the country. Humphrey Jennings' narrator in the Festival film *Family Portrait* would refer to inequalities created by industrialization as 'rifts in the family we are still having to repair'. Jennings also stretched the family metaphor to describe other 'families' or groupings that Britain was part of. 'We have to come within the family of Europe and the pattern overseas', said the narrator, referring to British involvement in the newly formed Council of Europe. The European Council had come about in 1949 from discussions about administering the Marshall Plan, US financial help for European postwar recovery. From 1949 Britain had also been part of the newly formed North Atlantic Treaty Organization (NATO), set up to ally key European countries with the USA against possible attack from outsiders. Metaphors of Britain as 'home' and the British as 'family' were used regardless of discord within the population – those for example, in Wales, Scotland or Northern Ireland actively seeking home rule.

Ideas of common ancestry were used in Festival discussions to suggest unity between the different races that were part of the British 'family'. Jennings' narrator in *Family Portrait* observed 'most of our family faces look back to Scandinavia, Germany, Italy …' Meanwhile archaeologist Jacquetta Hawkes, theme convenor for the South Bank People of Britain section, took visitors through sections devoted to 'The relics of our ancestors – How they Came Here – How They Lived.' Hawkes also described her display showing how 'different breeds of ancestors have contributed to the shaping of such a rare miscellany of faces as confronts the visitor in any London bus'.[17] She traced the evolution of the Britons from Celts, Romans, Anglo-Saxons and Danes, making an imaginative link between these people and their land. The ancient origins of the British as described in the 'People of Britain' section managed, however, to exclude generations of subsequent immigrants. The catalogue entry stated 'though the ancient dead are buried, it is the very blood they brought here that runs in us', suggesting no subsequent influx of immigrants worth mentioning.[18] And this, despite the well-publicised fact that *Empire Windrush* had docked at Tilbury in 1948, bringing nearly 500 Jamaican passengers to start a new life in the UK (in addition to many other recent immigrants from former colonies). This tone – and its use of the possessive 'us', 'our' and 'we' – was regularly repeated in Festival commentaries. Stepping inside the de-commissioned aircraft carrier the *HMS Campania*, visitors were immediately put in the position of imagining themselves as seafaring Britons of pre-history – 'You come upon our story just as our ancestors came upon this island – by the sea,' from 'Stone Age colonists', through Bronze Age people, 'bands of Celts', Anglo-Saxon 'pirates', to Vikings. The script blindly assumed designers and visitors were direct inheritors of the story being told.

Jennings' Festival film *Family Portrait*, made by an offshoot of the government Crown Film Unit, had pictured a Britain comfortably – even smugly – cohesive, without drawing a distinction between officials, families and individuals. Many films made privately saw things differently. *He Snoops to Conquer* (Marcel Varnel, 1944) and *Vote for Huggett* (Ken Annakin, 1948) both pointed to a deep cynicism about oppressive official controls, a lack of consensus in party politics. Comedy *Vote for Huggett* was about an aspiring local politician's attempts to curry favour locally while *He Snoops to Conquer* exposed local authorities' lack of attention to housing needs, with the family unit emerging triumphant. Similarly, films made in the 1940s and early 1950s at Ealing Studios, *Whisky Galore* (Alexander Mackendrick, 1947) and *Passport to Pimlico* (Henry Cornelius, 1949), for example, regularly showed families winning victories over starchy, colourless government apparatchiks. *The Happy Family* (Muriel Box, 1951) portrayed the salt-of-the-earth Lord family, holding out against the developers of the South Bank Exhibition who wished to demolish their family house and corner shop business. The film concluded with the Lords winning a victory against Whitehall officials, depicted as characterless bureaucrats. Mr Lord, delivering a soliloquy to family pet hare 'Winston' (only one sign of their political allegiance), declared 'Retirement, pension, peace, settling down with the family all around me. I've dreamed of Winston, and what he stands for. He will make everything all right.' The film strongly suggested the current Labour administration was anti-family, its wish to demolish a community nucleus in order to create an exhibition symbolic of this. This was underpinned by fact: parliamentary statistics showed 753 people had to be re-housed and 35 people to give up their businesses to make way for reclamation of the South Bank site.[19]

The image of British people as a family and the Festival as 'family party' was constantly repeated in Festival material, to suggest popular support for government events.[20] This mock modesty in the Festival's public language masked a fierce sense of national pride with the veneer of jovial diffidence. The British were to be 'at home to the world' during 1951, a conceit of polite, genteel domesticity which likened the Festival to a drinks party and Britain to a nation of hosts and hostesses, welcoming their neighbours by throwing everything across the country open to view.[21] In Festival rhetoric, being 'at home' was presented as a universal national ideal. Women were, however, consistently represented in the Festival as housewives and homemakers, while their husbands went out to work.

The idea of British women as hostesses and housewives was sustained by the employment of 'Festival hostesses' to work at exhibition sites to show off the 'beauty and star quality of British women'. These women were competitively selected to resemble the cast of a 'Hollywood musical', not, it was emphasized, like 'Paris Metro ticket collectors'.[22] At the South Bank's Telecinema only red-headed usherettes were employed, to co-ordinate with their Hardy Amies-designed green uniforms. Selecting women for their looks would become *de rigueur* from 1951: the first Miss World beauty pageant was held in London in July 1951 under the Festival banner. Devised by impresario Eric Morley, the 'Festival Bikini Contest', as it was originally called in honour of the new, two-piece swimsuit, was originally planned as a one-off but met with such an enthusiastic response that it would become an annual event, emulated worldwide. America – or Hollywood – offered the most vivid model for glamour in 1951. British magazine *Woman* ran a series of covers in May 1951 showing 'Festival Beauties', made up to look like Hollywood film stars.[23] Gerald Barry knew the power of Hollywood, visiting as part of his pre-Festival tour of the US, and dining with Charlie Chaplin and other stars.[24] The Festival Office tried to import a bit of this sparkle. 'Spot-Dance' competitions were held on a floodlit area in front of the Dome, with film and radio stars at the microphone. US-born actress Constance Cummings awarded winners a bouquet that had been donated by British-born Hollywood movie star Michael Wilding and sent direct from Hollywood, according to publicity. Evening dancing in a spot studded with twinkling lights in the trees and fiery fountains captured the imagination of contemporary journalists who wrote stories urging people that Hollywood glamour had come to London. Such uninhibited behaviour was surely not homespun.

HOMES IN THE FESTIVAL OF BRITAIN

Homes and housing were represented in a variety of forms at the Festival. At London's South Bank, Homes and Gardens was the largest section of the Festival dedicated solely to representing the home. Elsewhere, the Lansbury Live Architecture Exhibition contrasted well-built homes with 'jerry-built' ones. Both travelling exhibitions took up the homes theme: The People at Home section of *HMS Campania* included 'Homes and Gardens', while the Land Traveller Exhibition showcased domestic inventions and seven room-sets. House plans were also part of the Edinburgh Living Traditions Exhibition, the Belfast Farm and Factory Exhibition and the Welsh Dolhendre Rural Reconstruction Scheme.[25]

Representations of home in the Festival were meant to appeal to female visitors. Lack of female interest was, inversely, given as the reason for low visitor numbers at the exhibitions outside London, focused as they were on industry and books, subjects that could not, it was assumed, be of interest to women.[26] 'The history of the home is the history of women in the house' wrote James Laver in a 1947 essay tracing the English home from its earliest origins. This idea was not challenged in the Festival: women were assumed to be in the home in pre-Festival discussions and their likes and dislikes surmised by men, rather than through research or co-operation.[27] By 1951, 31 per cent of the national workforce was, in fact, women.[28] Conspicuously few women contributed to Festival organization: there were none on the Festival's Executive Committee, Presentation Panel, Architecture and Planning Committee, or Science and Technology Committee.

After the First World War a new generation of professional women architects was emerging in Britain but they were integrated into the mainstream system very slowly. A small number became associates of the RIBA during the 1920s; very few won any high profile commissions, most were from a professional background, often with an architect relative and usually working for female clients.[29] This was still largely the case by the time of the Festival of Britain; although by 1951 more women were coming through the architecture school system, few had been awarded notable commissions. A small number of women were members of the Modern Architectural Research Group, including Jacqueline Tyrwhitt, Jane Drew and housing consultant Elizabeth Denby; their role in debates about rebuilding Britain becoming increasingly important. At the Festival only two women architects were listed as contributing to the South Bank exhibitions and both were in partnership: Jane Drew with Maxwell Fry and Ursula Bowyer with Gordon Bowyer; while 22 year-old Angela Ryan was noted as 'the only girl working in the Architect's Department' of the Festival.[30]

The aim of the South Bank Homes and Gardens section was to show people how to create 'the very *best* home' possible.[31] Architects Bronek Katz and Reginald Vaughan designed a stone clad building, surrounded by gardens designed by Gordon Cullen, its external walls mounted with pot plants on trellises creating an intimate feeling of house and garden. Planting continued inside the building, reflecting the revived interest in plants as interior decoration.[32] The Festival Office did not intend to promote particular named or priced domestic products. No prices were given and designers were told that style as a subject should be avoided.[33] The focus was instead on creating a 'cosy, liveable atmosphere' in houses that were short of space. 'The key to homemaking is use of space', declared an introductory panel. To achieve this 'a variety of tastes' were to be represented in the rooms. This way the quality of home life was to be promoted above all, rather than show-homes with a 'building centre' or 'shop-fitting' atmosphere.[34] Room sets were the main vehicle for showing these ideas.

The COID were theme convenors for the section, advising on room contents from a list of 20,000 approved items known as 'The Stock List'.[35] Collaborative working between architects Katz and Vaughan and many room-set designers, under the direction of Director of Architecture Hugh Casson, restricted COID's ability to pursue single-mindedly their agenda for 'good' or 'quality' design.[36] Despite this, the COID wanted to showcase 'appropriate' styles through the Festival exhibitions. A letter from COID's Mark Hartland Thomas to his colleague S.D. Cooke, starting his work on Festival homes, warned him to avoid 'wishy washy contemporary design that was (quite rightly) in fashion in the late '30s'. A contemporary article in *Architectural Review* about the work of COID, which also reviewed their contribution to the South Bank exhibition, criticised their propensity 'to favour the merely fashionable' and suggested this was twinned with a 'lack of high aesthetic standards', singling out two sideboards from the exhibition to make their point: one by Gordon Russell was seen as 'subtly creative', the other by Robin Day for S. Hille & Co dismissed as 'pretentious and vulgar'.[37]

The Festival's designs, organized around solving 'problems' that might be found in the home, were underpinned by technical research into building and social science, and advice given by an expert panel of economists, a housing centre worker, a social historian from the London School of Economics (LSE) and a Board of Trade official. To qualify for the full design fee, section designers had to demonstrate they had carried out a large amount of social science research into ideal environments in which families could function, and design research into issues such as how to heat a room cost-effectively. Once they had reported back on their findings, they would be given the go-ahead to design the layout of their sections. This removed the immediate focus from what was fashionable or affordable, on to supposedly universal problems such as dripping teapots and draughty windows. This problem/solution paradigm was also central to homes at the Festival's Land Traveller and *HMS Campania* exhibitions. Solutions were all related to design of products and to management of the home, focusing displays on how people used rooms. The South Bank's Homes and Gardens started with the new-born baby in the home, and invited visitors to work their way through stages of child and adulthood, ending with the parlour, echoing the lives of its family inhabitants and their patterns of use, rather than comparing specific products. Issues of production – of producing home – were again at the fore, just as they had been in exhibitions of farming and industry.

REFURBISHING THE SOUTH BANK PARLOURS

The conflicting interests of the different groups organizing the Festival – the Festival Office, individual designers and the Council of Industrial Design – are revealed by an argument over how to design the South Bank parlours. In June 1951, a few weeks after the Festival of Britain opened at London's South Bank, the seven parlour rooms designed as part of Homes and Gardens by Eden and Bianca Minns, were closed and boarded up. The Festival Presentation Panel's recommendation to close them followed criticism of the designs from within the Festival Office – including from Gerald Barry, who felt strongly about it – and from elsewhere.[38] Senior Festival officials brought in new design teams to replace the seven original rooms with five refurbished parlours. A debate over how to replace the parlour rooms ensued at the highest level: between Gerald Barry, Hugh Casson, officials at the COID, and section designers.

From early in planning, the parlour had been included as one of several room-types in Homes and Gardens. The last section visitors would come to, the parlour was demarcated in discussions as a place for occasional use by important visitors, decorated with the household's most highly prized possessions, as opposed to the area for daily use or 'living room' displayed in 'Home Entertainment', rooms designed by Robin Day. Day had originally been offered the job of designing the parlours, but turned it down, at which point the work was awarded to husband and wife design team, Eden and Bianca Minns. AA-trained architect Eden Minns had worked since the early 1930s at Gordon Russell's workshop at Broadway in Worcestershire, alongside designers Robert Goodden, Neville Ward, Frank Austin and Cyril Rostgaard. Minns designed cabinet radios for Murphy, other furniture, and produced a television projector for the 'Britain Can Make It' future design section, which never went into production.[39] He had also been involved with advising and designing for the Utility Furniture Scheme in the early 1940s, before being called up for Navy service. His wife, Bianca Minns had a close association with society decorator John Fowler, working with him on the Department of Decorative Furniture at the Peter Jones department store in London from the late 1920s and afterwards at Fowler's Chelsea paint studio, designing wallpaper and textiles.

Festival organizers acknowledged the difficulty of designing a contemporary parlour. Parlours had a number of social functions, being 'a neutral zone' for visitors, a place of entertainment, an 'artistic outlet' and a place of privacy.[40] Ultimately the idea of the parlour was in transition in 1951. The South Bank Guide stated,

> The 'parlour' has long lost its original meaning as a place where people could sit and converse. To-day the very word has a frowsty sound. Yet, quite often, when architects have provided a family with a larger living-room instead of a parlour, one corner has been turned nostalgically into a token parlour substitute.[41]

The room's inclusion was at odds with overriding concerns of the section's designers with economy of space. The parlour did not fit with the future-vision of architects and planners, whose design manuals advocated flexible, open living space and clearly delineated functions in space-deficient homes. One planner had announced in 1949 'the parlour should go'.[42] Nor was the parlour in keeping with models being persuasively promoted by modernist architects, who had reassessed 'space needed for living purposes', dispensing with old room definitions in favour of multi-functional living and dining space.[43] The call to embrace open-plan amounted to the declaration of a manifesto, enjoining people to reject all the trappings of Victorian life. The parlour was closely identified with the lifestyle and visual excess of the Victorians. The horrifying nineteenth-century associations of the parlour were vividly described in Marghanita Laski's story *The Victorian Chaise-Longue*, published a couple of years after the Festival. This depicted a woman living with her husband in a Victorian house in postwar London, falling asleep on an old chaise and awaking to find herself in a Victorian parlour of 1864, becoming 'rigid with unimaginable terror', above all at the decorative excesses of that period.[44] British homes magazines contemporary with the Festival were at pains to show how far domestic life had progressed since the Victorians. *Homes and Gardens* for May 1951 ran a story about two sisters visiting the South Bank. Ann, living in 1951, had come up from the suburbs for the day while Amelia had travelled in a time machine from 1851. Comparing their reactions to the South Bank's Homes and Gardens, the author inevitably concluded that contemporary life was infinitely preferable. Other homes magazines used the Festival as an occasion upon which to show how much progress had been made in domestic design since 1851.

Despite contemporary admiration for open-plan internal space, Festival organizers believed in the importance of a separate, defined space for showing off decorative objects. One explained that 'Parlours in the past have been ridiculed by some, but to most it remains the place to display one's best.'[45] The inclusion of parlours signalled a continuation of ideas about creating particularity of place in homes. Even in entirely new housing the existence of ornaments and trinkets with strong sentimental associations were considered to make places distinctive. These ideas were in keeping with those espoused since the mid-1940s by *Architectural Review*. People should mix old and new design in their homes because of 'equally legitimate sentimental value', wrote editor Hastings. 'An interior to be successful should be *the result of growth, of attachments formed over years* to things old and new. *The fear of one's modern cupboard clashing with the Victorian atmosphere* of a room, or one's Victorian chandelier looking out of place in an Aalto environment is *wholly unjustified.*'[46]

Eden and Bianca Minns – the team appointed to design the Homes and Garden's parlours – disregarded the direction to underpin their designs with research into people's needs. Instead they sought to emphasize style above all. The Minns made decisions based on what looked good, rather than on what was widely available. Items in their original seven parlours were hard to find, in some cases one-offs. While Eden Minns designed and commissioned furniture for the rooms, which would be unavailable to the general public, his wife Bianca designed floral wallpapers for the exhibition, reproduced on short print-runs through John Line's Limited Editions. Bianca Minns' choice of décor was both Londoncentric and elite, with decorative items bought from small shops used to serving wealthy clients in London's Kensington and Chelsea.[47] Looking with alarm at the result, the Festival's organizers judged the Minns' parlours to be 'wide of the mark and not worthy of the rest of the excellent Homes and Gardens pavilion'. The Minns' colouring and furniture were singled out for criticism, courting such disapproval that they had to be closed while the Festival was already in full swing.[48]

At a hastily called meeting in June 1951, it was agreed the rooms should be re-dressed. The seven would be replaced with five new parlours, to be opened less than a month later, in mid-July.[49] This time all would be overseen by the Council of Industrial Design, treated as a 'normal COID furnished rooms exercise', and signed off by Gordon Russell before re-opening. The COID had seen the Minns' original rooms as a direct challenge to their work and mission. COID's Paul Reilly wrote, 'Personally, I think [the closure of the Minns' parlours] was a proper move for the schemes did damage (to our cause at least) every day they were on view.'[50] The design standard, COID officers believed, 'ran directly counter to much of the Council's propaganda'. 'The designer had been asked to step, as far as possible, out of the contemporary idiom. His solution had, however, proved a most unhappy compromise between old and new.'[51]

Three new design teams were quickly appointed and this time they were given clear specifications. Each setting was to be either urban or rural, and the class and gender of imagined inhabitants was specified. Two parlours would be for 'lower-class occupants', one 'country' and one 'town', designed by interior designer John Hill. Two parlours would be for 'middle-class

occupants', one 'country' and one 'town', designed by Neville Ward and Frank Austin (who had worked with Eden Minns at Gordon Russell's workshop), with Mary Ward, using only tax-free furniture and furnishings. The last parlour would be 'of more luxurious character', designed by Eden Minns, this time without the involvement of Bianca Minns. These changes reflected Festival organizers' anxiety to ensure exhibited items were within financial reach of the visiting public, being mass-produced and widely available, possibly following the bruising experience of 'Britain Can Make It' where the COID had been criticised for showing things which were not yet being manufactured. By displaying room sets that officials calculated would be within direct reach of the specified groupings the exhibitions suppressed aspirational tendencies, showing what they thought could be achieved, rather than a glamorous fantasy.

In the Minns' rooms, displays had shown mainly traditional feminine hobbies: sewing, piano-playing, shell decoration and everlasting flower arrangements made by the 'Rt. Hon Elizabeth, Countess of Bandon'. Devices that suggested the momentary absence from the room of a wealthy woman were also used, a 'ladies wrist watch in a display case', ebony and silver cigarette boxes, a powder compact, furs, handbags and hats. All put conspicuous leisure on display and endorsed a culture in which the female inhabitant was principally responsible for choices made in decorating the house. The Minns had favoured an affluent look associated with society designers Colefax and Fowler, Bianca Minns' employers for over a decade: floral patterning, muslin or taffeta curtains, murals, pelmets, tassels and trellis-work wallpaper.

The replacement parlour rooms represented a shift away from this decorative language. Formal flower-displays, sewing chest, piano, hats and handbags were removed. For the refurbished rooms, designers were asked to use the same suppliers as the Minns, wherever possible, but objects could be swapped with others from their stock. What was retained and what returned revealed the change of emphasis favoured by Festival officials. Two marble fireplaces were replaced with a radiator and gas fire from the same supplier. In the

7.1 HOMES AND GARDENS, ORIGINAL PARLOURS
(facing page)
designed by Eden and Bianca Minns
(Above, left) Scene I;
(Above, right) Scene III;
(Middle, left) Scene IV;
(Middle, right) Scene V;
(Bottom) Scene VI.

Minns' Scene 1 butterflies were mounted symmetrically in four oval frames and spaced above an upright Broadwood piano, against a striped floral paper. Butterflies were also used by Ward and Austin, but the four oval butterfly pictures were swapped for four rectangular mounted butterfly species from the same naturalists' shop. Brought together with a butterfly net and a wall-chart showing butterfly species, they implied the presence of a keen amateur lepidopterist, rather than someone who had used butterflies as part of a formal, decorative scheme.

The adjustments represented a change of class construction away from the formality of a middle-class parlour, towards the informality of the universal practice of home hobbies, which in a 1941 essay George Orwell had described as central to the national character: 'We are a nation of flower-lovers, but also a nation of stamp-collectors, pigeon fanciers, amateur carpenters, coupon snippers, darts players, crossword-puzzle fans.'[52] The refurbished parlour implied the presence of hard-working inhabitants, with a comfortable home, and spare time enough to pursue personal hobbies, which the final caption in the Homes and Gardens section declared 'play so large a part in TURNING THE HOUSE INTO A HOME.' This would take the parlours closer to the rooms originally imagined by James Gardner, who had specified that any hobbies featured in the homes should be 'in touch' with those 'practised by the ordinary people'.[53]

The new parlours, by comparison with the old, appeared plain. Austin and Ward's town parlour had unpatterned walls painted in darkish shades, with sober looking basalt urns and Portland vases in the wall niches, plain contemporary furniture and floors in brown, moorhen grey, peat brown and sedge green felts. John Hill's country parlour, meanwhile, had a claustrophobic feel: crowded with indoor plants, knick-knacks, a wicker magazine rack, sewing table and two sewing cabinets, pelmeted patterned curtains. Eden

7.2 HOMES AND GARDENS, REFURBISHED PARLOURS
(facing page)
(Above, left) Austin and Ward's Country Parlour for 'middle-class occupants';
(Above, right) Austin and Ward's Town Parlour for 'middle-class occupants';
(Middle, left) John Hills's Country Parlour for 'lower-class occupants';
(Middle, right) John Hills's Town Parlour; for 'lower-class occupants';
(Bottom) Eden Minns's Parlour 'for a Hampstead batchelor'.

Minns' refurbished parlour designed for a 'Hampstead male', was a bachelor pad, well-stocked with a drinks trolley for entertaining guests. Chintzy floral patterning and naturalist prints were replaced in the new rooms with plain, geometric abstract patterns or painted walls, aligning home decoration with the industrial design profession and away from the elite style of society interior decorators promoted by Bianca Minns.[54]

Ultimately, the refurbished parlours made little impact on the visiting public who were frustrated that exhibits still appeared out of financial reach and that no prices were given. A social scientist carrying out research in the section reported 'Very many people ask the cost of an article before they ask anything else.'[55] And despite all the strong feelings exchanged in correspondence between senior designers, most were unimpressed by the refurbished rooms. One COID officer wrote, 'It is easy to be wise after the event but it might have been a better idea when scrapping the first parlours to have built up the rooms of a house in a New Town and furnished them suitably.'[56] Hugh Casson wrote to COID's Paul Reilly,

Dear Paul,

I looked in on the re-vamped parlours today and am bound to say that I do not think that Mr John Hill's efforts look like being much better than their predecessors. The two bathroom lamp brackets in the first room are in my opinion disastrous, both ugly and out of character with the room. Is nobody keeping an eye on what is being done?

Yours despairingly,
Hugh Casson[57]

The two 'bathroom lamp brackets' Casson referred to – wall light fittings by Courtney Pope Ltd. – were among the only conspicuously contemporary items in the room, which otherwise paid homage to the Georgian with truncated columns, neo-Gothic clock, Staffordshire dogs and a marble bust. Paul Reilly was more enthusiastic about Austin and Ward's efforts, declaring 'I feel like moving in there every time I pass …'[58]

Festival parlours had become a battleground for conflicting ideas of how to represent the modern home. Festival organizers wanted to reflect people's situation after the war with homes that were within their reach. This was all surmised from research, however, rather than directly negotiated with consumers, as it was in new housing schemes elsewhere.[59] Despite the attempt to give people what it was assumed they needed, it seems on the whole that

Festival organizers got it wrong. Visitors regularly concluded that what was on display was still out of reach. The 'us' and 'them' division between Festival organizers and visitors was illustrated in an anecdote by social scientist Stephen Morse Brown, who interviewed visitors to Homes and Gardens. He reported one man saying,

'I don't suppose even you people have homes like these.'

'Some of us have,' Morse Brown replied. 'Intelligent mass production could turn the minority into a majority.'

But the man shook his head. 'You should make it look more within our reach,' he said. 'My house is still empty looking because I know what is good but cannot get it at the price I can afford.'[60]

Not all parts of the home were illustrated through room sets. Kitchens were shown in what appeared like a technology showroom, with unwieldy white goods mounted in rows and sinks tipped at 90° angles to show details rather than the feel of them. A wall banner announced: 'THE PROBLEM OF STORAGE IN THE KITCHEN IS LARGELY THE PROBLEM OF SAVING SPACE'. Making home in the Festival was refocused away from issues of consumption, of buying items and of choosing 'good' or 'quality' design, to making people producers of their homes, and contemporary design was put forward as compatible with comfort and homeliness.

FESTIVAL RESTAURANTS AND CAFÉS

Cafés and restaurants were among the most popular Festival interiors. They allowed architects to experiment with buildings and to showcase contemporary products without getting caught up in the complications of sticking to themes and scripts. Young architect Leonard Manasseh won one of the two South Bank design competitions and was commissioned to build the celebrated '51 Bar, an elevated glass box with sweeping roof and a striking view over the Thames and riverfront (Manasseh had originally won the commission for a luxury restaurant, which was not in the end built). Elsewhere, ACP designed the Fairway Café, F.H.K. Henrion The Dairy Bar, Trevor Dannatt The Whistle at the Power and Production pavilion and Basil Spence The Skylark. The Regatta Restaurant, designed by Misha Black with his DRU architect colleague Alexander Gibson lay at the end of the Bailey Bridge. With capacity for 500 people, the space had a panoramic view of the Thames and Westminster beyond. It was decorated with furnishings and tableware derived

7.3 *FESTIVAL FOOD AND DRINK*
(Above) The Garden Café at Homes and Gardens with mural by Marek Zulawski;
(Below, left) First floor of Regatta Restaurant by Alexander Gibson and Misha Black from DRU, with a decorative pattern developed by the Festival Pattern Group;
(Below, right) Milk Bar in the Country section selling pints of chilled milk with packaging designed by F.H.K. Henrion.

from patterns taken from crystallography as identified by the distinguished Festival Pattern Group led by Cambridge crystallographer Helen Megaw. X-ray crystallography – the study of matter at a sub-microscopic level that made visible the arrangement of atoms within molecules – was a branch of science in which Britain was leading the world in 1951. Its representation at the Festival – albeit in this extraordinarily contorted form on carpets, textiles and tableware – fitted with the focus on showing British discoveries at the Festival.[61] Chairs designed by Ernest Race for the Festival, the Antelope and Springbok constructed of steel rods stove-enamelled white, filled the cafés and restaurants of the South Bank.[62] They were also dotted through the landscapes of both the Festival at South Bank and in Belfast. Used internally and externally in exhibitions, they removed the barrier between indoor and outdoor furnishings.

Beyond remembering colour, which amounted to sudden liberation of vision, many Festival visitors fondly remember the experience of eating and drinking at the exhibitions. At a time of continued food rationing, visitors were free to eat candyfloss and Neapolitan ice creams, to picnic on sandwiches in the open air. At a time when few households had fridges, visitors could drink chilled milk at the Country pavilion's Milk Bar. The exhilaratingly liberating experience of drinking a glass of wine in an open-air café – something previously only thought possible in Continental Europe – was helped by the extension of licensing hours until 2am for the Festival months.

The international reputation of British food had sunk to an all-time low by the year of the Festival of Britain, with sugar, eggs, tea, cheese and meat rationing continuing. The situation was so dire that writer Raymond Postgate felt he must try to rally the general public into writing about their experiences of catering, to bring pressure to bear. He published these views as the first *Good Food Guide* in 1951. At the Festival, the cost of food and drink had been fixed under agreement in contracts with Festival Office. Many caterers did not stick to the agreement, causing one MP to point out in Parliament that afternoon tea at the South Bank cost five shillings, one shilling more than the Ritz Hotel charged.[63] Several visitors later recalled the terrible quality of Festival food. Architect Albert Richardson was taken by some chartered surveyors to lunch in the restaurant at Royal Festival Hall in July 1951. He recorded in his diary:

Being priveleged persons we were allowed a table next to the glass front. A poor lunch for 7/6 Cocktail (Tomato Juice) The soup was bill poster paste (a bilge) The Vol au Vent fairly good, The ice cream fair. Coffee not at all good. The best thing was the roll.[64]

Despite Richardson's – and many others' – displeasure at the food they were served at the South Bank, there had been an earnest attempt to provide varied types of food and drink, catering for every perceived type of visitor, to serve it in congenial surroundings and to introduce new tastes. Gerald Barry insisted, for example, that all possible British cheeses be available.[65] At the Belfast Farm and Factory Exhibition, the experience of eating and drinking new things in the open-air restaurant was central to visitors' experience of the Festival as the start of a new world.

PLANNING FOR NEIGHBOURHOODS

Displays of Festival homes showed people ways to improve their living space. Gerald Barry wanted displays of housing and planning to do something similar, to give people an opinion on how to improve the areas outside their homes. *Architectural Review* had argued a direct comparison should be made between planning of rooms in the home and planning of the urban environment several years before the Festival. Hubert de Cronin Hastings' 1944 article 'Exterior Furnishing', illustrated with a sketch by Kenneth Rowntree, showed how interior decorations should be echoed in the 'decoration' of the street outside, making parallels between wallpaper and furniture in the home and wall textures and street 'furniture' outside. Hastings envisaged the wider environment providing a homely, sympathetic atmosphere, a form of Picturesque. The vision set out in *Architectural Review* for principles of home organization shaping organization outside influenced the approach taken at the Festival.

The Exhibition of Live Architecture was built at Poplar, a blitzed area of east London. It centred on the development of the Lansbury Estate, named after local Labour MP and social campaigner George Lansbury. The Exhibition became part of the Festival of Britain after the organizers decided a display of town planning, originally intended for the South Bank, should be moved to east London due to restricted space at the South Bank. Co-ordinated by the LCC as part of the Stepney-Poplar Redevelopment Area set out in Abercrombie's *Greater London Plan 1944*, only 30 of the 2,000 acres had been developed by the time the Festival opened. Around 500 people were displaced to make room for the permanent redevelopment of the neighbourhood, in the hope that three times as many could be provided with new housing by the time the exhibition opened.[66] The exhibition's focus was on 'live' or 'living' communities, and visitors were invited to witness 'live architecture' through work in progress, seeing houses being completed during the period of the exhibition.

Other blitzed sites across the country were redeveloped under the Festival banner. At Liverpool the Festival's opening ceremony involved a midnight fireworks display from barges on the Mersey, while diggers went ceremonially on to bombed-out city centre sites for the first time. At Canterbury, Belfast and in many other towns across the country the Festival was celebrated through the symbolic demonstration of live reconstruction. These live exhibitions were seen as an opportunity for people to see themselves as participants in the ongoing process of rebuilding Britain.

Festival exhibitions in the New Towns also allowed the public to witness the spectacle of reconstruction in progress. The programme included tours to 14 New Town sites in the process of being built. The New Towns Act of 1946 had enabled development corporations to be appointed by the Minister of Local Government and Planning, with the task of planning and building towns using capital in the form of repayable government loans. The New Towns were planned as self-contained places where those otherwise living in crowded conditions in London, or travelling long distances from outer suburbs to work, could find homes and employment. Transfer of suitable industries was an integral part of the New Towns plan. Eight such towns were built in a ring outside London's Green Belt from the late 1940s onward.[67] By 1951, they were also being built elsewhere, all aimed at offering solutions to problems created by the needs of industry.[68] A guide to all New Towns on show for the Festival stressed the 14 underway were built around existing, relatively small communities. It highlighted the historic features that remained within new developments. The Crawley brochure photographed 'ancient buildings', next to new housing, set in ample green space and flanked by old trees. At Stevenage, visitors were taken on a coach tour of work in progress with a technical guide and an exhibition of the engineering features of the construction of the town, which also highlighted topographical, soil and meteorological conditions of the town. All emphasized continuity between the historic past and new developments.

This was in keeping with the way new housing developments were presented through contemporary architectural journals. An element of *Architectural Review*'s campaign for a revived Picturesque had focused on the way old buildings, ruined by wartime bombs might be integrated into reconstruction schemes. A 1944 article had proposed keeping ruins of bombed churches in London as open space, with appropriate planning.[69] This mid-twentieth century interest in ruins was different from the detached enjoyment of ruined follies the original proponents of Picturesque had revelled in. The appreciation of ruins after the Second World War sprang from an imagination deeply transformed by the experience of war. Preserved ruins were now imagined as public monuments: functions or carriers of public memory, to remind citizens of wartime suffering and warning against its reoccurrence. Ruins were not imagined simply as eye-pleasers. This was revealed in Hugh Casson's seminal 1945 book *Bombed Churches as War Memorials*, based on the 1944 article. In it he appealed for the preservation of the ruins of some churches whose rebuilding in the centres of congested cities could not be justified, but whose disappearance would sever people's link with their past.

One model uniting Festival displays of housing and new homes was that of the village. 'The village', Gerald Barry stated, 'is the guardian still of the deepest truths of the British way of life'. This admiration was strongly shared by Hugh Casson, as well as by many contemporary planners and architects who saw the village as popular model for conceptualising the future development of large urban areas.[70] This was bolstered by a prevailing belief that the Industrial Revolution had devalued and undermined the structure of the village, something that must be set right through new housing developments. Postwar housing minister Aneurin Bevan had admiringly likened housing estates to 'modern villages', where all classes would live in harmony.[71]

Lansbury, the Poplar development that formed part of the Festival, was planned as one of eleven 'neighbourhood units', an idea advanced by planner Patrick Abercrombie as a model for structuring tight communities within larger planning masses.[72] 'Neighborhood Units' had been introduced into North American planning debates in 1929 by planner Clarence Arthur Perry and adopted in interwar Britain. In the British context, 'neighbourhood units' became imagined as linked villages. Planners such as Sharp in his *Anatomy of the Village* had sought to encapsulate the spirit and atmosphere of the village in order that it could be transferred to new, urban developments.[73]

If British planners were interested in finding usable community models, the interests of other international modernists were also shifting beyond the earlier simplistic functionalist agenda to models for creating community focus and cohesion. From 1947 MARS was led by J.M. Richards, editor of *Architectural Review*. Richards was at the forefront of the magazine's campaign for a twentieth-century Picturesque. In his leadership of MARS, Richards shifted the group's direction from its prewar functionalist concerns toward his own philosophical interests in the aesthetic appeal of modern architecture to what he described as the 'Common Man'.[74] Richards' increasingly populist approach was typified by his much-maligned 1946 *Castles on the Ground*, which was about the allure of the suburban home. Richards' book was a thinly veiled attack on superior people – such as those from COID – who sought to educate people out of 'bad' taste. Painter John Piper's South Bank mural 'The Englishman's Home', with its mish–mash of homes of varying sizes, styles and periods, was driven by a similar attachment to home, without the snobbish discrimination against certain building types (Victorian buildings, for example) and against suburbia that was being voiced by some contemporaries. For many years Piper had been closely associated with Richards and *Architectural Review*. Piper's mural depicted houses close to his heart, including a red brick Victorian villa that featured on the original dust jacket of Richards' *Castles on the Ground* with a much-loved monkey puzzle tree standing beside it. The mural depicted many other buildings that Piper admired including a Regency square in Brighton, a station cottage, an Oxford church, and the dome of Castle Howard.[75]

The British contingent of CIAM, dominant at this period through their organization of 1947 and 1951 meetings in England, were not isolated in showing increasing interest in what the populace needed. The character of the Europe-wide group had altered considerably after the Second World War. War had limited opportunities for travel to meetings, meaning groupings had splintered along national lines, and refocusing CIAM's members on a dominant social agenda. From its first postwar meeting in 1947, discussions of CIAM moved away from their original 'functional city' model until, by 1951, the year of the Festival of Britain, the group's concerns were with creating the 'core' or 'heart of the city'. Presentations at CIAM 8 in 1951 from prominent British, Swiss, Spanish and Scandinavian members addressed subjects such as 'Satisfying Human Needs at the Core', showing a shared concern with community cohesion .[76] But there was no consensus over how to expedite this. This is particularly clear when Le Corbusier's solution to collective living is compared with that of his British contemporaries'. The form of his 1946–52 'Unité d'Habitation de grandeur conforme' or 'neighbourhood unit of the proper size' was in stark contrast to the neighbourhood units designed by those of his British contemporaries. In Le Corbusier's scheme, the rough concrete slab-block with its 337 duplex units sat alone in its 35,000 metre square site, intended to maintain family privacy whilst also containing collective services, such as day-care centres. In Britain the trend was for low- and medium-rise buildings dotted over the contours of the site. Both shared a common concern with building 'successful' communities and providing collective services, but the way green space was integrated into the schemes was significantly different. Across the members of CIAM, many other models for integrating buildings and landscape were also explored.

Several of those key to representing Britain in 1951 CIAM discussions were also engaged with designing Lansbury. Town planner Jacqueline Tyrwhitt (1905–83), an active contributor to CIAM and the MARS Group (organizing and co-editing proceedings of CIAM 8) was scriptwriter of the Lansbury Exhibition. It is no coincidence that the Lansbury 'Live Architecture' Exhibition included 'The Heart of the Town' as one of its six sections, which focused on rebuilding new town centres that had qualities of being 'the heart of the new community', issues that no doubt Tyrwhitt had been discussing with CIAM and Festival colleagues.[77] Tyrwhitt was more interested in defining community models than on structural issues. In a 1951 lecture on 'The Neighbourhood Unit idea', she revised Perry's definition of the 'Neighborhood Unit' as follows:

1. Make the elementary school the focus of the neighbourhood. 2. Eliminate through traffic from the neighbourhood and reform local streets to serve the residents. 3. Localize and segregate the shopping at the corners of the neighbourhood. 4. Provide minimum standards for open space and neighbourhood parks.[78]

In line with Tyrwhitt's vision, schools were integrated at the heart of the Lansbury community: Ricardo Street Nursery and Primary School designed by Yorke, Rosenberg and Mardall (YRM) was particularly visually striking (mirroring their innovative work for the Hertfordshire Schools Programme, in particular the Barclay School at Stevenage, 1947–51). Social housing in the Lansbury 'neighbourhood unit' mimicked the atmosphere of an intimate village by setting housing in leafy areas, many with their own gardens or else immediate to green space, predominately low-rise and small-scale.

The anxiety to demonstrate that architectural modernity was compatible with historical continuity was also a feature of the Festival's exhibitions of public housing. The Lansbury Estate was built on a site that had been almost completely devastated during the Blitz due to its proximity to London's docks. But a belief in the existence of a continuing character or *genius loci* embedded in place, regardless of its current appearance, influenced the LCC's instruction

7.4 FESTIVAL EXHIBITION OF LIVE ARCHITECTURE, LANSBURY (facing page)
(Above) Mrs Snoddy with daughter Jean and mother-in-law Mrs Ball in the kitchen of their new flat in Gladstone House, Lansbury, the first block completed on the site; (Below) The Snoddys in the living room of their new flat.

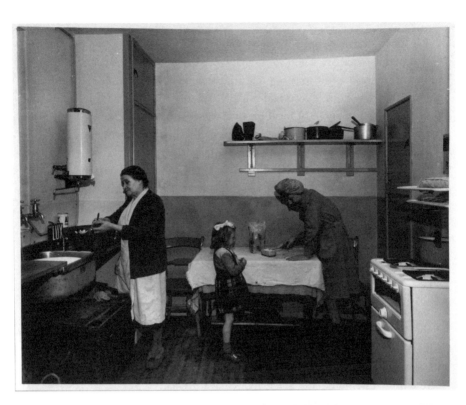

to Lansbury's various contributing architects to focus on using the purple grey slate, London stock brick and stone that were native to that part of east London and to preserve the few existing mature trees, wherever possible. In addition, the way that new housing was laid out at Lansbury reflected this preoccupation with maintaining a sense of local particularity. At Bridgwater and Shepheard's Pekin Close, for example, houses were set in two-storey terraces made from brick with tiled, pitched roofs, each with gardens, set in a pedestrianized cul-de-sac, cut off from traffic by bollards. Architectural writer Ian Nairn would later be particularly enthusiastic about Pekin Close, 'this is what building for people, real people, means'.[79] The very first tenants at Lansbury, Mr and Mrs Albert Snoddy, their two children and pet tortoise, moved from No. 6 Yattan Street, Poplar, into a three-bedroom flat in Gladstone House on 14 February 1951.[80] They were welcomed into their new home by the Mayor of Poplar and the Chairman of the LCC's Housing Committee.[81] Lansbury Estate residents, in a radio programme about LCC housing, praised its 'pleasant and friendly architecture' and its 'village feel'.[82] These houses sat in the shadow of the Roman Catholic Church of St Mary & St Joseph (designed by Adrian Gilbert Scott, built 1950–9), a building of monumental size. Access between clusters of houses was through a succession of green, landscaped spaces that were closely integrated and acted like village greens.

Just as at the South Bank, Casson had described architects working with a written brief in one hand and a plan in the other, Lansbury was designed from a developed script sketching out the character of each area. This was remarked on in an article about Lansbury written by planner William Holford who regarded attempts to create a model neighbourhood as something that could only be fulfilled through following a written brief. 'Town planners have a good deal in common with novelists', he wrote. 'Their designs are drawn in front of a vast background, and both deal ultimately with the lives of the individual and of society,' he likened Abercrombie and Forshaw, authors of the *London Plan*, to novelists.[83]

Much of the focus of Lansbury was on the external environment around housing, but some interiors were also shown. 'The Lansbury Show House', designed by the COID, was a flat with imaginary tenants: a dockworker father, a housewife mother and four children. This interior, like others in the Festival, did not question family formulations or gender roles within the home, putting women firmly in the home while their husbands went out to work. Nor did interiors focus on issues of taste or 'good' design instead emphasizing the prime importance of family, the practical use of space, and lightening the load of women by introducing labour- and time-saving devices. One Lansbury 'Live Exhibition' visitor, himself an East Ender, later recalled 'Mum, Dad and children "oohing" and "aahing" at the new kitchen with modern cookers and appliances. Compared with the scullery back home and the kitchen coal range this really was like the Hollywood films. A bathroom to yourself? No queuing on Saturday morning at the public baths, for these lucky tenants. Oh, and just look at that, a toilet inside!'[84]

Mod cons were not only shown at Lansbury. A spacious kitchen was part of *HMS Campania's* homes section. The guide excitedly declared 'this typifies the efforts which are now being made to bring the housewife back into the social life of the family, while still letting her work in the kitchen'.[85] A show house at East Kilbride New Town was exhibited for the Festival, designed by the Scottish Committee of COID and using tax-free utility furniture. Alastair Borthwick, organizer of the Glasgow Festival show explained that 'The wilder examples of modern design had been avoided. It was not the kind of thing most people buy, but it looked a wonderful house to live in ... More than 1,000 "assorted housewives" trooped through in one day, and nearly all of them liked it'.[86]

The Lansbury Estate, at least in spirit, was a fulfilment of the 'Twentieth Century Picturesque' promoted by *Architectural Review*. In appearance, however, it fell short of the mark, being criticised by J.M. Richards – who had been on the planning committee – as 'completely orthodox in construction' and having a 'dull, less characterful external appearance that followed in a nineteenth century building tradition, so lacking the required innovation'.[87] Gibberd himself, writing later, suggested he had not been happy with Lansbury, being 'too modest and lacking in exciting "architectural statements"'. This may, he thought, have been because its architects had been particularly keen to prioritise community needs above all. He concluded 'it was immensely important, and I suppose everyone who was in any way involved in the rebuilding of Britain was influenced by it'.[88]

Creating environments for fully functioning communities in newly rebuilt areas was the major focus of Festival housing. The idea of 'mixed development' was also a focus for experimentation at the Festival. This idea – of which Festival architect Frederick Gibberd was a strong exponent – owed a lot to Swedish experimental planning models. It saw new estates populated with a cross section of age groups and a variety of groupings including families, couples and single people. Gibberd believed mixed buildings allowed for a social cross-section and produced an appropriate visual impact. 'Buildings with quite different formal qualities such as blocks of flats, maisonettes and bungalows are needed to provide "contrast" and "variety" in the "composition" of an area', wrote Gibberd.[89] The impact of this preference can be seen in his schemes at Somerford Estate in

Hackney (1947), Harlow New Town (1951), and the Lansbury Estate. At Lansbury the mixed development comprised of two-storey terrace houses with gardens; three-storey houses; houses with a flat over or maisonettes with a flat below; four-storey maisonettes; and three- and six-storey flats. LCC planner Percy Johnson-Marshall recalled later how difficult it had been working under restrictions imposed by the LCC Housing Committee at Lansbury, where no flats were allowed to be over six-storeys.[90]

The predilection for low-rise buildings at Lansbury also characterised other public housing schemes singled out as having special merit in the Festival of Britain's 1951 Architecture Awards. The Awards set out to stimulate the 'creation of beauty', which its organizers saw as 'an appropriate form for celebrating the Festival throughout Great Britain'.[91] Award-winning schemes included Jury's Old People's Housing in Glasgow (designed by Glasgow City Council, 1949–50) where single-storey dwellings were set amongst mature trees with steeply-pitched, tiled roofs. Low-rise buildings set in green space were also the favoured form for housing at Stevenage (the earliest tranche of housing contemporary with the Festival being two-storey houses, the next being model flats three-, four- and seven-storeys high, designed by Yorke Rosenberg and Mardall). Partners Tayler and Green also won Festival awards for five groups of terraced houses in Norfolk, all of colour-washed brick with low roofs.[92]

Low-rise was also the preferred form at Harlow New Town. In its earliest stages, Gibberd's only high-rise building was The Lawn (1951), a nine-storey point block. Standing, as it did, in isolation, The Lawn was more akin to a viewing-tower allowing a view down onto the Harlow Estate for those inside it, and a visual feature – like the 'eye stoppers' used as landscaping devices – for those below. This newly completed building formed the centrepiece of Harlow New Town's Festival Exhibition. Visitors were invited to climb to the ninth floor to view models, maps and drawings, stepping out onto the penthouse balcony to compare models with work-in-progress on site. In the same spirit, Gibberd inserted a clock and viewing tower into his Festival designs for Lansbury's Chrisp Street Market Place, explaining that a clock tower, rising above the otherwise low rise buildings of the market square, 'closes the long vista down the road leading to the square, and provides a contrast to the comparatively low shop buildings', blocking the view to the desolate and unsightly stretch beyond.[93] From the top of the five-storey tower there was a good view of the local area and beyond: westward towards the City and Tower Bridge and southward to the Docks and the Thames. This was a 'practical folly' made to give pleasure, as Gibberd explained.[94] It was perfectly in keeping with the new Picturesque that the Festival's architects were taking an active role in reviving. Indeed, Nikolaus Pevsner would later single out Gibberd's Harlow Town Centre as the epitome of 'Picturesque Principles applied to urban conditions', the very fulfilment of *Architectural Review*'s agenda towards reviving Picturesque for the twentieth century.[95]

In the Festival, homes and the areas surrounding them became grounds for experimentation with appropriate visual expressions of British identity and the nation became likened to a 'family' in Festival rhetoric. Home in the Festival became an important locus for what it meant to be modern and British, while at the same time holding tight to things from the past.

8

'WISH ME LUCK AS
YOU WAVE ME GOODBYE'

It may have taught the men who are building our cities something. It may have given impetus to new building here in Britain. But for ordinary people it was fun.

Hugh Casson, *Brief City*

The closure of the Festival, on the last day of September 1951, was marked by a service at Royal Festival Hall. The Archbishop of Canterbury gave the closing address. 'Every joy must be worked for. All work should be productive of joy, and both joy and work are essentially cooperative in character,' he preached, underlining the close link between pleasure and productivity that was the Festival gospel. Afterwards Archbishop Fisher broadcast to the nation, standing in for the King who was unable to make an appearance, being by then critically ill with a lung condition. It was a demure occasion and Fisher's broadcast set the tone. He noted the King's absence and wished him well, saying modestly that the Festival, this 'brightening up the family home', 'has been achieved at little cost', extending the metaphor of Britons as family and Britain as home to people listening across the nation.[1] This somber tone also inflected Gerald Barry's end of Festival broadcast where he mused that although the Festival's purpose was serious, 'it has not been done solemnly, but with gaiety'.[2]

Afterwards many flocked to a closing ceremony on the brilliantly floodlit Fairway of the South Bank. Geraldo's orchestra played the dance tunes that had become a major draw but the crowds were so tightly packed that only 'rhythmic movement' was possible.[3] Gracie Fields sang a rendition of her wartime favourite *Wish Me Luck As You Wave Me Goodbye*. The BBC Choral Society led the crowds in singing popular songs: *It's a long way to Tipperary*, *Danny Boy*, and *Loch Lomond*, winding up with *Abide with me* and the *National Anthem*. While lights were dimmed, the Brigade of Guards beat the Retreat and Tattoo, the Union Jack and Festival flag were lowered, and through the loud speakers came the words: 'This is the Festival announcer, wishing you goodnight for the last time'.

On Monday 1 October, only a few hours after closing, the work of packing up and dismantling began. Bunting was the first thing taken down: the party was over. Meanwhile, army teams erected barbed wire fences and sealed up pavilions to secure the site. The Country pavilion was cleared to become an auction room and the Land of Britain to become a general object store.[4] The first large exhibit to leave the South Bank was John Cobb's Railton Special car from outside the Dome of Discovery. Trees were uprooted from outside Transport to make it possible to move large exhibits, including a railway engine, shipped to India for use on the Indian Government Railway.

The Times featured several valedictory pieces marking the South Bank's closure. Noting ponds had immediately been emptied and fountains had 'ceased to play', a journalist remarked that small boats were being removed from a lake in the Sport section 'where a number of ducks were swimming, serenely unconscious that two Government departments were discussing their fate.' Officials of the Ministry of Works had been lobbying for the South Bank ducks to be moved to London parks. Officials of the Ministry of Agriculture declared there was a high risk that the ducks could be carrying diseases and that they should first receive a certificate. 'The battery fowls in the Agriculture Pavilion had no such powerful champions', the journalist noted. 'They were slaughtered by their owners on Monday and sold at 10s. each to workmen on the site.'[5]

This work carried out by a demolition contractor was sanctioned and directed by the Demolition Working Party, instructed to remove all 'industrial and non-industrial exhibits by 31 December 1951'. So intensive was their programme of work, focused on 'disposing of all exhibits as quickly as possible', that they met daily for many weeks.[6] Minutes record the Group as pleasantly surprised that exhibitors were co-operating with their rapid programme. Pavilions were cleared first of valuable and large exhibits, allowing for the removal of smaller portable items and for electricity, gas and water to be cut off as soon as possible. A doorway was cut in the wall of the Dome of Discovery in October 1951, to allow large items to be released. Internal platforms were then cleared and removed, one-by-one, and materials sold on to contractors for re-use elsewhere. Neglected and forgotten in cold buildings, indoor plants started to wilt and the demolition gang had to bring in electric radiators to save them.

In October the Conservatives returned to power with a narrow majority. Winston Churchill was Prime Minister once more and David Eccles was appointed as Minister of Works. The demolition and clearance of the South Bank site became more urgent, as correspondence shows. Barry was forced to argue with Eccles to be kept on just beyond the end of the year to tie up loose ends. In their last exchange, Eccles gave Barry the following mealy-mouthed compliment: 'Of course I did not see at first hand all you did, but I am sure that the Festival will remain a landmark in the history of exhibitions, and your name will always be associated with it.'[7]

If the desire to rid the South Bank of the Festival of Britain was driven by its association with the ideals of Clement Attlee's government, the incoming Conservative government also considered it a symbol of Labour's financial mismanagement, their 'squandermania'. Churchill wrote to Herbert Morrison in November 1951 telling him that they would be keeping Battersea Pleasure Gardens open for a bit longer, as Morrison had suggested. Headed '**SECRET**', Churchill wrote 'Out of our love for you we are going to do what you wish — also to try to get a little of the money back that was wasted. Yours sincerely, WSC.'[8] In order further to recoup money spent on the Festival, several auctions were held to sell off exhibits and equipment; the first was in December, a Colonel playing auctioneer. Outdoor chairs and plaster doves from the Lion and Unicorn were sold in a special sale. Plastic-covered Springbok chairs commanded the highest price at 50/- each, wooden seated Antelopes and metal perforated chairs went for 40/-, fragile plaster doves sold off at 20/- apiece.

When the Festival closed there was still the possibility that other South Bank buildings would be retained, in addition to the permanent Royal Festival Hall. A plan was mooted for the Festival Office to retain the South Bank's downstream area. Early in October, as the Festival was dismantled, Gerald Barry wrote, 'What about the future of the South Bank? There could be no more ironic monument to the future than that the site should again become derelict and an eyesore,' still optimistic at this stage that some buildings could be kept. The Thameside Restaurant with its magnificent views was, he declared, one of his favourites.[9] But once the Conservative government came to power, in late October, the retention of any section of the South Bank was declared impractical by the Ministry of Works and LCC. Wells Coates' Telecinema building was retained as there was a solid plan: it was to be rented by the British Film Institute as a film theatre. The Dome and Skylon were both dismantled in April 1952. Aluminium was carefully removed panel by panel from the Dome's roof to be sold on, while the Skylon was sold off for scrap. Press News Agency photographs from late April showed staff foreman Mr Killerman being hoisted up in a bucket to inspect the Skylon before starting work. The Dome and Skylon had existed only very fleetingly but they would become memorialised as the great Festival symbols, emblematic of this summer-long national celebration, which had set out to give people a glimpse of the future, while being proud of the present and rooted in the past. By May 1952, with many of the Festival's buildings demolished, photographs began to appear in the press of a new South Bank Riverside Walk under construction in front of Royal Festival Hall.

The Festival – this gaiety with a serious purpose – stood on the brink of Britain's Cold War. After closure, two Festival sites were turned over to fighting this war. In Northern Ireland the Castlereagh exhibition site was turned over to become a munitions factory. Run by Short Brothers and Harland it produced armaments to equip troops in Korea. Even more symbolically potent was the immediate reuse of *HMS Campania*, home to the Festival's Sea Travelling Exhibition, for nuclear testing. Early in 1952 the *Campania* was fitted out, exhibition displays replaced by workshops, laboratories, offices and cabins, ready to carry scientists and members of the navy to Montebello in Australia for the first British nuclear test codenamed Operation Hurricane.

A 1952 edition of *Picture Post* showed 'Festival in the Junk Yard', with photos of Festival detritus found at a builder's yard at Gospel Oak. 'Amid the junk of a builder's yard at Gospel Oak, London, the last, sad remnants of the South Bank Exhibition await a buyer,' the article ran. 'The dummy hotels, the miniature lamp post, the roundabouts and switch-backs which once graced the sea-side section, have proved popular among rock gardeners and other souvenir hunters, at two to three guineas an item'.[10] Festival designer Clifford Hatts stumbled upon a Lewisham scrapyard selling off Festival exhibits.[11] An exhibition display-box on leprosy – its glass windows smashed and photographs of leprosy sufferers half-visible – lay upended in a muddy heap. Chipped plaster casts of the English Eccentrics salvaged from the Lion and Unicorn pavilion, were being sold off for 10 bob each.[12] A large, rusting metal version of Abram Games' Festival emblem was tied to a railing outside, waiting to be sold off. In another part of the yard, an exhibition display box lay broken up and shattered. After looking more closely, Hatts realised that it had been part of a display about the nuclear pile he himself had worked on for the Dome of Discovery; internal lighting in the boxes had been removed, to be sold-off separately. Some of its written descriptions were still legible:

What the pile produces

A large quantity of heat. A new fissile element, plutonium. Radioisotopes. Neutrons for experimental work. Highly radioactive fission products.

Only a year after the Festival, displays about leprosy and the pile – forgotten along with the 'story' they had told – seemed little short of impenetrable gobbledygook. But they had already done their job of showing people a new Britain.

'AFTER THE BALL IS OVER'

More than one in three Britons had attended the Festival, over eight million to the South Bank alone. Many fewer visitors than hoped for had come from America, due partly to the impact of the Korean War on national prosperity and fears about travelling in Europe, but tourist traffic to Britain in 1951 had been higher than estimated.[13]

As soon as the Festival's doors closed for the last time, Gerald Barry tried to weigh up all this frenetic nationwide activity. The Festival had given people a chance to use their eyes again to see new shapes and unfamiliar colours, he thought, and there had been two styles at the Festival: at South Bank there was 'contemporary' and at Battersea 'fantastical and 'pastiche'.[14] 'Contemporary', a term denoting clean, modern design, was associated with the modern movement of the 1920s and 1930s in Britain and the USA. The Festival of Britain had brought contemporary design squarely into the public consciousness and with it this term would come into common currency in Britain.[15] Another term – 'Festival style' – would also soon be assimilated into popular vocabulary. Often used pejoratively, 'Festival style' suggested something whimsical, derived from atomic patterning, perhaps highly patterned and in strong colours. By all accounts, the Festival had given people who were starved of colour, even beauty, a feast for the senses. Journalist Marghanita Laski wrote 'one remembers with such pleasure, the beauty – the yellow flock wallpaper in

---

8.1 FESTIVAL IN THE JUNKYARD (facing page)

Remnants of Festival displays found in a Lewisham junkyard in 1952

(Above) The Festival emblem;

(Below) Displays about leprosy from the Dome of Discovery.

the Lion and Unicorn, the shining loaves of bread, the fruits of agriculture, the pearls-against-velvet mystery of the planetarium.'[16] This was not, she pointed out, beauty normally associated with opulence and pomposity. Instead, it was elegance for the people, a universal beauty; the glimpse of a world where designers worked on things that were within everyone's reach, rather than just for the old elites.

Barry made great claims for the Festival's impact on exhibition design. The 'old departmental method of display' had been swept away, he said, establishing the narrative exhibition as 'the technique of the future'.[17] Soon after the Festival, Misha Black also declared the Festival a landmark in exhibition design. It had given designers the opportunity to 'prove their capabilities in the full orchestration of a major national display'.[18] But Black also recognized the flaws in the Festival as exhibition. These information exhibitions, which tried to show the whole of British history and achievement, had been over ambitious, he admitted. 'Everything that could be said would be said: there would be brown owls and flatfish, a locomotive and aircraft, Anglo Saxons and Romans, chemistry, physics and nuclear science ... Polar dogs, public health and the White Knight'. In the process, they were far too reliant on text, which was alienating and impossible to take in. 'Tens of descriptive words were carefully, and sometimes brilliantly, written and edited', he wrote. 'The theme convenors, who were responsible for the content of the exhibition, were determined that everything should be shown and explained.'[19] Much of its proposed impact would, Black thought, likely have been lost on visitors. 'Only a fraction of this verbosity was read', he reflected. Richard Levin, evaluating his own designs for the Festival's Land Travelling exhibition, later said '... we were trying to tell too involved or technical a story. The mixture of instruction and amusement was not always easy to maintain.'[20]

This earnest attempt to communicate ideas of national importance was the most notable difference between the Festival's exhibitions and other innovative collaborative shows such as those being mounted at the newly founded Institute of Contemporary Arts (ICA).[21] The exhibition 'Growth and Form', put on by Richard Hamilton in 1951, shared common visual territory with the Festival, creating a complete environment through which to illustrate the growth of natural forms, with images drawn from all sorts of natural phenomena from sea urchins to crystal growth. But Hamilton as artist was driven by an idea of integrating art forms – art, architecture and sculpture – as an end in itself and not as an instrumental means to an end, as at the Festival.

The Festival was the last great British propaganda exhibition. It was held at a moment when exhibition remained a medium of extraordinary potency for communicating ideas through image and word. By the end of the 1950s the majority of British people would have access to a television and this, alongside radio, would become the ubiquitous medium for mass communication in Britain. Exhibition as a means for communicating public information was soon to become outmoded. This was borne out by the commissions undertaken by Misha Black and Milner Gray's consultancy DRU, for example. In the three years after the Festival, DRU took on a few further international exhibition commissions, designing UK pavilions for the Colombo Exhibition in Ceylon and the Rhodes Centenary Exhibition in Bulawayo, Southern Rhodesia, as well as an exhibition for UNESCO and the World Health Organization. But essentially, by the mid-1950s, this kind of exhibition design was no longer in demand and their focus had moved towards other sorts of work. In 1955 Richard Levin, designer of the Festival's Land Traveller Exhibition, now Head of Design at the BBC, appointed many DRU members to work with him. The BBC's early look owed a lot to the Festival of Britain and its endorsement of the role of designers in shaping public culture. As TV – this medium of condensed clarity with sound and vision combined – became more universal, information exhibition design was increasingly seen as a redundant form of visual communication. More importantly for a designer like Misha Black, who was also a savvy businessman, exhibitions were no longer where the money was.

The Festival of Britain had done something more profound than influencing styles or modes of communication; it had legitimised the very role of the designer. Discussion of the design of things had, before the Festival, been only for an elite. After the Festival it was more universal. The Festival's organization, whereby architects, exhibition and graphic designers and landscape architects had collaborated had broken down some of the barriers – largely of class – within the design profession and launched a new generation of British designers. The young designers who had been prominent in designing the exhibitions themselves: Hugh Casson and Powell and Moya and many dozens of others, would flourish post-Festival in partnerships and practices. Many fledging designers who visited the South Bank as students also saw the Festival as their springboard. Product designers Terence Conran, who worked as an assistant on the Festival and David Mellor and fashion designer Mary Quant attributed their interest in pursuing a career in design to early experiences at the Festival.

What of the Festival's impact on architecture? Writing in *Architectural Review* in 1953, critic Reyner Banham reflected on international reactions to the Festival.[22] Comment had appeared in over twenty foreign architecture magazines on the South Bank Exhibition. They divided into three types: first, 'criticism of fittings and furniture'; second, 'of individual buildings'; and third, 'of the whole scheme, urbanistically'. *Spazio* of August 1950 had called into question the originality of structures like the Skylon and proposed Italian precursors such as the exhibition stands of Zavanella. *Décor d'Aujourd'hui* and *Art et Décoration* praised the exhibition, detecting a strong Italian influence but differed as to whether the other major influence was Scandinavian or Victorian. Norwegian, Danish, German, Swiss and Swedish journals had all reported on the Festival. Phrases common to most included 'neue Stadtlandschaft' (new urban landscape), 'Phantasie' (imagination), 'räumliche Gestaltung' (spatial design) and 'Selbstironie' (self-irony). Nearly all foreign critics were, Banham reported, 'captivated' by the Sea and Ships, 'which received on all hands praise exceeded only by that lavished on the Lion and Unicorn'. Madrid-based *Revista Nacional de Arquitectura* had carried a piece contrasting 'North and South' as being characterized by 'the Architecture of Humanism' and 'the Architecture of Technology' respectively. While Rome-based *Rassegna Critica di Architettura* had called Festival architecture 'Northern and anticlassical, but emphatically part of the English tradition'.

Festival Director of Architecture Hugh Casson skirted round the issue of the Festival's architectural legacy in his post-Festival film *Brief City*, saying 'It may have taught the men who are building our cities something. It may have given impetus to new building here in Britain. But for ordinary people it was fun.'[23] Casson and his Festival colleagues would, in subsequent assessments, conclude the Festival achieved what it had set out to do: to give people a good time, while at the same time showing them building which was modern, without being unpalatably so. The Festival had shown the British public modernism need not be an alien concept. It put forward a visual compromise, a tempered modernism – this new Picturesque – new building, in new materials that was at the same time imbued with a sense of the past. The visual forms associated with the new Picturesque continued to be applied after the Festival. 'Mixed development', this form of visual planning strongly associated with the Festival moment in Harlow and Lansbury, was used to notable Picturesque effect at the LCC's first development on the Roehampton Estate at Alton East, London. Built between 1952 and 1955, Alton East was set over an important high-lying 130-acre site overlooking Richmond Park, where there already existed a number of significant eighteenth-century houses and gardens. Designed by the LCC's architecture department, Alton East set a mix of 11-storey point blocks, five-storey maisonettes and two-storey terraced housing, along with community buildings and shops, amongst mature trees, while retaining the original shape of the landscaped parkland. Alton East, having been an eighteenth-century private park, now owned by the LCC, was a perfect fulfilment of the new Picturesque ideal of public authorities taking on the mantel and inheritance of private landlords in their custodianship of public land. Lansbury's influence was also seen in the development of New Towns that continued to be built until the late 1960s and, to a lesser extent, in housing schemes in redeveloped urban areas.

Picturesque revival continued to be promoted for a few years after the Festival as a necessary element of British reconstruction, most prominently by Pevsner who made this the subject of one of his 1955 Reith lectures.[24] His approach was strongly and satirically attacked by contemporaries such as art historian Basil Taylor in a series of broadcasts he gave in 1953. Taylor criticised those in positions of authority in government arts, architecture and design agencies for their uncritical admiration for the Picturesque, mockingly suggesting Herefordshire squires Payne Knight and Uvedale Price would have been quite at home in this postwar world.[25]

The impact of the new Picturesque was, ultimately, short-lived. The centralising influence of public authorities as landowners broke down when the new Conservative administration took power in 1951, reversing Labour's nationalization policies, including those affecting building controls. This led to a professional exodus into private architectural practices, where there was increased design autonomy and meaning the potential for implementing an official national aesthetic was curtailed. Disillusionment soon set in with a vehicle of new Picturesque experiments, the New Towns building programme. J.M. Richards criticised new communities like Harlow only two years after the Festival when he castigated the New Towns as places of community dysfunction, producing 'lop-sided and amputated suburban communities'.[26] Mrs Snoddy, Lansbury's celebrated first resident, later admitted she would like to have stayed in their old house, but had felt she had no choice but to take the Lansbury flat.[27] Mrs Snoddy was not the only Lansbury resident who felt forced to accept new housing that was seductively modern, while at the same time isolated from friends, family and work. Having been moved to the estate from homes sometimes a few miles away, many new residents missed familiar extended groupings of friends and family they had enjoyed before. Although having modern amenities such as indoor bathrooms, residents at Lansbury also had to pay substantially more rent, with two in three having to find double their original rent by the end of 1951, while at the same time having to travel further afield to find work.[28]

Many young people were inspired by the example of the Festival to train as architects.[29] Others considered it to be laughably parochial, an example to be strongly rejected. A group led by critic Reyner Banham and architects Peter and Alison Smithson vociferously ridiculed the architectural ideals associated with the Festival. Characterizing themselves as a new generation, they rejected the work of their forebears, who had been hung up on promoting historic styles, and set out a manifesto for the future: The New Brutalism, an architecture that rejected historicism, an 'architecture of our time'.[30] The experiments of Festival architects with Picturesque, Banham claimed, were an escape from the real problems and opportunities of urbanization, 'an overwhelming demonstration of the superiority of the English Picturesque tradition over all other planning dogmas'. Further, they were a symptom of a xenophobia that he and his contemporaries were at pains to distance themselves from and utterly irrelevant, relating more to the aesthetics of an older generation.[31] A broader sense of dissatisfaction about the direction that international modern architecture was taking would lead in 1954 to the creation of the new international group 'Team 10', which aimed to renew the connections between collective social transformation and avant-garde urban architecture, believed by its members to have been absent in architectural discussions since the war.[32]

Comparing Basil Spence's winning design to rebuild Coventry Cathedral and young architects Alison and Peter Smithson's competition entry, both in 1951, reveals the generation gap. Spence, having completed work on the Festival's Heavy Industry Exhibition at Glasgow and Sea and Ships at the South Bank was reaching the height of his career. He designed a single building that rose out of the Cathedral's ruins, set in the landscape and forming a vista from afar, framed from the city's centre. The Smithsons, then in their twenties, set all the functions of their Cathedral on a platform above the sloping site, in an anticlastic concrete shell. By doing so they created a building that sat above the landscape, rather than giving any illusion of becoming part of it. The generational divide that the Smithsons felt so acutely now appears rather more like an evolution, less like the revolution they claimed it was; after all, both were bidding to work on a reconstruction of the same Cathedral, where construction would inevitably have a relationship with the remaining historic fragment. Architectural working practices were changing rapidly from the time of the Festival. While many architects continued to thrive in enlightened local authority architects' departments well into the 1960s and 1970s, private practice and international projects not subject to the same building licences drew some away.[33]

The Festival had shown that landscaping design could create a visual relationship between new buildings, roads and technologies being incorporated into the environment. The Festival's experimentations with landscape launched a new generation of landscape architects, a number of whom – such as Sylvia Crowe and Brenda Colvin – went on shortly after the Festival to take this idea to another level; landscaping the areas around nuclear power stations.

The closure of the Festival of Britain marked the end of Attlee's government and the dying embers of George VI's reign. The King finally succumbed to long-term illness early in 1952 and was succeeded to the throne by Elizabeth II. Within months, Festival designers such as Hugh Casson and Misha Black would be called upon to design a momentous new national event: the Queen's Coronation in 1953.

The Festival had not simply been a celebration. It had helped British people make sense of their country in the wake of war and industrialization, to see a glimpse of a new country that was not at odds with the old one. In order to help people experience the Festival as the start of a new world, a break with the past, this celebration was both fun while it lasted and lingered in the imagination after the ball was over. In retrospect there appears a mismatch between Festival visitors' memories of colour, pleasure and exhilaration and the earnest intentions of the Festival. As Misha Black commented the 'official version' of the Festival was different from what visitors experienced, enjoyed and remembered.[34] But this was all part of the work of reconstruction that the Festival had set out to do.

Looking back fifty years on, at the age of 90, one Festival architect told me, 'The Festival was enormously thrilling and almost makes me cry to think about it, because the future seemed so possible and so benign.'[35] Whether the vision of the future set out in the Festival of Britain came to be is irrelevant. But it did what it set out to do: to inspire hope in a generation that the future would not be as terrible as the recent past, that Britain would go from strength to strength and that the people would again be able to embrace their land.

Postscript

60 YEARS AFTER '51

In the six decades since the Festival of Britain the South Bank has become a bustling hubbub with the addition of the Queen Elizabeth Hall, the Hayward Gallery, the new National Film Theatre and, a little further along the Thames, the National Theatre. As the only remaining monument to the Festival of Britain, the metropolitan Royal Festival Hall has become synonymous with these celebrations that tried so hard to be nationwide.

My work on this book ends at the close of the Festival's sixtieth anniversary, a year that has seen a major revival of interest in these events, spear-headed by a five-month celebration mounted by Southbank Centre. Held from April to September 2011, events were loosely based around themes drawn from the original South Bank Exhibition: 'People of Britain', 'Land', 'Power and Production' and 'Seaside', the programme packed with shows, gigs and talks that paid homage to 1951. Multi-coloured seaside huts were dotted along the Thames-side walk, a reference to the original Seaside section and bunting again fluttered up and down the riverfront. The dancing after dark of 1951 became an outdoor tea dance; a floral bicycle parade was revived. With a royal wedding during the first week of celebrations – the marriage of William and Kate – and towns and villages up and down the country also smothered in bunting, it felt uncannily like the Southbank Centre and Middle Britain were as one.

Abram Games' emblem was again emblazoned on everything but only after a makeover by global advertising agency Saatchi and Saatchi. Games' original colouring, the 'loyal' red, white and blue, as one contemporary had referred to it, the colours of the Union Jack, became light blue and acid green to complement sponsor Mastercard's orange and red logo. Britannia's feminine profile with her delicate pointed nose was squared off and masculinized: a bloke with a helmet, the original reference obscured. Festival Gardens were created on the roof of Queen Elizabeth Hall, with a nod to the original Festival Pleasure Gardens at Battersea. The new Gardens included a swathe of lush grass nestled on the roof of one of London's best-known Brutalist buildings, with a dramatic view towards St Paul's and Westminster.

What these celebrations revealed, as well as the wealth of articles, books, radio and TV broadcasts produced in 2011, was that the Festival is very much alive in the national imagination – in the memories of people who look back on it with pleasure, or those who keep souvenirs that have become the Festival's most important fragments. For many the Festival, which helped a nation to leave behind the shattering experience of war, remains the rainbow bridge that reconnected the prose in us with the passion.

NOTES

INTRODUCTION

.

1   *Festival Office Information Leaflet* (London: HMSO, 1951).
2   Kelvin Hall is still used for exhibitions and sports.
3   John D. Stewart, *Ulster Farm and Factory Exhibition Guide: A Guide to the Story It Tells* (London: HMSO, 1951), p. 5.
4   Ralph Tubbs' 1951 Dome of Discovery was 365 feet wide, while Richard Rogers' 2000 Dome referenced it, being 365 metres.
5   Editorial, *The Guardian*, Saturday 29 January 2000.
6   In trying to show the Festival's deep relationship with wider cultural sensibilities this book has had to leave out much that has been dealt with elsewhere. See, amongst others, Festival accounts by Becky Conekin, Margaret Garlake, Barry Turner, Lesley Jackson and Paul Rennie.
7   Vera and Jack's photograph album was found by my friend, Retronaut Chris Wild, www.retronaut.co.uk.
8   Photographs given to the author by Derek Baker.
9   Kathleen Cant, 13 February 2002. Available http://www.museumoflondon.org.uk (accessed 6 February 2006).
10 Janet Johnson, 13 February 2002. Available http://www.museumoflondon.org.uk (accessed 6 February 2006).
11 Marghanita Laski, *Observer*, 6 July 1952.
12 Ian Mackenzie-Kerr, 14 February 2002. Available http://www.museumoflondon.org.uk (accessed 6 February 2006).
13 Ruari McLean, *True to Type* (London: Werner Shaw, 2000), p. 92.
14 *South Bank Exhibition Guide* (London: HMSO, 1951), p. 6.
15 Auden introduction to John Betjeman, *Slick but not Streamlined* (Doubleday & Co, NY, 1947). Auden refused to be included under this definition of 'topophils' but he shared Betjeman's deep love of the English landscape as expressed in his talks and poems. Gaston Bachelard would later use 'topophilia' to describe 'space that may be grasped, that may be defended against adverse forces, the space we love' during his philosophical exploration of the space of home in the very

different context of his introduction to *The Poetics of Space* (Paris: Presses Universitaires de France, 1958).

16 Art historian Kitty Hauser has defined 'topophilia' in relation to a generation of 1930s and 1940s British artists and writers as requiring 'a visual imagination, but also a wilfully parochial outlook and a reluctance to engage with the homogenizing forces of urban modernity', Kitty Hauser, *Photography and the Archaeological Imagination, Britain c.1927–1951* (DPhil Thesis, Oxford University, 2003), p. 1. My understanding of topophils in this period is different: that they were engaging with urban modernity in its most formalized groupings (as active members of CIAM and MARS) but that this was not considered at odds with the past. David Matless describes these architects as 'planner preservationists', looking to build a modern nation while wanting to preserve the past, *Landscape and Englishness* (Reaktion, 1988), p. 202.

CHAPTER I

1   The Bank of England and civil aviation were nationalised in 1946; coal, cables and wireless followed in 1947; transport and electricity in 1948; gas in 1949; iron and steel in 1951. Figures from Alan Sked and Chris Cook, *Post-War Britain* (London: Pelican, 1979), p. 30.

2   *The Times*, Tuesday September 11, 1945, p. 5, Issue 50244, col E. Letters to the Editor, 'An Exhibition in 1951'.

3   *News Chronicle*, Friday September 14 1945, p. 2.

4   Speech delivered at SIA Dinner on Tuesday 16 October 1951, transcript in Gerald Barry (GB) family archive. *The Ambassador* magazine published Black's drawing in 1946.

5   *News Chronicle*, Tuesday 25 September 1945, p. 1.

6   Board of Trade Report of the Committee appointed by the Secretary for Overseas Trade under the Chairmanship of the Lord Ramsden to consider the part which exhibitions and fairs should play in the promotion of Export Trade in the Post-War Era and to advise on the policy and plans to be adopted to derive the maximum advantage from such displays. Presented by the President of the Board of Trade to Parliament by Command of His Majesty, March 1946 (London: HMSO).

7   Bernard Donoughue and G. W. Jones, *Herbert Morrison: Portrait of a Politician* (London: Weidenfeld, 1973), p. 493.

8   House of Commons debate, 5 December 1947, *Hansard*, Vol. 445, cc.691–5.

9   As Morrison explained in House of Commons debate, 12 July 1949, *Hansard*, Vol. 467, cc.12–3W.

10 Son of a clergyman, GB had been educated at public school and Cambridge, serving in the Royal Flying Corps during the First World War and after being demobilised. GB had started his journalistic career on the *Saturday Review*, then *The Weekend Review*, before joining the *Chronicle*. He took up his Festival appointment in March 1948, on a civil servant's salary of £3,000 per annum.

11 A competition for an ideal secondary school run in *News Chronicle* in 1937, for example, was won by AA-trained Denis Clarke Hall for a design that married functionalist principles with progressive building science.

12 Having previously been referred to as the '1951 Exhibition' or 'Centenary Exhibition'.

13 Phrase used GB, first statement to Festival Council, 31 May 1948.

14   This exclusive focus on Britain is discussed by Becky Conekin in *Autobiography of a Nation* (Manchester: MUP, 2003) and Jo Littler in 'Festering Britain: The 1951 Festival of Britain, decolonisation and the representation of the Commonwealth', in Simon Faulkner and Anandi Ramamurthy Anandi (eds.) *Visual Culture and Decolonisation in Britain* (London: Ashgate, 2006). There were those on the Festival Council who thought the whole point of the Festival should be to demonstrate the foundation of the British Empire (see National Archives WORK 25/44, 28 July 1948). During the planning of this exclusively British Festival, the 1948 Olympic Games (the so-called 'Austerity Olympics' because of continuing rationing) were staged in London, with the participation of 59 nations, including several British colonies and first-time competitors. Defying critics who had not wished to see resources being diverted away from the business of rebuilding Britain, the Games were a brilliant success, making a modest profit to boot.

15   Barry Turner discusses the possible sites in *Beacon for Change: How the 1951 Festival of Britain Shaped the Modern World* (London: Aurum, 2011), pp. 45–9.

16   Abercrombie and Forshaw's *County of London Plan 1943* (London: Macmillan and Co, 1943) and *Greater London Plan 1944* (HMSO, 1945) developed in some detail the potential of the South Bank.

17   Phrase used by Misha Black in *Design 149*, May 1961, p. 51.

18   Gielgud was knighted in 1953. I.I.I. Ebong's PhD thesis, *The Origins, Organisation and Significance of the Festival of Britain, 1951* investigates Festival administration (University of Edinburgh, 1986).

19   Statement of 31 May 1948, GB family archive.

20   Stephen Tallents, *The Projection of England* (London: Faber & Faber, 1932), pp. 34–5.

21   Although the EMB was a short-lived body dissolved in 1933.

22   As argued by Philip M. Taylor in *The Projection of Britain: British Overseas Publicity and Propaganda 1919–1939* (Cambridge University Press, 1981), pp. 122, 125.

23   The goods shown in Paris correlated closely to British exports to France.

24   Article 27, Universal Declaration of Human Rights. Available www.un.org/en/documents/udhr/index.shtml (accessed 5 January 2011).

25   GB, 'Festival of Britain 1951', *Britain To-Day*, June 1949, p. 9.

26   For example, Sir W. Smithers, House of Commons debate, 24 October 1949, *Hansard*, Vol. 468, cc.1006–7. Questions also raised the Festival diverting resources and slowing the rebuilding programme, House of Commons debate, 16 November 1950, *Hansard*, Vol. 480, c.1884.

27   Rt Hon Herbert Morrison, 'Something to shout about', in *Illustrated*, 2 December 1950, p. 11.

28   The Organization for European Economic Co-operation (OEEC) was founded in 1947 to handle distribution of Marshall Aid among European states. In 1949 M. Schumann, French Finance Minister, introduced proposals for a European Coal and Steel Community. These developments had received little attention in the British Parliament.

29   House of Commons debate, 18 September 1950, *Hansard*, Vol. 478, cc.1550–1.

30   Draft for *English Speaking World*, GB family archive.

31   Draft for *Flair* Magazine, September 1950, GB family archive.

32   *Listener*, Thursday August 3 1950, Vol. XLIV, No. 1123, pp. 147–8.

33   As recalled by Max Nicholson to Mary Banham and Roy Strong, in preparatory conversation for the V&A's *A Tonic to the Nation*, 1976.

34   Draft for *Picture Post*, 15 December 1950, GB family archive.

35 Paul Wright interview with the author, 3 June 2004. See Harriet Atkinson obituary Sir Paul Wright, *The Independent* 23 July 2005. For more on GB's house see Jeremy Melvin, *FRS Yorke and the Evolution of English Modernism* (Chichester: Wiley-Academy, 2003).

36 1 (of 3) Cantor Lectures given by GB, RSA, 12 May 1952, *Journal of RSA*, 4880, 22 August 1952. GB's stepson Richard Burton commented on his love of Sussex countryside.

37 Nikolaus Pevsner claimed this, for example, in 'Festival of Britain', reproduced in *Visual Planning and the Picturesque* (LA: Getty Research Institute, 2010), p. 197.

38 GB chose EM Nicholson's *Birds and Men* and American marine biologist and nature writer Rachel Carson's *The Sea Around Us* as his two books for 1951, for *The Observer*'s end of year round up.

39 Paul Wright, interview with author, 3 June 2004. Swann and Edgar advertising agency was contracted to work on Festival publicity.

40 Abram Games, *Over My Shoulder* (London: Studio Books, 1960). For more on the evolution of the Festival symbol see Naomi Games (et al.), *Abram Games* (Aldershot: Lund Humphries, 2003) and Naomi Games, *A Symbol for the Festival* (London: Capital, 2011).

41 Paul Reilly, 'The Printed Publicity of the Festival of Britain', *Penrose Annual: A review of the Graphic Arts* 1952, Vol. 46, p. 23.

42 Description written by Games in his personal album, begun 1950, courtesy Estate of Abram Games and thanks to Naomi Games.

43 Paul Wright, 'Projecting the Festival of Britain', *Penrose Annual* 1951, Vol. 45, pp. 60–1.

44 Kneebone collection, Museum of London.

45 The relationship between the Festival Office and the BBC had deteriorated when it was decided there would no longer be a BBC TV studio on the site.

46 Cultural historian Dick Hebdige characterises the twin 'obsessive' debate within Britain about popular culture and popular taste during the three decades from the 1930s as revolving around the twin themes of Americanization and the levelling down process in *Hiding in the Light: On Images and Things* (Routledge, 1988), p. 62. Details of GB's trips to the USA are in his unpublished diaries, GB family archive.

47 'One Man's Week', *The Leader*, 9 July 1949.

48 Sir Paul Wright, interview with author, London 2004. The advertisement appeared in *Life*, January 22nd 1951, pp. 17–20.

49 The Executive Committee included Festival Directors of Architecture, Exhibitions, Science & Technology and also Directors of the British Film Institute and Council of Industrial Design. The Presentation Panel was chaired by GB and included Cecil Cooke as Director of Exhibitions, exhibition designers Misha Black, James Gardner and James Holland, George Campbell as Director of Finance and Establishments, Hugh Casson as Director of Architecture, Ian Cox as Director of Science and Technology, A.D. Hippisley Coxe and M. Hartland Thomas of the Council of Industrial Design, and architect Ralph Tubbs, with Peter Kneebone as Secretary.

50 See Volker M. Welter, in Iain Boyd Whyte (ed), *Modernism and the Spirit of the City* (London: Routledge, 2003).

51 Casson's drawing is at National Archives WORK 25/ 195 FOB 1001 and Holland's at WORK 25/ 195 FOB 1002.

52 Charles Plouviez, *A Tonic to the Nation* (London: Thames & Hudson, 1976), p. 165.

53 Hugh Casson 'The 1951 Exhibition', *RIBA Journal* April 1950, p. 208.

54   Dylan Thomas 'The Festival Exhibition', *On the Air with Dylan Thomas: The Broadcasts* (New York: New Directions, 1992), p. 246.

55   Richard Burton, interview with author, 2006.

56   As described by Bevis Hillier in *A Tonic to the Nation*, p. 15.

57   Alan Powers, 'Casson, Sir Hugh Maxwell (1910–1999)', *Oxford Dictionary of National Biography*, Oxford University Press, 2004. Available www.oxforddnb.com/view/article/72656 (accessed 25 September 2005).

58   *Festival of Britain 1951 May-September Information Summary* (Issued by Information Office, Festival of Britain, 1951).

59   Misha Black in *International Lighting Review*, Vol. 1950/51, No. 6, p. 2.

60   *South Bank Guide*, p. 8 and *Festival Ship Campania Guide-Catalogue*, p. 4.

61   Basil Taylor, *Official Book of the Festival of Britain* (produced under direction of Lund Humphries & Co. Ltd for HMSO, 1951), p. 4.

62   *Festival of Britain 1951* (HMSO, 1951), p. 3. Cultural historian Barry Curtis discusses the story-telling presentation of the Festival in 'One Continuous Interwoven Serial Story', *Block* 11, 1985–6.

63   Ian Cox, 'Three years a-growing', *A Tonic to the Nation*, p. 62.

64   Ian Cox, Ibid., p. 62.

65   Hugh Casson, 'Period Piece', *A Tonic to the Nation*, p. 78.

66   'Relay' was an idea developed by Roland Barthes in 'The Rhetoric of the Image', *Image Music Text* (London: Fontana, 1977) to describe equal weighting of meaning between differing media. Festival text also performed the simple act of 'anchorage' by explaining displays in Festival exhibitions.

67   Misha Black, *International Lighting Review*, p. 4.

68   DA File 5183, paper of 31 March 1949.

CHAPTER 2

1   *South Bank Exhibition Catalogue of Exhibits* (HMSO, 1951), pp. 2–3.

2   Graphic designer Ashley Havinden believed the MOI's Exhibitions Branch 'had laid the foundation for modern exhibition technique as we know it today', *Advertising and the Artist* (London: Studio Publications, 1956), p. 12.

3   Information from National Archives website. Available www.nationalarchives.gov.uk/theartofwar/inf3.htm (accessed 22 June 2010).

4   Valerie Holman, 'Carefully Concealed Connections: The Ministry of Information and British Publishing, 1939–1946', *Book History*, Vol. 8, 2005, pp. 197–226.

5   DA, F.H.K. Henrion collection (Exhibitions box).

6   DA, photographs of 'The Army Exhibition', F.H.K. Henrion collection (Exhibitions Box).

7   Ashley Havinden, *Advertising and the Artist*, p. 12.

8   Havinden, Ibid., p. 33.

9   Posters had been used in Britain for political propaganda for a century by 1951, most usually in support of election campaigns. Their use during the First World War, for example, to inspire people to enlist, had been particularly powerful.

10   Austin Cooper, *Making a Poster* (The Studio, 1945), pp. 24, 95.

11   Eric Newton, catalogue essay for AIA exhibition 'Poster Design in Wartime Britain' at Harrods.

12   Abram Games, *Over My Shoulder* (Studio, 1960), pp. 8, 12.

13   Adrian Forty describes the Festival's design grouping as a 'technocracy' in 'Festival Politics', *A Tonic to the Nation*. Clifford Hatts, interview with author, 2003.

14   Christopher Frayling, *Art and Design: 100 Years at the Royal College of Art* (London: Collins & Brown, 1999), pp. 253–4.

15   COI was formed on 1 April 1946.

16   Sir Stafford Cripps, foreword to the *Britain Can Make It Exhibition Catalogue*.

17   Cecil Cooke made a major contribution to mid twentieth-century exhibition design as Director of the Exhibitions Division at the MOI and COI, then as the Festival's Director of Exhibitions. Cooke's next role was as Director of Exhibitions for the British Government Pavilion at the 1958 Brussels Expo. His final significant job was Commander General of the British Pavilion of the 1962 Seattle World's Fair. 'COOKE, (Roland) Cecil', *Who Was Who*, A & C Black, 1920–2008; online edition, Oxford University Press, Dec 2007. Available www.ukwhoswho.com/view/article/oupww/whowaswho/U171804 (accessed 13 August 2010). Dr Charles Plouviez, Cooke's Festival assistant, in an interview with the author in March 2003, commented that Cooke deserved much of the credit for shaping the thematic drive of the Festival but was not good at self-publicity so is largely forgotten.

18   Patrick Maguire and Jonathan M. Woodham (eds), *Design and Cultural Politics in Post-War Britain: The Britain Can Make It Exhibition of 1946* (London & Washington: Leicester University Press, 1997), p. 19.

19   The year after 'Britain Can Make It', designer James Gardner would work on an equivalent Board of Trade show for Scotland, 'Enterprise Scotland' 1947, with architect Basil Spence; both would design parts of the later Festival.

20   Ashley Havinden, *Advertising and the Artist,* p. 41.

21   Misha Black, *Exhibition Design* (London: Architectural Press, 1950), p. 11.

22   Ibid., p. 21.

23   Adrian Thomas, *Exhibition Design*, p. 118.

24   Ibid., p. 119.

25   Black would later describe the MARS exhibition, with the South Bank exhibition, as the two greatest influences on building styles within Britain, 'Notes on 1951' in Misha Black collection, V&A AAD/ 1980/3/4 File 2/3.

26   Black lectured regularly on the subject of exhibition design, showing his awareness of the history and evolution of the exhibition form and his interest in examples of recent innovation through his book *Exhibition Design*.

27   'For Liberty' exhibition catalogue, AIA, 1943.

28   Misha Black's interest in collecting was described by his daughter Julia in discussion with the author in July 2010. Cadbury-Brown's interest was described by Elain Harwood in a note to 'A Good Time-and-a-half was had by All', *Twentieth Century Architecture 5: Festival of Britain (Journal of the Twentieth Century Society*, 2001), p. 60.

29   Eva Rudberg explains that some had their first experience of Swedish functionalism at Alvar Aalto's 1929 Turku exhibition in *The Stockholm Exhibition 1930* (Stockholmia Forlag, 1999), p. 22 and pp. 60–1.

30   P.M. Shand, 'Gunnar Asplund', *AR*, May 1941.

31   J.M. Richards, *Modern Architecture* (Penguin, 1960), p. 91.

32   English planners envied Sweden's progressive approach to town planning. An 1874 Act had been passed in Sweden regulating reconstruction and town extensions several decades before it was in place in England (English Town Planning Acts were passed in 1901 and 1919). See guide to the International Cities and Town Planning Exhibition (Gothenburg, Sweden, 27 July–12 August, 1923), p. 5.

33   *Architects' Journal*, 20 January 1949, p. 71.

34   *AR*, Vol. 101, June 1947, pp. 199–204 and Vol. 103, January 1948, pp. 180–2.

35   Young architect Michael Grice, who would go on to be Architects Co-operative Partnership's lead member on the Festival, had been an apprentice under Asplund in the 1930s, living with him while he worked on the Stockholm Cemetery, something that would profoundly shape the direction of Grice's work, as he explained to me in interviews in 2003 and 2004.

36   Reyner Banham, *The New Brutalism* (Architectural Press, 1966).

37   Black, *Exhibition Design*.

38   Black, Ibid., p. 11.

39   *Architects' Journal*, 13 January 1949, p. 28.

40   Kenneth W. Luckhurst, *The Story of Exhibitions* (London & NY: The Studio Publications, 1951), p. 168.

41   Misha Black and Ralph Tubbs wrote a report to the Presentation Panel (49) 42, Kneebone Collection, Museum of London.

42   Report of a roundtable discussion organized by *Architects' Journal*, Vol. 109, No. 2815 (20 January 1949), p. 74.

43   Ivor Montagu, *What happened at Wrocław* (London: British Cultural Committee for Peace 1949), p. 4.

44   Kingsley Martin, *The New Statesman and Nation*, 4 September 1948, pp. 187–8.

45   Katarzyna Murawska-Muthesius, 'Modernism between Peace and Free: Picasso and Others at the Congress of Intellectuals in Wrocław, 1948', in Crowley and Pavitt (eds), *Cold War Modern* (London: V&A, 2008).

46   In Britain, a Royal Commission had dealt with international exhibitions policy until 1912 when an exhibitions branch of the Board of Trade was established to oversee this work (a responsibility taken on by the Department for Overseas Trade in 1918). British involvement in international exhibitions was never a given but agreed on an *ad hoc* basis and commercial and cultural elements were never fully integrated. See Philip M. Taylor, *The Projection of Britain*.

47   See David Dean, *The Architect as Stand Designer 1895–1983* (London: Scolar Press, 1985).

48   *Architects' Journal*, 20 January 1949, p. 68.

49   Black in Robert Gutmann and Alexander Koch, *Exhibition Stands* (Verlagsanstalt Alexander Koch GMBH Stuttgart, 1954), p. 11.

50   Philip M. Taylor, *The Projection of Britain*, p. 90.

51   Deborah Ryan, *Daily Mail Ideal Home Exhibitions* (Hazar Publishing, 1997).

52   Gutmann and Koch, p. 18.

53   Gio Ponti said exhibition designers in Italy had trained through the Milan Triennali, in Gutmann and Koch.

54   Report to Presentation Panel (49) in Kneebone collection, Museum of London archives. Paul Wright went to Rome in Holy Year, 1950, and talked to city officials about the problem of large crowds. It wasn't an exact parallel, but it was the nearest thing he could think of, he told me in 2004.

CHAPTER 3

1   *South Bank Exhibition Guide* (London: HMSO, 1951), p. 6.

2   A Festival church committee was set up under the leadership of the Church of England, including reluctant representatives of churches in Wales and Scotland. Northern Ireland had separate and independent church arrangements co-ordinated by the Government of NI. The Roman Catholic Church chose not to sit on the central committee. The Lambeth Palace exhibition 'Art in the Service of the Church' showed church objects made by contemporary artists and designers. 'The Faith of Britain' exhibition showed the Christian tradition in Britain. Christianity was strongly aligned in the Festival with a tradition of British liberal politics, asserted to show the difference between Britain and non-democratic states. Professor Butterfield pursued this line in his introductory essay 'Christianity and Western Ideals' for the catalogue *The Church and the Festival 1951*. Other religions were not referred to across Festival sites. The limited representation of Judaism was justified in a letter from the Archbishop of Canterbury to the Chairman of the Council of Christians and Jews, '... after all it is Christianity which has been the religion of this country and formative of its tradition and not Judaism, and if the Festival is to be typical of England the religious contribution must be Christian' (Letter from Archbishop Fisher to Rev W.W. Simpson of Council of Christians and Jews, 18 July 1950, Church of England Archive, Vol. 85, Fisher 1951, ff. 1–228). Despite the limited focus on Judaism within the exhibitions, many outstanding contributions to the exhibitions were made by Jewish people, as recorded in the *American Jewish Year Book* (1952, p. 278), which stated 'Outstanding contributions to the Festival were made by Jews in all fields. The symbol of the Festival itself (...) was designed by Abram Games (...) At (...) the south bank (...) the work of Jewish designers and architects like Mischa (*sic*) Black, Leonard Manasseh, Bronek Katz, H.J. Reifenberg, Manfred Reiss and H.A. Rothhols (*sic*) were represented. Jacob Epstein's great female figure ... was the chief Jewish contribution to the nation's sculpture'.

3   GB, 'The Festival of Britain' for *Adelphi*, 2nd Quarter 1951, p. 206. Sir George Alwyn, Lord Mayor of London briefed local authority leaders on the Festival at London's Guildhall in June 1948.

4   Sketch in private collection. Lee drew a regular cartoon called 'London Laughs'.

5   Playwright Michael Frayn mocked the phrase 'spontaneous expressions of citizenship' as 'Soviet', seeing the organizers coercing the 'citizenship' to respond to the festivities, 'Festival', in Michael Sissons and Philip French (eds), *Age of Austerity* (London: Hodder and Stoughton, 1963). 'Spontaneity' was a word with significant currency in 1951. For planners and architects it described the way that environments and buildings were taken up for use by the public. At CIAM's meeting at Hoddesdon in 1951, Le Corbusier raised the issue of how to provoke 'spontaneity' in new city centres, part of an increased concern within CIAM with anticipating public reactions.

6   *Official Book of the Festival of Britain* (London: HMSO, 1951), p. 64.

7   GB private diary, Thursday 15 February 1951.

8   John Moore, *The Dance and Skylark* (London: Collins, 1950), p. 60.

9   Sketch in private collection.

10 Evelyn Waugh, *The Sword of Honour Trilogy* (first published Butler & Tanner, 1965), p. 793. Prologue to the Trilogy is sometimes called 'Festival of Britain'.

11 Wyndham Lewis, *Rotting Hill* (London: Methuen & Co, 1951), preface, not paginated.

12   'Song for a Festival' commissioned by Arts Council of Great Britain, 1951, words by Cecil Day-Lewis, music by George Dyson. 'The Festival of Britain (This Grand Old Land of Mine)', words by Tommie Connor, music by Horatio Nicholls.

13   *South Bank Exhibition Guide*, pp. 8–9.

14   *Festival Office Information Leaflet*.

15   The phrase 'magical city' was used by Misha Black in 'FoB+51' in *Design*, Council of Industrial Design, No. 149, May 1961, p. 51 and 'brief city' by Patrick O'Donovan and Hugh Casson in *Brief City*, produced by Richard Massingham, 1951.

16   Peter Mandler, *The Fall and Rise of the Stately Home* (New Haven: Yale UP, 1997); Copley in Stephen Copley and Peter Garside, *The Politics of the Picturesque: Literature, Landscape and Aesthetics Since 1770* (Cambridge University Press, 1994), p. 208. Andrew Ballantyne, *Architecture, Landscape and Liberty: Richard Payne Knight and the Picturesque* (Cambridge, 1997) and Ballantyne, in Daniels and Watkins (eds.), *The Picturesque Landscape* (University of Nottingham, 1994).

17   Christopher Hussey, *The Picturesque* (London: Frank Cass & Co, 1927), foreword to 1967 reprint, p. 66.

18   As described in *A Short Story With A Hundred Pictures And About As Many Morals: Your Inheritance: The Land: An Uncomic Strip* (London: Architectural Press, 1942), which was probably by H. de C. Hastings.

19   This is discussed at length in Erdem Erten's PhD, 'Shaping the Second Half Century' (MIT, 2004).

20   *AR*, May 1944, pp. 125–9.

21   'The Editor', 'Exterior Furnishing or Sharawaggi', *AR*, January 1944, pp. 2–3.

22   Nikolaus Pevsner, 'The Genesis of the Picturesque' *AR*, December 1944, p. 139; repeated in *The Englishness of English Art* (London: Architectural Press, 1956), p. 162. H. de C. Hastings (owner of Architectural Press) had in fact commissioned Pevsner to write a book on town planning and the Picturesque in 1942. This has recently been published posthumously. See also Christopher Woodward, *In Ruins* (London: Chatto & Windus, 2002), pp. 119–21. Alan Powers very generously helped me with formulating my early thoughts on this.

23   'Townscape: A Plea for an English Visual Philosophy Founded on the True Rock of Sir Uvedale Price', *AR*, December 1949, p. 354; 'Townscape Casebook' *AR*, December 1949, p. 363. These ideas culminated in the Cullen's book *Townscape* (London: Architectural Press, 1961).

24   The idea of 'new Picturesque' serves as useful shorthand. But there are clearly problems with critiquing a period using a phrase that had itself spawned similar ones ('the New Empiricism', 'the New Humanism', etc) within its contemporary architectural press. Other commentators have also coined phrases to denote a stylistic revival of Picturesque in the twentieth century: art historian Frances Spalding's 'neo-picturesque', cultural historian Barry Curtis's 'utility picturesque' and architectural historian Alan Powers' 'Revived Picturesque', while Pevsner had referred to a 'Twentieth Century Picturesque'. My 'new Picturesque' owes a debt to architectural critic Reyner Banham who argued that his phrase 'The New Brutalism' denoted an 'ethical' agenda akin to a manifesto. This 'New Brutalism', he said, was different from the existing phrase 'Neo Brutalism', which had served as a stylistic assessment, largely pejorative. Similarly, 'the new Picturesque' is used here to point to the reuse of Picturesque principles as in a deeper sense ideological: specifically, principles associated with private property being reclaimed and mobilized for use in the reconstruction of the British public realm after the Second World War.

25   *Ministry of Health Housing Manual* (HMSO, 1949), p. 35.

26   Brenda Colvin, *Land and Landscape* (London: John Murray, 1947), p.xxi. Colvin was landscape architect of East Kilbride New Town.

27   Brenda Colvin, Ibid.

28   John Ratcliff, *A Tonic to the Nation*, p. 110.

39   GB, 2 (of 3) Cantor Lectures, RSA.

30   Barry Evans. Available www.museumoflondon.org.uk (accessed 30 September 2010).

31   Black in conversation with Mary Banham in 1975, in preparation for *A Tonic to the Nation*.

CHAPTER 4

1   King George VI and Queen Elizabeth, Queen Mary, Princess Elizabeth and Prince Philip, the Duke of Edinburgh, attended the ceremony.

2   GB, *Radio Times*, 18 April 1951.

3   Ismay, *The Memoirs of General the Lord Ismay* (London: Heinemann, 1970), p. 451.

4   The first bonfire to be lit was outside St Paul's.

5   Nigel Nicolson (ed), *Harold Nicolson, Diaries and letters 1945–62* (London: Fontana, 1971), entry for 4 May 1951, pp. 190–1.

6   *Life*, 14 May 1951, p. 36.

7   *The Times*, 9 May 1951, p. 3, issue 51996, col A, 'So Far so good at Festival'. The first overseas visitor to arrive at the South Bank was Mrs A.M. Robertson from Wellington, New Zealand and the first home visitor Mrs N. Oliver of Parkhurst Road, London N7, photographed looking at the displays together.

8   Clifford Hatts described 'doing a ghoster', interview with author, January 2010. Misha Black also described working all night and killing rats at 4 am on opening day. Charles Plouviez illustrated the fact that the South Bank exhibitions were not complete upon opening by telling a story of King George VI walking round a section on interior lighting in the Homes and Gardens pavilion in total darkness. The King, turning to Attlee, said 'Another of your power cuts, Prime Minister?' (*A Tonic to the Nation*, pp. 165–6). Clifford Hatts said that many rather intricate machines designed to tell a part of the Dome's story could not stand up to thousands of visitors. A machine to show Robert Hook's work on colour theory using overlapping colour wheels broke early on. So did a push button model showing Clark Maxwell's theory of transmitted and reflected colour light (Hatts, interview with author, January 2010).

9   Ralph Tubbs, WORK 25/43.

10   Sir Philip Powell, interview with author, 2 April 2003.

11   The same link was made in the miniature version of the South Bank exhibition aboard *HMS Campania* where the first section, devoted to the 'Origins of the Island', led directly up a ramp into sections on 'Coal', 'Steel', 'Industry', 'Power', 'Transport' and 'Sea and Ships', so bringing together productivity of land with that of people through their control of industrial machinery.

12   As Peter Moro recalled, Peter Moro, 8 out of 15, *Architects' Lives, National Sound Archive*, 1996.8.01 and 1996.8.14 and 1996.9.05.

13   *AR*, June 1951.

14   *Stone On The South Bank: A Geological Walk Organized by The Geological Museum* (London: Geological Museum, 1979), p. 7.

15   Richard Dimbleby, broadcast on 16.1.1950 in National Archives, INF 12/ 255.

16   Professor Peter Youngman, interview with author, March 2004.

17   Robin Day was originally designer of this section but withdrew when the display changed, becoming more theatrical and demanding animated models, National Archives, WORK 25/48 Presentation Panel, 6 July 1949.

18   As Misha Black explained, National Archives, WORK 25/48, Presentation Panel 26 October 1949.

19   He was working at the same time on housing, lay out and hard landscaping for Harlow New Town, Professor H.T. Cadbury-Brown, interview with author, April 2003.

20   Professor HT Cadbury-Brown, interview with author, June 2006.

21   Rotter had previously illustrated the steel-making process using clever theatrical effects including lighting for the British Iron and Steel Federation for the Ideal Home Exhibition, 1949.

22   'A Map comes to Life', *Display: Design and Presentation*, July 1951, pp. 32–3.

23   Dylan Thomas, 'The Festival Exhibition', *On the Air with Dylan Thomas: The Broadcasts* (New York: New Directions, 1992), p. 249.

24   'The Exhibition as Landscape', *AR*, August 1951, pp. 85–6.

25   *Official Book of the Festival of Britain*, p. 8.

26   Dylan Thomas, 'The Festival Exhibition'.

27   Professor Peter Youngman, interview with the author, March 2004.

28   House of Commons debate, 14 November 1950, *Hansard*, Vol. 480, cc.129–30W.

29   Notes about tree planting in National Archives, INF 12/255. Peter Shepheard stated his belief in tree planting as an act of reconstruction in *Modern Gardens* (London: Architectural Press, 1953), p. 17.

30   Youngman, speaking to the author in 2004, attributed this idea to the contribution of landscaper H.F. Clark who had been influenced by Scandinavia, where he had travelled extensively after the war for work.

31   Sir Peter Shepheard, 14 out of 18, *Architects' Lives, National Sound Archive*, 1997.07.02 to 1997.08.12.

32   *Brief City.*

33   As in Presentation Panel, 27 July 1949 minutes, p. 5, point 13, 'South Bank excavation' in National Archives WORK 25/ 48.

34   London County Council, *South Bank Past & Present Exhibition*, May-September 1951.

35   Jacquetta Hawkes, *A Land* (Cresset, 1951), preface.

36   Jacquetta Hawkes, *A Land* (Penguin, 1959), p. 11.

37   Hawkes, *A Land*, Ibid., p. 9.

38   Record of meeting held on 31 Aug 1949 entitled 'Sculpture on the South Bank', Presentation Panel papers, National Archives WORK 25 48 (49) 62. Epstein was the other sculptor commissioned·directly by the Festival Office. 60 painters and 12 sculptors were commissioned by the Arts Council at the South Bank.

39   *South Bank Guide*, p. 90.

40   Many paintings shown in the Arts Council's '60 Paintings for '51' exhibition also took the land as subject. Edward Bawden's *Country Life* mural in the Lion and Unicorn depicted the ebb and flow of farming through the seasons. Farming was also the focus of Michael O'Connell's wallhanging in the Country pavilion, not mechanized farming but an image of a rural pastoral idyll: a man leading a horse through a field, hop buildings at a farm.

41   GB private diary, Friday 9 March 1951.

42   *Royal River*, a film about the River Thames shown in the South Bank's Telecinema, was the first British stereoscopic Technicolor film. A campaign for the Thames and its borders to become a national park had been run in *AR* and special edition issued on this subject in July 1950.

43   The Festival was repeatedly imagined as the work of an 'island people'. This island was 'Britain' and the fact that that Northern Ireland was also a part of the Festival was often, for the sake of rhetoric, conveniently forgotten.

44   As reported by Reyner Banham in 'Opinions of the Festival of Britain', *AR,* January 1953, pp. 62–3.

45   *AR*, August 1951, Vol. CX, No. 656, Special South Bank Edition.

46   As noted by Erdem Erten, 'Shaping the Second Half Century', pp. 58–9.

47   Hugh Casson letter to H. de C. Hastings, n.d., quoted by Susan Lasdun, and Hugh Casson interview with Lasdun, 1984, both quoted in Lasdun, 'H. de C. reviewed', *AR*, September 1996. J.M. Richards also acknowledged the Festival of Britain as realization of H. de C.'s ideas: 'It was the physical embodiment of townscape policy', according to Susan Lasdun interview with J.M. Richards, 1975. Michael Frayn believes that the South Bank's Picturesque was inspired by the layout of Oxbridge college quads ('Random Edition', BBC 4 broadcast 4 May 2011).

48   GB, 'One Man's Day', *The Leader*, 9 July 1949.

49   National Archives, INF 12/255.

50   *Brief City*.

51   Gordon Bowyer, interview with the author, 2004.

52   Peter Shepheard, *Modern Gardens* (Architectural Press, 1953), p. 17. Shepheard's book owed a clear debt to Christopher Tunnard's *Gardens in the Modern Landscape*, (London: Architectural Press, 1938), developed out of his articles in *AR*, which had addressed the issue of the 'functional' landscape.

53   As Casson explained in *Brief City*.

54   Even the internal spaces of the Festival Hall were seen through a Picturesque frame. Architect Peter Moro, for example, later commented on their 'lack of regularity', allowing 'a multiplicity of perspectives' (in Peter Moro, National Life Story Collection Architects' Lives, 8 out of 15, 28.43). Charles Plouviez, assistant to Cecil Cooke later commented 'What was best about the South Bank was just walking round it. It was a totally new experience and it was what we all hoped the New Towns would be like, and they mostly didn't make it .... Most people reacted to that more than to any individual exhibit.' 'It was a beautifully designed series of spaces, and as much as anything else people just enjoyed the ambiance and liked walking around the S.B. People didn't remember the story in any depth ... possibly some people did and read all the captions, but I don't think most people did, but I don't think that matters,' interview with the author, 2003.

55   E.A. Gutkind, *Architectural Design*, December 1951, pp. 349, 351.

56   C.G.E. Wingfield, *International Lighting Review*, p. 27.

57   *Illustrated London News*, special Festival edition, May 12 1951. GB knew the impact of nighttime spectacle. Richard Burton, his stepson, recalled GB taking him as a boy on to the roof of the *News Chronicle* building to see the Blitz in 1941. Burton recalled 'You could see St Paul's standing there and the flames lighting the sky behind where the docks were burning. Gerald was

very keen on that kind of thing. He knew what the effect of events were and how to use them,' Richard Burton, interview with author, February 2006.

58   As described in *Brief City*.

59   Ibid.

60   Professor HT Cadbury-Brown, interview with the author, June 2006.

61   The idea of an imaginative 'return' is developed by Marc Augé, *Oblivion* (Minnesota, 2004), p. 55.

CHAPTER 5

1   Food rationing continued until 1954.

2   David Kynaston, *Austerity Britain* (London: Bloomsbury, 2007), p. 407.

3   In March 1946 Black used the AIA Lecture to examine the possibility of holding an international exhibition, Misha Black Collection, V&A AAD/ 1980/ 3/ 4 (1 of 3).

4   Indeed the fact that the Festival marked 1851's centenary was all but forgotten until James Gardner designed a small pavilion in homage to the Crystal Palace, which stood on a platform next to the Shot Tower.

5   Paul Greenhalgh, *Ephemeral Vistas: The Expositions Universelles, Great Exhibitions, and World's Fairs 1851–1939* (Manchester University Press, 1988).

6   Nikolaus Pevsner, *High Victorian Design: A Study of the Exhibits of 1851* (London: Architectural Press, 1951) pp. 45, 49.

7   Although not focused on an end product, manufactured products were shown across Festival pavilions chosen from a Stock List put together by the Council of Industrial Design. Festival exhibitions also showcased the spectacle of production in ways familiar to visitors of other international shows where displays of technology had allowed countries to draw attention to their own strengths in particular areas of manufacturing. The 1924 Wembley Empire Exhibition with its Halls of Industry and Civil Engineering and Glasgow's Empire Exhibition 1938 where Misha Black had himself designed the UK Pavilion's section on Steel, Coal and Shipbuilding. Manufacturing machinery, as well as the final products – trains, tractors and ships – were put on display across the Festival sites.

8   John Gloag, *Men and Buildings* (London: Country Life, 1931), p. 195.

9   H.T. Cadbury-Brown, 'A Good Time-and-a-half', p. 64.

10   *Belfast News-Letter*, 17 May 1951.

11   Misha Black, *International Lighting Review*, pp. 2–3.

12   Reyner Banham, 'The Shape of Things: The Skylon', *Art News and Review*, p. 6. Mary Banham, in conversation with the author in 2011, described them instead as male and female: phallic and yonic symbols auguring a fecund second half-century.

13   Altering scale to help people understand difficult concepts was used regularly across the Festival. The Science Exhibition played around with sense of scale, using *Alice in Wonderland*'s adventures through shrinking or becoming enlarged as a theme through which to put the otherwise invisible building blocks of science, atoms and molecules on display at a visible size.

14   See Nicholas Bullock, *Building the Post-War World* (Routledge, 2002).

15   Diary of Albert Richardson, 5 July 1951 (original spelling), from Avenue House Collection, with thanks to Simon Houfe.

16 *Glasgow Exhibition of Heavy Industry Catalogue*, introduction.

17 From the 1970s Castlereagh developed a terrifying reputation after a police interrogation centre was opened there; it was the scene of many complaints of police brutality which are still being heard in appeals.

18 All other exhibitions were funded centrally from London.

19 Introductory Panel to Ulster Farm and Factory Exhibition.

20 John D. Stewart, *Ulster Festival Farm and Factory Guide* (London: HMSO, 1951), p. 5. BBC broadcaster Geoffrey Boumphrey comment from broadcast, 3 June 1951, transcript PRONI COM 4A/71.

21 By 1951 the constitutional relationship between the Westminster Parliament and that of Northern Ireland was complex. In the 1940s, financial and legislative responsibilities had largely been devolved to Stormont, accelerated in 1949 with the Ireland Act, while it continued formally to be a dominion of the United Kingdom.

22 Sir Roland Nugent, Speaker of the Northern Ireland (NI) Senate, led the NI Festival Committee, which has been characterised as a unionist elite by Northern Ireland historian Gillian McIntosh, *The Force of Culture: Unionist Identities in Twentieth-Century Ireland* (Cork University Press, 1999). The Countess of Antrim, whose husband was a wealthy landowner and Chairman of National Trust in Northern Ireland was a leading member, as was Professor E. Estyn Evans, whose writings on the topography and traditions of NI were strongly focused towards establishing the links and continuities between Ulster and the rest of the British Isles.

23 *Daily Mail*, preview of Festival Exhibitions, May 1951, pp. 70–1 (original emphases).

24 PRONI COM 4A/ 64, 'Briefing by Wm de Majo about exhibition', 4 October 1950.

25 Knox's statue is now in the park at Stormont.

26 *Architects' Journal*, 26 July 1951, p. 100. Ulster's postwar approach to meeting the housing shortage was shown by a Festival display of the Northern Ireland Housing Trust's new Cregagh Housing Estate.

27 Made by Trident Films, sponsored by the Government of NI and COI.

28 The exhibition building, now part of a trading estate, still stands on the corner of Craigavon and Alanbrooke Road, Castlereagh. Some of the exhibition's external landscaping is still recognizable.

29 Juliet and Perilla Kinchin, *Glasgow's Great Exhibitions* (White Cockade, 1988); Paul Greenhalgh characterised these exhibitions of people 'human showcases', dating the origins of the tradition to between 1889 and 1914, when people from all over the world were displayed for the 'gratification and education' of exhibition visitors, Greenhalgh, p. 82. See also Colin McArthur, 'The dialectic of national identity: The Glasgow Empire Exhibition of 1938', in Bennett (et al.), *Popular Culture and Social Relations* (Oxford UNiversity Press, 1986).

30 Robert W. Rydell, *All the World's A Fair: Visions of Empire at American International Expositions, 1876–1916* (University of Chicago Press, 1984).

31 GB, 2 (of 3) Cantor Lectures.

32 *Living Traditions: 1951 Festival Exhibition of Scottish Architecture & Crafts*, held at the Royal Scottish Museum.

33 *Belfast Telegraph and Northern Whig*, 12 July 1951 (PRONI COM/4/E/2/1 press cuttings).

34 E.E. Evans, *Mourne Country* (Dundalk: Dudalgan Press, 1951), pp. 178–80.

35 PRONI COM 4B/19, 'Story of the Tobacco and Cigarette Industry in Ulster'.

36 PRONI COM 4A/61, press release of 22 August 1951: 'Livestock Thriving and Milk Yield Satisfactory'.

37 PRONI COM 4B/19, correspondence of 16 August 1952.

38 National Archives WORK 25, F.H.K. Henrion's comments on the trials of live demonstrators, including the blacksmith he had employed.

39 *Ulster Farm and Factory Exhibition Guide-Catalogue*, p. 29.

40 Festival of Britain collection, archive at Mitchell Library, Glasgow.

41 Alastair Borthwick, *Scotland's SMT Magazine*, May 1951, p. 27.

42 Ibid.

43 Ibid. 'Whalen is a great admirer of his Celtic forebears and feels that the Celts in the functional and decorative use of their medium have very definite affinities with the Greeks.'

44 *Architects' Journal*, 9 August 1951.

45 Nikolaus Pevsner, 'Il Festival di Londra', Communita, 12 October 1951, pp. 48–51, reproduced in *Visual Planning and the Picturesque* Mathew Aitchison (ed.) (J. Paul Getty Trust, 2010), p. 197.

46 See, for example, *Your Inheritance: The land: An uncomic strip*.

47 *Official Book of the Festival of Britain*, p. 8.

48 M. Hartland Thomas, 'The gasworks in the landscape', *AR*, April 1947, pp. 136–8.

49 E.E. Evans, *Irish Heritage: The Landscape, The People and Their Work* (1942).

50 A legacy of the NI Festival was the founding of Cultra's Folk Museum, following a campaign spear-headed by Evans.

51 *Belfast Telegraph*, 28 August 1951, Letters, p. 117.

52 David Matless, *Landscape and Englishness*, p. 129. Evans can be characterised as 'organicist', in Matless's characterization of those who built up 'the region from geology and topography as a counter-modern unit'.

53 William Holt, 'Festival in Ireland', BBC broadcast, 13 April 1951, transcript, p. 4, PRONI.

54 *Belfast Telegraph*, 20 April 1951, PRONI.

55 'Farm of the Future', *AR*, September 1951, Vol. 110, pp. 191–2.

56 PRONI COM 4A/64 (Castlereagh Exhibition: General), July 1950.

57 Operating via a form of 'conservative modernity' to use Alison Light's term in *Forever England* (London: Routledge, 1991), p. 10.

58 William Holt, 'Festival of Britain', BBC General Overseas Service, 19 June 1951, 18.00, PRONI.

59 Wyn Griffith, *The Dolhendre Scheme: An Experiment in Rural Reconstruction* (Cambrian News Aberystwyth, 1951), p. 4.

60 Ling in 'Satisfying human needs at the core' at CIAM 8, 1951, in Tyrwhitt, Sert, Rogers (eds), *CIAM 8: The Heart of the City* (London: Lund Humphries, 1952), p. 96.

61 W.G. Holford, 'The Lansbury Neighbourhood', *Listener*, 29 March 1951. These ideas echoed planner Thomas Sharp's comments on how public authorities were taking over village planning from large landowners in *Anatomy of the Village* (London: Penguin, 1946), p. 31.

62 *Festival Science Guide-Catalogue*, p. 7. The Science Exhibition was the inaugural show held in the Science Museum's new wing.

63 Jacob Bronowski, *The Common Sense of Science* (London: Heinemann, 1951).

64 Margaret Gowing, *Independence and Deterrence: Britain and Atomic Energy, 1945–1952* (London: Macmillan, 1974).

65 Lockspeiser would be key to the 1954 establishment of CERN (the European Council for Nuclear Research) and its first president.

66   *Exhibition of Science Guide-Catalogue*, p. 7.

67   *Official Book of the Festival of Britain.*

68   *Glasgow Exhibition of Heavy Industry Catalogue* (London: HMSO, 1951), p. 45.

69   National Archives WORK 25/19 (FB Presentation Panel (49) 63.

70   *Festival Science Exhibition Guide-Catalogue*, p.xxviii.

71   National Archives, STAT 14/1759.

72   *Festival Science Exhibition Guide-Catalogue*, p. 17.

73   National Archives WORK 25/146.

74   Ministry of Defence, Directorate of Scientific Intelligence and Joint Technical Intelligence Committee: 'Unidentified Flying Objects'. Paper in private collection.

CHAPTER 6

1   Stephen Tallents, *The Projection of England.*

2   GB, *Books* (magazine of the National Book League), May 1951, proof, GB family archive, accompanied by letter of 9 April 1951.

3   GB, 'One Man's Week', *The Leader*, 9 July 1949, GB family archive.

4   *Picture Post*, 25 March 1944, Vol. 22, No. 13, p. 22.

5   The Society of Pure English was founded in 1913, Philip Dodd, 'Englishness and the national culture', in Colls & Dodd (eds), *Englishness: Politics and Culture 1880–1920* (Australia, Kent: Croom Helm, 1986), p. 15.

6   George Orwell, 'Politics and the English Language', *Horizon*, Vol. 13, 1946.

7   GB, *Books*, May 1951. Becky Conekin discusses this aspect of GB's rhetoric, linking GB's phrase 'language as missionary' to Britain's imperial endeavours and the belief that Britain had a role in influencing the minds of other peoples, *Autobiography*, pp. 184–5.

8   GB, *National Book League Annual Report 1950–1*, p. 1152.

9   GB statement to Festival Council, 31 May 1951, p. 10, GB family archive.

10   GB, *Radio Times*, April 18 1951.

11   2,700 BBC radio broadcasts were made during the Festival.

12   GB, *Radio Times*, April 18 1951.

13   Cultural historian Stuart Hall describes the 'Standard Voice' of the early BBC licensed to broadcast news in 1923 with its 'received' pronunciation, accent and tonal pitch. The voice set out to form a unified 'voice' for the nation, 'not of the state, the government, or even "the people", so much as the nation', controlling and subordinating regional and class difference, Stuart Hall 'Popular culture and the state', in Bennett, Mercer, Woollacott, *Popular Culture and Social Relations*, pp. 43–4. Contemporary commentators such as Ivor Brown had seen broadcasting diminishing the language, paring it away 'instead of enlarging verbal richness', 'The Glory of the Word', *This Britain: Tradition and Achievement* (Macdonald, London 1951).

14   Geoffrey Boumphrey, BBC 'Festival Notebook', 'Ulster Farm and Factory Exhibition', part 5, transmitted Sunday 3 June 1951, p. 4, PRONI COM 4A/71.

15   William Holt, BBC 'Festival in Britain', broadcast 19 June 1951, transcript, pp. 3–4.

16   Michel de Certeau describes two visions of the city-panorama, with one as 'itinerary', followed on the ground and another as 'voyeur god', *The Practice of Everyday Life* (University of California Press, 1988), p. 93.

17   Architect Clough Williams-Ellis debated the respective merits of being a 'foreigner' or a 'native' in a Festival article, *Britain To-Day,* Festival Number, May 1951, p. 18. One drawback, he said, was that 'unlike the foreigner and the overseas visitor, the poor native can never have the staggering experience of beholding our country suddenly and for the first time, with all the emotion and surprise of a discovery'. The ability to encapsulate English culture was sustained in writings of Leipzig-born architectural historian Nikolaus Pevsner, who had emigrated to England in the early 1930s. His many articles on English history and culture in *AR* and writings such as *The Englishness of English Art* (1956), made sweeping connections between national land, national climate and the temperament of English people, gathering assumed authority from his position as incomer. Émigré George Mikes's witty observations of the idiosyncrasies and inconsistencies of British postwar life, in *How to Be An Alien* (1946), derived from his declared position as foreigner, describing himself as 'the perpetual outsider'.

18   Charles Plouviez, assistant to the Director of Exhibitions Cecil Cooke, sensed around the Festival a fairly jovial but nevertheless tangible chauvinism. He recalled seeing a letter from someone at the Council of Industrial Design to someone at the Festival Office at Savoy Court about him (originally a French national) and a fellow worker, 'The person had put in brackets after our names "(I thought this was supposed to be a Festival of <u>Britain</u>)".' Dr Charles Plouviez, interview with author, 2003.

19   As seen in Society of Industrial Artists *Designers in Britain* publications from the late 1940s and trade journals such as *Display Design Presentation*.

20   Michael Middleton also wrote on 'Political Typography' in graphic design magazine *Typographica 2*.

21   Milner Gray, 'Notes on proposed research into improvements in the design, manufacture and siting of street lettering,' 26 May 1944, draft GB family archive.

22   Holford was Technical Adviser to the Ministry of Town and Country Planning in 1944 and Tallents was Principal Assistant Secretary to the Ministry of Town and Country Planning, 1943–6.

23   Gordon Cullen 'Townscape' section on publicity, *AR*, December 1949, p. 372.

24   Charles Hasler, Museum of the Domestic Interior (MODA), Box CH/4/5, described the original Festival titling as 'Festivalis bastorialis'.

25   Charles Hasler, *A Tonic to the Nation*, p. 114.

26   The poet Robert Southey first recorded the word 'Egyptian' in connection with the style in 1807 (Napoleon had returned from Egypt in 1799, sparking a wave of Egyptomania throughout Europe), and by the following decade all of the major British foundries had produced slab serif typefaces under different names that evoked the ancient world. Available http://www.typography.com (accessed 7 October 2011). Dick Negus was part of the team designing the Festival alphabet.

27   Nicolete Gray, *Lettering on Buildings* (Architectural Press, 1960), p. 94.

28   Paul Reilly, 'The Printed Publicity of the Festival of Britain', *The Penrose Annual: A Review of the Graphic Arts* 1952, Vol. 46, p. 23.

29   Indeed Harling was suggested as an addition to the Typography Panel (as shown in the Panel minutes) but in the interests of keeping the Panel small he was not invited to join.

30   Harling's quarterly *Alphabet and Image*, published through specialist publishing firm Art and Tecnics, only appeared for eight issues during 1946–8, becoming the independent journal of visual culture *Image*, 1948–52.

31   *Lettering on Buildings,* a survey of how lettering could be integrated into architecture, was the culmination of Gray's articles on lettering for *AR* (at the 1953 invitation of Nikolaus Pevsner), Gray, p. 166. Nicolete Gray was not formally a part of the Festival's organization as has been suggested in some other histories of the Festival.

32   Nikolaus Pevsner, *Visual Planning*, p. 198.

33   Pevsner 'Lettering and the Festival on the South Bank', *The Penrose Annual*, 1952, pp. 28–30.

34   Pauline Baines remembers this process being used for the Exhibition of Heavy Industry's text. Charles Hasler recalled this use of photographic reproduction and enlargement of lettering as a particular innovation of the Festival in later correspondence, Charles Hasler, MODA, Box CH/4/5.

35   Paul Wright in 'Projecting the Festival of Britain', *The Penrose Annual*, 1951, p. 62.

36   GB private diary, 'Monday February 26'.

37   Michael Hales, 7 July 2008. Available http://www.museumoflondon.org.uk (accessed 30 September 2010).

38   Maps are 'an entire logocentric construct' as art historian Irit Rogoff argues, *Terra Infirma* (Routledge, 2000), p. 96.

39   To make the 'bipolar distinction between "map" and "itinerary"' described by de Certeau, *The Practice of Everyday Life*, p. 93.

40   Being the 'voyeur gods' that de Certeau described, Ibid.

41   650,000 Guides were published, Ruari McLean *True to Type*, p. 89. Advertising agent George Rainbird has initially conceived the idea of guidebooks linked to the Festival and it was Rainbird who chose the editorial team, see Tim Cockin 'The About Britain Series', *Book and Magazine Collector*, No. 88, July 1991.

42   Grigson wrote *About Britain* guides to *West Country* and *Wessex*; natural historian R.S.R. Fitter, whose bird books were particularly popular, wrote *Home Counties*; local historian R.H. Mottram wrote *East Anglia*; social historian W.G. Hoskins (whose 1955 *The Making of the English Landscape* would have a profound influence on people's understand of the evolution of the English countryside) wrote *Chilterns to Black Country* and *East Midlands and the Peak*. Poet W.J. Gruffydd wrote the two Welsh guides; novelist Leo Walmsley wrote about Lancashire and Yorkshire; mine-worker and occasional contributor to *The Coal Magazine* Sid Chaplin wrote *The Lakes to Tyneside*; social and cultural historian John R. Allan about *The Lowlands of Scotland*; Scottish novelist Alistair M. Dunnett about *The Highlands and Islands of Scotland*; while E.E. Evans wrote the guide to NI.

43   A type of literature aptly described by David Matless as 'motoring pastoral' in *Landscape and Englishness*, p. 63.

44   Another important series of this period was 'Vision of England' published by Paul Elek and edited by Clough and Amabel Williams-Ellis, between 1946 and 1950, which celebrated the historic landscape and buildings of Britain.

45   *About Britain No 10* (London: Collins, 1951), p. 57.

46   McLean discussed this role in *True to Type*, further illuminated in correspondence with the author, February 2006. McLean supervised the design of the books' cartouche titles, which were drawn by his fellow tutor at RCA, John Brinkley, while McLean's RCA students E.W. Fenton and Sheila Robinson both contributed illustrations for title pages.

47   Adam's photographs were mainly of sweeping scenery seen from a distance, while Cash's photographs were more often of people carrying out work that was particularly distinctive to

that area, such as peat cutting or seaweed gathering. Landscape photographer Bertram Unné (1913–81), who specialised in documenting people and scenes of the Yorkshire Dales, folk activities and the landscapes of farming and coastal communities, took many of the pictures featured in *Lancashire and Yorkshire*. His photographs included many standard scenes of the counties, including well-known abbey ruins and coastal views.

48   GB, letter to the editor of *Flair* magazine, October 1950, GB family archive.

49   In 1951, the first volumes of Pevsner's *The Buildings of England* series were published by Penguin, covering Cornwall, Nottinghamshire and Middlesex. Dating, categorising and recording for the first time all buildings of note in these counties, the *Buildings* series were not topographical accounts or a tourist's reference series but part of a wider project to record buildings after the Second World War, realising that their destruction either by aerial bombing or by hasty planners had become a distinct possibility. Design commentator John Gloag observed 'England is a living guide-book to over two thousand years of civilization', suggesting that exploration of England, or Britain, would illuminate history and that England was a text to be 'read', as it was explored. John Gloag, *2000 Years of England*, (London: Cassell & Co, 1952). Other guides to Britain also flooded the market in 1951, including Denys Val Baker's *Britain Discovers Herself* published by Christopher Johnson, Adam de Hegedus's *Home and Away* published by Hutchinson and an essay collection *Our Way of Life*, published by Country Life.

50   The first commercial aerial photography agency, Aerofilms (founded in 1919 by a former First World War pilot to take vertical photographs) was recruited to fly reconnaissance missions during the Second World War. Many of the aerial photographs of the Festival's South Bank site both under construction and, indeed, destruction, were by Aerofilms.

51   Colin Banks, Production Assistant to McLean on the *Guides*, foreword to *True to Type*, p. xi.

52   *Britain To-Day Festival Number*, May 1951, pp. 20–1.

53   GB, transcript, 'Films in 1951', for BFI, dated 28 March 1951, GB family archive. 25 minute *Family Portrait* commissioned for the Festival from Wessex Films. Jennings had spent the Second World War working for the Crown Film Unit (CFU) and his film collaborations – *Words for Battle* (1941), *Listen to Britain* (1942) and *Fires Were Started* (1943), etc – had been focused towards boosting morale during war.

54   CFU colleagues John Grierson, Paul Rotha and Basil Wright all shared this interest. Other Festival films included *David* (a study of Wales through the experiences of a caretaker of a school on the edge of the coalfields) and Basil Wright's film on the Port of London Authority, *Waters of Time*.

55   National Archives INF 12/255.

56   Jennings, like contemporaries such as Marxist art historian F.D. Klingender, saw the division of the country and city as symptomatic of the impact of the Industrial Revolution, expanded upon in his collection *Pandaemonium 1990–1886: The coming of the machine as seen by contemporary observers* (London: Andre Deutsch, 1985).

57   GB, 'Films in 1951', for BFI, transcript, GB family archive.

58   GB private diary.

59   John Taylor 'Picturing the Past: Documentary realism in the 30s' in *Ten.8*, No. 11, 1983, p. 24.

60   Morrison had spoken on 'Books and the Festival of Britain' at a luncheon, 4 October 1949, as noted in *NBL Annual Report*, 1949–50.

61 *NBL Annual Report*, 1950–1, p. 1151.

62 Jeremy Aynsley, *Graphic Design in Germany 1890–1945* (Thames & Hudson, 2000), pp. 138–56.

63 Eva Rudberg, *The Stockholm Exhibition 1930* (Stockholmia Forlag, 1999), p. 121.

64 Called the 'Centre of Knowledge and Research', designed by architect MM Alix.

65 *Exposition Internationale: Arts and Crafts in Modern Life, Paris 1937 Official Guide* (Éditions de la Société pour le Développement du Tourisme, 1937), p. 32.

66 Set up as the National Book Council in 1925, re-launched as the National Book League in 1944 along the lines of a quasi-public body, but funded by the book trade.

67 *NBL Annual Report*, 1950–1, p. 1151.

68 National Archives WORK 25/44/A5/A3, papers 4 October 1949 and 31 March 1949.

69 In Festival book exhibitions, designers worked alongside curators who chose content. At London's V&A, the Festival Exhibition of Books held in Gallery 45 (a space with high status in the Museum's layout, being between the main entrance and central courtyard area), was divided into 14 sections. NBL Director John Hadfield co-ordinated the exhibition, supported by a central Festival Book Committee that, in turn, took advice from 74 scholars and critics, advising on the content of each sub-section.

70 *The Bookseller*, 28 April 1951, p. 1007.

71 Quoted in NBL report 'Books in the Festival of Britain', p. 4. Priestley had also written a comic novel on the Festival: *Festival at Farbridge* (1951).

72 Catalogue of *Exhibition of Books*, pp. 6–7.

73 *The Official Book of the Festival of Britain*, p. 20.

74 *Sunday Pictorial*, 23 February 1951.

75 GB speech to Churches Meeting, Nottingham, 20 September 1951, GB family archive.

76 A 'Hobbies and Reading' show, according to NBL, attracted the largest crowd: 8,200 visitors in 57 exhibition days, but little more is known about how these exhibitions were received.

77 NBL report, 'Books in the Festival of Britain', p. 7.

78 *South Bank Exhibition Guide*, pp. 67–8.

79 Becky Conekin discusses this in her analysis of the absence of British Empire in Festival events, *Autobiography*, p. 96.

80 *Exhibition of Books* catalogue, p. 6.

81 Jonathan Rose, *The Intellectual Life of the British Working Classes* (Yale UP, 2001), p. 231; Angus Calder, *The People's War: Britain 1939–1945* (Jonathan Cape, 1969), p. 512; Ross McKibbin, *Classes and Cultures: England 1918–1951* (OUP, 1998), Ch XIII 'The Community of Language'. In his 1962 *Communications*, Raymond Williams had traced the development of popular reading habits, showing how by 1955 there had already been a major increase through the Second World War. Per capita sales of books were to increase by 50 per cent from 1938–44, and over the longer period from 1918–51 increasingly large numbers of books and newspapers began to be sold and enjoyed.

82 Day-Lewis, 'Do we read better books in wartime?', *Picture Post*, 25 March 1944, pp. 22–6.

83 'Reading in Tottenham: A report on a survey carried out by Mass Observation on behalf of the Tottenham Borough Council,' not paginated, June 1952.

84 The show was presented with the co-operation of The Publishers' Association, The Booksellers' Association and NBL. See Deborah Ryan, *Daily Mail Ideal Home Exhibitions*, p. 97, for discussions of the 1951 exhibition, p. 97. Ideal Home had a full-page advertisement in *TLS*, 2 March 1951, p. 131, announcing the book exhibition as central.

85 Juliet Gardiner on TV, *From the Bomb to the Beatles* (Collins and Brown, 1999), p. 8, and Arthur Marwick on cinema going, *British Society Since 1945* (Penguin, 1990), p. 71. In 1946, at the peak of cinema's popularity, a third of the population went once a week.

86 DA File 5181, Morse Brown, 5 July 1951. The Telecinema (as it was listed in the South Bank Guide) was also at times called the 'Telekinema'.

87 According to NBL, the V&A Book Exhibition attracted 63,219 visitors and 17,000 catalogue sales during its five-month existence while The Ideal Home Book exhibition had been visited by an astonishing 250,000 people in 22 days, Edmund Penning-Rowsell, *The Bookseller*, 14 April 1951, p. 920. Meanwhile, a mere 5,770 had attended the Glasgow books exhibition and a pitiful 2,738 the Edinburgh one, NBL Annual Report 1950–1, p. 9.

CHAPTER 7

1 *South Bank Exhibition Guide*, p. 69.

2 The 1927 Tudor-Walters report had set out minimum standards for providing space for new houses.

3 Gilbert and Elizabeth Glen McAllister (eds), *Homes, Towns and Countryside: A Practical Plan for Britain* (Batsford, 1945), introduction, p. xxix.

4 Ibid., p. 101, in Chapter 7, 'Space Standards in Planning'.

5 John R Gold, *The Experience of Modernism* (London: E&FN Spon, 1997), p. 142.

6 Elizabeth Darling, *Re-forming Britain: Narratives of Modernity before Reconstruction* (London: Routledge, 2007).

7 William Henry Beveridge, *The Beveridge Report on the Social Insurance and Allied Services* (London: HMSO, 1942).

8 And indeed much of the rest of Europe, as argued by Betts and Crowley in 'Domestic Dreamworlds: Images of Home in Post-1945 Europe', *Journal of Contemporary History*, 30 April 2004.

9 First published in Graham Greene, *Nineteen Stories* (Viking Press, 1949).

10 *South Bank Exhibition Guide*, p. li.

11 Clare Langhamer, 'The Meanings of Home in Postwar Britain', *Journal of Contemporary History*, 30 April 2004, pp. 341–62. Penny Sparke argues the 1950s saw a 're-energised domestication of women', *As Long as its Pink* (Pandora, 1995), p. 166.

12 DA File 5181, notes on Shelter, 'Homes and Gardens'.

13 DA File 5181, paper dated 23 April 1949.

14 Osbert Lancaster, *Homes Sweet Homes* (London: John Murray, 1939), p. 9 (original emphases and wording).

15 Ismay, 'Welcome to the people of all lands', in *Daily Mail* Festival Preview, p. 80.

16 DA File 5183, 31 March 1949, probably written by A.D. Hippisley Coxe. Architect Denis Clarke Hall had been invited to design the Family section but the idea was abandoned in 1950, at a late stage in planning despite being well-researched and designed, because it was not upbeat enough, putting a 'rather grim aspect' on the break-up of the family post-Industrial Revolution (DA File 5183, Memo of 30 June 1949). The importance of bolstering family life was central to Ralph Tubbs' vision of reconstruction in his 1942 book *Living in Cities*.

17 *South Bank Exhibition Guide*, p. 63.

18   Becky Conekin discusses this further in *Autobiography*, p. 193. *South Bank Exhibition Guide*, p. 65.

19   House of Commons debate, 14 November 1950, *Hansard*, Vol. 480, cc.129–30W.

20   Geoffrey Fisher, Archbishop of Canterbury, 'The Closing of the Festival of Britain', *Listener*, Vol. 46, No. 1179, 4 October 1951.

21   These phrases also pointed to the milieu of the Festival's organizers: almost all living in London, mainly middle class, many public school-educated and mostly left-wing, though with differing degrees of radicalism, willing to champion a progressive social programme that represented liberal rhetoric and values. Michael Frayn aptly characterized them as do-gooding 'herbivores' in his 1963 essay, as opposed to right-wing 'carnivores', such as Evelyn Waugh. Architect Jim Cadbury-Brown raised the seeming contradiction for him of having an establishment background and also left politics, interview with author, June 2006. Many of these architects had got their Festival jobs through an old-boys' network. The cover of *The Festival Post*, the Festival's first newsletter, proclaimed 'Mr and Mrs John Bull request the Pleasure of Your Company in the UK for the summer of 1951.' Using the national personification represented in the figure of John Bull to suggest honest, down-to-earth British values.

22   National Archives, WORK 25/48, Presentation Panel papers 1950–1.

23   Janice Winship argues that magazines such as *Woman* reinforced traditional notions of femininity after the war, 'Nation Before Family: Woman, the National Home Weekly 1945–1953', in *Formations* (London: Routledge and Kegan Paul, 1984).

24   GB private diary.

25   Model housing had been central at international exhibitions from the 1851 Great Exhibition onwards. At Crystal Palace, architect Henry Roberts had designed a popular display of model working-class housing for four families, two on each floor, with open staircases, and inside lavatory. It illustrated how housing might be reformed to offer improved living conditions. The 1867 Exposition Universelle in Paris had also put workers' housing on show. Such models drew attention to the virtues of architects as designers rather than to the ability of inhabitants to use places to best advantage.

26   Alastair Borthwick, Heavy Industry Exhibition organizer, and the Provost of Glasgow both expressed this opinion in relation to the Glasgow exhibition.

27   James Laver 'Homes and Habitat', Ernest Barker (ed), *The Character of England* (OUP, 1947), p. 462.

28   As set out by Sean Glynn and Alan Booth in *Modern Britain: A Social and Economic History* (London: Routledge, 2003), p. 45. This study shows that single women formed the largest percentage of the workforce, with married and widowed women less active, but numbers of working married women were rising.

29   See Lynne Walker, in Rendell, Penner and Borden (eds), *Gender Space Architecture* (London: Routledge, 2000), p. 253.

30   National Archives (WORK 25/205) holds a photograph of 22 year-old Angela Ryan, with the caption 'the only girl working in the Architects' Department of the Festival of Britain Office', 17 March 1951. A small number of women were listed as designers, again in partnership: Patience Clifford with Neville Conder. Other women listed on their own were married to significant designers. The most prominent of these was Margaret Casson, wife of Hugh Casson, a successful architect in her own right. Other female contributors included Mary Ward, wife of designer Neville Ward, and Veronica de Majo who made contributions

at Belfast under the direction of her husband Willy de Majo. At Lansbury, key parts of the exhibition were designed by women: architect Judith Ledeboer worked in partnership with David Booth on housing and open spaces, planner Jacqueline Tyrwhitt helped organize the Lansbury show and wrote the script for a Town Planning pavilion, and Sadie Speight collaborated with Leonard Manasseh on the Rosie Lee Cafeteria. Women were, however, leading the field in the embryonic profession of landscape architecture: Brenda Colvin, Sylvia Crowe, Marjory Allen and Susan Jellicoe were making their mark through landscaping schemes and through publishing their writings on postwar landscaping. At the South Bank Exhibition Maria Shephard – who would go on to build an important career as a landscape designer – assisted Frank Clark with landscaping. Writer and archaeologist Jacquetta Hawkes, as theme convenor of The People of Britain, and Barbara Jones, as designer of the Seaside section (both at the South Bank), made significant contributions. Other female contributors included influential crystallographer Helen Megaw, leading the Festival Pattern Group and textile designers Lucienne Day and Jacqueline Groag.

31   DA File 5181.

32   Plants were described by gardeners Jones and Clark as a 'picturesque' home furnishing tool, Clark and Jones, *Indoor Plants and Gardens* (Architectural Press, 1952).

33   DA File 5181, meeting 18 May 1948.

34   DA File 5181, memo James Gardner to A.D. Hippisley Coxe at COID, 24 November 1949, about structure of 'Homes and Gardens'.

35   The COID 'Stock List' became the basis of the South Bank 'Design Review' section.

36   Jonathan M Woodham, 'Managing British Design Reform I: Fresh Perspectives on the Early Years of the COID' in *Journal of Design History*, Vol. 9, No. 2, 1993. Nor was the Festival about showcasing new goods across price range and house-type as at the 1946 'Britain Can Make It' show, with its driving concern to promote so-called 'good' design. This differs from defining concern for 'quality', which Cheryl Buckley has shown dominated design discourse from 1930–51, *Designing Modern Britain* (London: Reaktion Press, 2007), p. 106. The COID's role in the Festival has been overstated, partly because COID wrote some of the first histories of British design.

37   Letter in DA File 5429 'Parlours', 11 June 1951. *AR*, December 1951, 'COID Progress Report', p. 354.

38   DA File 5429 'Parlours'. A letter of 9 August 1951 from Paul Reilly to Industrial Officers at COID shows GB felt strongly about this too.

39   Gordon Russell, *A Designer's Trade* (London: George Allen and Unwin Ltd, 1968), pp. 131, 201, 211.

40   DA 5429 'The Parlour' theme paper.

41   *South Bank Exhibition Guide*, p. 69.

42   Stanley Gale, *Modern Housing Estates* (Batsford, 1949), p. 181.

43   F.R.S. Yorke's 1934 *The Modern House* and Yorke and Frederick Gibberd's 1937 *The Modern Flat*, for example. *Ideal Home*'s series 'Planning for the Future', which ran across 30 instalments from 1941 to 1943, promoted designs such as Mary Crowley and Ernö Goldfinger's open-plan bungalow. Lionel Brett's *The Things We See: Houses* (Penguin, 1947) had suggested one 'lump' of space for a living room was preferable to 'small packets', although conceding that modern designers of the 1930s had achieved 'spaciousness' at the expense of 'cosiness' and this imbalance was recently being realigned.

44   Marghanita Laski, *The Victorian Chaise-Longue* (London: Persephone Books, 1999). Thad
     Logan's *The Victorian Parlour* (Cambridge University Press, 2001) interrogates parlour as
     'synecdoche' for Victorian culture, exploring the anti-Victorian reaction in the twentieth
     century. The fear of Victoriana also characterised many writings on architecture and
     design contemporary with the Festival by John Gloag, Ralph Dutton and Ralph Tubbs. The
     revival of interest in the Victorian was signalled by Hugh Casson's 1948 study *Victorian
     Architecture*, followed a decade later by foundation of The Victorian Society by, among
     others, John Betjeman and Nikolaus Pevsner, a body that fought for preservation of
     Victorian buildings.

45   DA File 5181, memo from Hippisley Coxe to Ian Cox, 5 October 1950. This need to display
     trinkets was also acknowledged in the Land Traveller Exhibition's section on 'The Best Room',
     introduced with 'The Victorian parlour gradually disappears, but our desire for ornaments
     remains', *Land Traveller Exhibition Catalogue* (HMSO, 1951), p. 23.

46   *AR* January 1944, p. 6.

47   The *South Bank Exhibition Catalogue* lists the origin of every item on display.

48   DA File 5429, 11 June 1951, letter from Paul Reilly at COID to Cecil Cooke, Festival Director
     of Exhibitions.

49   DA 5429. At the 19 June meeting a budget of £650 was to be spent on replacing the Minns'
     work (repapering five rooms, a screen to shield them from view temporarily, essential structural
     alterations and wallpaper). In a later meeting it was stated the Festival Office would contribute
     £500 and COID £750.

50   DA File 5249, 11 June 1951, Reilly to Cooke.

51   DA File 5429, 29 June 1951, and note of unlabelled and undated meeting.

52   George Orwell, 'The Lion and the Unicorn', 1941 in Sonia Orwell and Ian Angus (eds), *The
     Collected Essays, Journalism and Letters of George Orwell,* Vol.II (London: Secker and Warburg,
     1968), p. 58.

53   DA File 5181, letter of 26 January 1950 from James Gardner to Bronek Katz.

54   The clash between society designers and other designers seen in the parlours incident was
     also evident in the conflict between interior designers Roger and Robert Nicholson, who
     had initially worked with Fry and Drew and the Bowyers on the South Bank Sports section
     but left acrimoniously part-way through to work on Homes and Gardens. Gordon Bowyer
     later commented 'They were absolutely designers, in the narrowest sense ... I remember one
     of them saying: "Colour is easy – all you have to do is paint every wall a different colour,"'
     interview with author, 2004.

55   DA File 5181, Morse Brown, 4 July 1951.

56   DA File 5429, memo 15 August 1951, Miss Stewart to Mr Reilly.

57   DA File 5429, letter 13 July 1951.

58   DA File 5429, letter from Reilly to Austin and Ward, 25 July 1951.

59   The conflict between popular taste and the official 'good design' agenda was felt acutely
     elsewhere, for example in New Town housing as described by design historian Judy Attfield in
     her study of Harlow New Town interior decoration where women, negotiating the unfamiliar
     space of New Town housing came head-to-head with architects, anxious to implement their
     vision of a 'new society', see Judy Attfield, 'Inside Pram Town: A Case Study of Harlow House
     Interiors, 1951–61', in Judy Attfield and Pat Kirkham (eds), *A View from the Interior: Women and
     Design* (The Women's Press Ltd, 1989).

60 DA File 5181, Morse-Brown.

61 Lesley Jackson, *From Atoms to Patterns* (Richard Dennis, 2008). Only three years after the Festival crystallography would result in the discovery of DNA.

62 Antelope had a ply seat and Springbok had a sprung seat. See Hazel Conway, *Ernest Race* (The Design Council, 1982).

63 'South Bank Exhibition (Catering Prices)', House of Commons debate, 9 May 1951, Vol. 487, cc.1952–4.

64 Diary of Albert Richardson, 5 July 1951 (original spelling), from Avenue House Collection, with thanks to Simon Houfe.

65 Paul Wright, interview with author, June 2004.

66 House of Commons debate, 14 November 1950, *Hansard*, Vol. 480, cc.129–30W, states 533 people were displaced to make way for permanent housing for 1,624.

67 Basildon, Bracknell, Crawley, Harlow, Hatfield, Hemel Hempstead, Stevenage and Welwyn Garden City.

68 At Newton Aycliffe and Peterlee in County Durham and Corby in Northamptonshire. A Welsh New Town, Cwmbran in Monmouthshire, and two Scottish ones, East Kilbride and Glenrothes, were all built to serve local industry.

69 *AR* editor J.M. Richards' *Bombed Buildings of Britain* (London: Architectural Press, 1942) had discussed the spectacular damage wrought on Britain by the Blitz. John Piper's article 'Pleasing Decay' enthusiastically asserted 'Bomb damage has revealed new beauties in unexpected places', *AR*, January 1944, pp. 13–17; John Piper, *AR*, CII, Sep 1947, p. 38. These sentiments were amplified in Piper's *Buildings and Prospects* (London: Architectural Press, 1948). Hugh Casson, *Bombed Churches as War Memorials* (Cheam: Architectural Press, 1945).

70 GB, 'What is the Festival?' article sent to the Bishop of Southwell, 15 August 1950, in GB family archive.

71 Alison Ravetz, *Council Housing and Culture* (London: Routledge, 2001), p. 96.

72 Planner Abercrombie had earlier asserted that England had invented the village, in *The Preservation of Rural England* (London: Hodder & Stoughton, 1926). Villages were repeatedly cited as a model of virtuous community for British planning and loosely defined as a small cluster of houses with the central focus of a church, area of common land or pond.

73 Thomas Sharp, *Anatomy of the Village* (London: Penguin, 1946). See also, Cecil Stewart, *The Village Surveyed* (London: Edward Arnold & Co, 1948).

74 Eric Mumford, *The CIAM Discourse on Urbanism 1928–1960* (Cambridge, Mass: MIT, 2002), p. 177. Richards set out these beliefs in a talk at CIAM 6. H. de C Hastings had questioned what might appeal to 'the Man in the Street' in 'Exterior Furnishing', *AR*, January 1944.

75 Frances Spalding *John Piper, Myfanwy Piper: Lives in Art* (Oxford University Press, 2009), p. 7. With many thanks to Conor Mullan, see also Alan Powers, 'Piper's Mural: Home from Home', *History Today*, Vol. 61, issue 5, May 2011.

76 Mumford, p. 164.

77 *1951 Exhibition of Architecture Poplar Guide*, pp. 42–3.

78 Jacqueline Tyrwhitt, 'The Neighbourhood Unit Idea', in *Programme of Lectures on Principles of Town Planning, University of Toronto*, Fall Term 1951, typescript, The CIAM Collection, Special Collections in the Frances Loeb Library, Harvard University (SC/CIAM Collection, Folder E5).

79 Ian Nairn, *Modern Buildings in London* (London Transport Board, 1964), pp. 24–5.

80   Mrs Snoddy later said that the tortoise met an untimely death soon after the family arrived at Lansbury, when it was decapitated by a sliding glass door (Mrs Snoddy in an interview with Catherine Croft).

81   'The Lansbury Estate: Introduction and the Festival of Britain exhibition', *Survey of London: volumes 43 and 44: Poplar, Blackwall and Isle of Dogs* (1994), pp. 212–23. Available www.british-history.ac.uk/report.aspx?compid=46490 (accessed 21 September 2010).

82   Macdonald and Porter, *Putting on the Style* (Geffrye Museum, 1990), 'Lansbury' section.

83   W.G. Holford 'The Lansbury Neighbourhood', *Listener*, Vol. XLV, 29 March 1951, pp. 493–5.

84   David Garred, 14 February 2002. Available Museum of London Festival of Britain website archive (30 September 2010).

85   *Land Traveller Exhibition Guide-Catalogue*, p. 26.

86   Alastair Borthwick 'Furniture', *Scotland's SMT*, December 1951, p. 8.

87   J.M. Richards, 'Lansbury', *AR*, December 1951, pp. 361–2.

88   Gibberd, 'Lansbury: the Live Architecture Exhibition', *A Tonic to the Nation*, p. 138.

89   Frederick Gibberd, 'The design of residential areas', *Design in Town and Village* (London: HMSO, 1953) Part II, p. 24.

90   Percy Johnson-Marshall, *Rebuilding Cities* (Edinburgh University Press, 1966) pp. 226–36.

91   National Archives WORK25/44/A5/A4, 4 December 1948.

92   Elain Harwood and Alan Powers, *Tayler and Green, 1938–1973* (Prince of Wales's Institute, 1998).

93   Frederick Gibberd, *Town Design* (London: Architectural Press, 1953), p. 170.

94   Gibberd, *A Tonic to the Nation*, p. 141.

95   Pevsner Reith lectures, 1955 published as *The Englishness of English Art* (Architectural Press, 1956), p. 168.

CHAPTER 8

1   Geoffrey Fisher, *Listener*, 1951, Vol. 46.

2   GB broadcast for *Saturday Review*, Saturday 29 September 1951, GB archive, LSE.

3   *The Times*, 1 October 1951, p. 4.

4   *The Times*, 3 October 1951, p. 2. The Council of Industrial Design took over the Health pavilion and Fairway Café as stores.

5   *The Times*, 3 October 1951, p. 2.

6   National Archives, WORK 25/59 'Report of Demolition Working Party'.

7   Letter from Eccles to GB, 28 Dec 1951, GB family archive.

8   National Archives WORK 25 letter of 12 November 1951 from Churchill to Morrison marked at top 'for statement in House by Ministry of Works, 14.11.51' and in top right corner 'Exhibitions and Fairs'. Battersea Pleasure Gardens were to stay open for five years longer. National Archives T267/6 'Treasury Historical Memoranda No. 2. The Festival Pleasure Gardens'.

9   GB, 'After the Ball is Over', *The New Statesman and Nation*, 13 October 1951. Indeed the Thameside Restaurant lasted until 1962.

10   'Festival in the Junk Yard', *Picture Post*, 28 June 1952.

11   Clifford Hatts generously gave me these photographs.

12   'Bob' was a slang phrase for a shilling, a form of currency which is no longer used.

12   A number of foreign correspondents were sent by their countries to report on Festival events. 'Breakdown of Foreign Correspondents in London since May 3', paper in GB family archive, records correspondents sent 'expressly to report on the Festival' as follows: 12 were from USA, 65 from Western Europe (including 32 from Scandinavia), 12 from the Commonwealth and Empire, 3 from the Middle East.

13   GB 'After the Ball Is Over', *The New Statesman*.

14   Lesley Jackson, *'Contemporary': Architecture and Interiors of the 1950s* (London: Phaidon, 1994).

15   Marghanita Laski, *The Observer*, 6 July 1952.

16   GB in speech to SIA, Tuesday 16 Oct 1951, GB family archive.

17   Gutmann and Koch, *Exhibition Stands* (GMBH Stuttgart, 1954).

18   Avril Blake (ed), *The Black Papers on Design* (London: Pergamon Press, 1983), pp. 133–4. James Gardner criticized the wordiness of exhibitions in *Exhibition and Display* (Batsford, 1960).

19   Richard Levin, *A Tonic to the Nation*, p. 151.

20   Herbert Read founded the ICA in 1947, its first exhibition, entitled *40 years of Modern Art: A Selection from British Collections*, was held in 1948.

21   The contemporary preoccupation with integrating the arts was underlined by an ICA discussion on 13 September 1951 entitled 'Are Architecture, Painting and Sculpture properly correlated on the South Bank?', chaired by GB, with contributions from Misha Black, Hugh Casson and Victor Pasmore.

22   Peter Reyner Banham, 'Opinions of the Festival of Britain', *AR*, January 1953, pp. 62–3.

23   Pevsner's 1955 Reith Lectures published as *The Englishness of English Art* (Architectural Press, 1956).

24   Basil Taylor, 'English Art and the Picturesque', for BBC Third Programme, November 1953. Programme 1 (of 3), transcript p. 7, BBC Archive.

25   J.M. Richards 'The Failure of the New Towns', *AR*, July 1953, p. 28. These thoughts were endorsed by sociologists Michael Young and Peter Willmott, *Family and Kinship in East London* (research published in 1954), focusing on the impact of moving east London families from slum dwellings to new housing in the early 1950s. They concluded that old, dense communities were more effective than the new ones residents had been moved to.

26   Paul Addison, *Now the War is Over* (London: Jonathan Cape: 1985), p. 77.

27   Jessica Allen, *Contested Understandings: the Lansbury Estate in the Post-war Period* (PhD, University of London, 1994).

28   Richard Burton (of Ahrends Burton Koralek) told me that the influence of the Festival of Britain had encouraged him to pursue an architectural training. At the AA architects like Leonard Manasseh, who had cut their teeth at the Festival, taught him.

29   Banham, *AR*, Vol. 118, December 1955, pp. 354–61.

30   Banham, 'Revenge of the Picturesque', in John Summerson (ed) *Concerning Architecture* (London: Penguin, 1968).

31   Mumford, p. 7.

32   The Time-Life building, New Bond Street (1951–3), for example, was an extraordinary collaborative project that allowed many Festival designers to experience working in private practice. The building was designed by Michael Rosenauer, while Hugh Casson and Misha Black co-ordinated interiors. Leonard Manasseh and Ian Baker designed a restaurant, Hugh Casson and Neville Conder a café, Jim Cadbury-Brown a meeting room interior, Robert Goodden a staircase, and Peter Shepheard a terrace. Conceived as a monument to Anglo-

American friendship, it was paid for in dollars, so was not subject to the same licensing or material restrictions and consequently lavish materials could be used – metal and timber finishes that had been rationed at the Festival.

33   Avril Blake, *Misha Black* (Design Council, 1984), pp. 44–5.

34   Professor H.T. Cadbury-Brown, interview with author, 15 April 2003.

SELECT BIBLIOGRAPHY

Works quoted in the text that do not appear in the bibliography are cited with full publication details in the notes. This applies particularly to shorter articles and works briefly referred to.

Banham, Mary and Bevis Hillier (eds), *A Tonic to the Nation* (London: Thames & Hudson, 1976).

Burstow, Robert, *Symbols for '51: The Royal Festival Hall, Skylon and Sculptures on the South Bank for the Festival of Britain* (London: Royal Festival Hall, 1996).

Conekin, Becky, *'The Autobiography of a Nation': The 1951 Festival of Britain* (Manchester: Manchester University Press, 2003)

Curtis, Barry, 'One Continuous Interwoven Story (The Festival of Britain)', *Block* Issue 11, 1985–6, pp. 209–20, reproduced in *Block Reader in Visual Culture* (London: Routledge, 1996).

Frayn, Michael, 'Festival', in Michael Sissons and Philip French (eds), *Age of Austerity* (London: Hodder & Stoughton, 1963).

Games, Naomi, *A Symbol for the Festival* (London: Capital, 2011).

Garlake, Margaret, *Artists and patrons in post-war Britain* (Aldershot: Ashgate, 2001).

Garlake, Margaret, *New Art, New World: British Art in Postwar Society* (New Haven: Yale University Press, 1998).

Glendinning, Miles (ed), *Rebuilding Scotland: The Postwar Vision 1945–1975* (East Linton: Tuckwell Press, 1997).

Goodden, Henrietta, *The Lion and the Unicorn* (Norwich: Unicorn Press, 2011).

Harwood, Elain and Alan Powers (eds), *Festival of Britain* (London: Twentieth Century Society, 2001).

Jackson, Lesley, *From Atoms to Patterns: Crystal structure designs from the 1951 Festival of Britain* (Shepton Beauchamp: Richard Dennis, 2008).

Matless, David, *Landscape and Englishness: Picturing History* (London: Reaktion Books, 2001).

McIntosh, Gillian, *The Force of Culture: Unionist Identities in Twentieth Century Ireland* (Cork: Cork University Press, 1999).

Rennie, Paul, *Festival of Britain Design* (Woodbridge: The Antique Collectors' Club, 2007).

Royal Festival Hall, *Royal Festival Hall 1951–2001 Past, Present, Future* (including essays by Bryan Appleyard, Richard Morrison, Adrian Forty et al.) (Royal Festival Hall, 2001).

Turner, Barry, *Beacon for Change: How the 1951 Festival of Britain Shaped the Modern World* (London: Aurum, 2011).

INDEX

Page numbers in italics refer to illustrations.